International Political Economy Series

General Editor: **Timothy M. Shaw**, Professor of Commonwealth Governance and Development, and Director of the Institute of Commonwealth Studies, School of Advanced Study, University of London

Titles include:

S. Javed Maswood
JAPAN IN CRISIS

Ananya Mukherjee Reed
PERSPECTIVES ON THE INDIAN CORPORATE ECONOMY
Exploring the Paradox of Profits
CORPORATE CAPITALISM IN CONTEMPORARY SOUTH ASIA (*editor*)
Conventional Wisdoms and South Asian Realities

Cecilia Ng
POSITIONING WOMEN IN MALAYSIA
Class and Gender in an Industrializing State

Ian Scott (*editor*)
INSTITUTIONAL CHANGE AND THE POLITICAL TRANSITION
IN HONG KONG

Mark Turner (*editor*)
CENTRAL–LOCAL RELATIONS IN ASIA-PACIFIC
Convergence or Divergence?

Fei-Ling Wang
INSTITUTIONS AND INSTITUTIONAL CHANGE IN CHINA
Premodernity and Modernization

International Political Economy Series
Series Standing Order ISBN 0–333–71708–2 hardcover
Series Standing Order ISBN 0–333–71110–6 paperback
(*outside North America only*)

You can receive future titles in this series as they are published by placing a standing order.
Please contact your bookseller or, in case of difficulty, write to us at the address below with
your name and address, the title of the series and one of the ISBNs quoted above.

Customer Services Department, Macmillan Distribution Ltd, Houndmills, Basingstoke,
Hampshire RG21 6XS, England

Corporate Capitalism in Contemporary South Asia

Conventional Wisdoms and South Asian Realities

Edited by

Ananya Mukherjee Reed

Associate Professor, Department of Political Science, York University, Canada

First published 2003 by
PALGRAVE MACMILLAN
Houndmills, Basingstoke, Hampshire RG21 6XS and
175 Fifth Avenue, New York, N.Y. 10010
Companies and representatives throughout the world

PALGRAVE MACMILLAN is the global academic imprint of the Palgrave Macmillan division of St. Martin's Press, LLC and of Palgrave Macmillan Ltd. Macmillan® is a registered trademark in the United States, United Kingdom and other countries. Palgrave is a registered trademark in the European Union and other countries.

ISBN 0–333–97720–3

This book is printed on paper suitable for recycling and made from fully managed and sustained forest sources.

A catalogue record for this book is available from the British Library.

Library of Congress Cataloging in Publication Data
Corporate capitalism in contemporary South Asia : conventional wisdoms and South Asian realities / edited by Ananya Mukherjee Reed.
    p.   cm. — (International political economy series)
Includes bibliographical references and index.
ISBN 0–333–97720–3
1. Corporations—South Asia—Finance. 2. Capitalism—South Asia.
I. Mukherjee Reed, Ananya. II. International political economy series (Palgrave (Firm))

HG4236.C67 2003
338.0954—dc21

2003040468

10   9   8   7   6   5   4   3   2   1
12   11   10   09   08   07   06   05   04   03

Printed and bound in Great Britain by
Antony Rowe Ltd, Chippenham and Eastbourne

– dedicated to a hope for change

Contents

List of Tables

List of Figures

List of Acronyms

ACMA	Automotive Components Manufactures Association of India
AL	Awami League
APTMA	All Pakistan Textile Mills Association
AT	Asset Turnover
BCs	Backward Castes
BNP	Bangladesh Nationalist Party
CMIE	Center for Monitoring Indian Economy
CEC	Cotton Export Corporation
DCCI	Dhaka Chamber of Commerce and Industry
DFIs	Development Finance Institutions
EFF	Extended Fund Facility
EF	Electric Furnace
EPZ	Export Processing Zone
FDI	Foreign Direct Investment
FERA	Foreign Exchange and Regulation Act
GDP	Gross Domestic Product
GVW	Gross Vehicle Weight
HBI	Hot Briquetted Iron
HCL	Hindustan Computers Limited
HM	Hindustan Motors Limited
IFIs	International Financial Institutions
IMF	International Monetary Fund
IDBP	Industrial Development Bank of Pakistan
IPR	Industrial Policy Resolution
IPR	Intellectual Property Right
ISO	International Organization for Standardization
JLCV	Japanese Light Commercial Vehicle
JP	Jatiya Party
JV	Joint venture
MBCs	Most Backward Castes
MRTPA	Monopolies and Restrictive Trade Practices Act
MUL	Maruti Udyog Limited
NASSCOM	National Association for Software & Services Companies
NEC	National Economic Council
NCBs	Nationalized Commercial Banks
NDIL	Nippon Denro Ispat Limited

OGL	Open General License
OHF	Open Hearth Furnace
ORG	Operations Research Group
PAL	Premier Automobiles Limited
PNA	Pakistan National Alliance
PBC	Pakistan Banking Council
PICIC	Pakistan Industrial Credit and Investment Corporation
RIP	Revised Investment Policy
ROA	Return on Assets
RECP	Rice Export Corporation
SBOP	State Bank of Pakistan
SAIL	Steel Authority of India Limited
SCs	Scheduled Castes
SIEL	Shriram Industrial Enterprises Limited
SKOP	Sramik Karmachari Oikka Parishad
SOEs	State-owned enterprises
SSA	Social structures of accumulation
SVM	Shareholder value maximisation
TCS	Tata Consultancy Services
TELCO	Tata Engineering and Locomotive Company Limited
TFP	Total Factor Productivity
TVS	TV Sundaram
UTI	Unit Trust of India
VAT	Value Added Taxation

Acknowledgements

'Capitalist Maturity and Corporate Responses to Liberalization: The Steel, Automobile, and Software Sectors in India' by Anthony P. D'Costa is reprinted with permission from *Contemporary South Asia* (2000), 9(2), pp. 141–63.

An earlier version of 'Corporate Capital in Contemporary Sri Lanka' by Don K. Embuldeniya, was published in *Contemporary South Asia* (2000), 9(2), pp. 165–79.

An earlier version of 'Legitimization, Patrimonialism, and Regime Consolidation: The Myth of Market Reform in Bangladesh' by Fahimul Quadir was published in *Contemporary South Asia* (2000), 9(2), pp. 197–212.

An earlier version of 'The Politics of Accumulation in Small Town India' by Elisabetta Basile and Barbara Harriss-White was published in the *Bulletin of the Institute of Development Studies*, 30(4), pp. 31–8 (Special Issue 'Politics in Development: Essays in Honour of Gordon White).

Preface

These are difficult times for South Asia. On the one hand there is increasing violence and the deepening spectre of 'terrorism'. On the other, there is increasing uncertainty about the twin experiments of globalisation and domestic economic reforms. In the light of this, it is important to engage in an analysis as to why the experiments are failing, and how, if at all, a more stable trajectory of political and economic change can be identified.

Several dichotomous and overdetermined discourses now dominate the discussion of South Asian development, and development in the 'South' in general. The most pervasive of these is the one between all forms of state-led development (including narrow economic nationalism) and an almost state-less form of development, the agents of which are an anthropomorphised vision of globalisation and a benign and fair Anglo-American model of capitalism. Yet another (false) dichotomy is represented by the debate on path dependency and convergence. The notion of convergence, which has been extensively critiqued in the context of advanced capitalist economies, continues to be readily advocated for developing countries; in the case of the latter, convergence is posited as an unmitigated 'good' which should be engineered in order to improve economic performance. As is well known, this view of convergence very often is based on the problematic notion that the obstacles to convergence (and growth) emanate from elements of 'tradition', viz. caste, religion, ethnicity and so on. Needless to say, all these discourses are nested within the rather grand meta-narrative of globalisation, envisioned as a process emanating from the North – of which the 'South' is a passive recipient.

In this volume we have made an effort to move beyond these false binary oppositions in several ways. While the different authors have approached the problem differently, the collaborative outcome has been to question a set of conventional wisdoms about South Asia – and to arrive at a comparative and contextually specific analysis of the politics of accumulation in South Asia. It is my hope that we have been able to realise our efforts to some extent.

The discussions in this volume point us to an area of future research with respect to South Asia. This concerns the changes occurring in corporate economies as a result of the on-going *War on Terror*. In particular, it seems highly pertinent to explore the relationship between the corporate economy and the imperatives of the national security discourses that have emerged in South Asia since September 11. What kind of structures of accumulation can flourish in highly militaristic economies? What in fact are the structural affinities between firms geared towards profit and states geared towards defence, construed in conservative realist terms? Needless to say, active collaboration amongst South Asian scholars is necessary to engage in further research into these issues. It is my hope that this volume would be a modest contribution in this direction.

As to the birth of this volume, I am especially thankful to Apurba Kundu, the editor of *Contemporary South Asia*, who agreed to publish a special thematic issue of the journal. An earlier version of some of the chapters in this volume was published in that thematic issue. I am also very grateful to Professor Timothy M. Shaw, editor of the *International Political Economy* series for Palgrave Macmillan, who first suggested that we convert the journal issue into a volume. Last but not least, I would like to thank my family to whom I am grateful for much more than I will ever be able to articulate.

Ananya Mukherjee Reed
Toronto

Notes on Contributors

Elisabetta Basile is Professor of Agricultural Economics at Rome University, 'La Sapienza', and has completed fieldwork for a doctoral thesis on accumulation trajectories in South India with Barbara Harriss-White at Oxford University, UK.

Ali Cheema completed his doctoral degree in Economics from Cambridge University in 1999. He returned to Pakistan and is now Assistant Professor, Faculty of Economics, at the Lahore University of Management Sciences. He is also a consultant to the Task Force on the Restructuring of the Central Board of Revenue, Government of Pakistan and has previously worked as consultant to the Asian Development Bank's country mission to Pakistan. He was a Rhodes Scholar at Oxford University from 1989 to 1992.

Anthony P. D'Costa is currently Associate Professor, University of Washington, Tacoma, USA. He is the author of *The Global Restructuring of the Steel Industry* (1999). He is currently working on India's software sector. In 1997 and 1998, he held Senior Fellowships with the National University of Singapore and the American Institute of Indian Studies respectively.

Don K. Embuldeniya is a doctoral candidate in the Department of Political Science at York University and a Research Associate at the Canadian Centre for Philanthropy, Canada. His current research focuses on international trade policy, international development, civil society and social movements.

Barbara Harriss-White is Professor of Development Studies, in Oxford University's Centre for International Development, Queen Elizabeth House. She has been carrying out field research on local level accumulation in India intermittently since 1972. Books on this subject include *A Political Economy of Agricultural Markets in South India; Masters of the Countryside* (1996) and *How India Works: The Economy from the Ground* (forthcoming).

Fahimul Quadir received a PhD in Political Science from Dalhousie University after which he served as Assistant Professor of Political Studies at Queen's University, Canada. He has taught International Development Studies at Dalhousie University and Political Science at the University of Chittagong, Bangladesh. He also has participated in several large-scale development and research projects both in Canada and Bangladesh. His research interests include globalisation, democratisation, governance, civil society, NGOs, micro-finance, development, regionalism, and human security. He has recently published on these topics in *Contemporary South Asia, New Political Economy, South Asian Studies, Development Review, Thomas and Wilkin* (eds), *Globalization and the South, Gills* (ed.), *Globalization and the Politics of Resistence* and *Poku and Pettiford* (eds), *Redefining the Third World*. He has just co-edited a volume entitled *Crises of Governance in Asia and Africa* (2001). He has received several awards and fellowships including a Fulbright Scholarship, Killam doctoral and postdoctoral fellowships and Canada in the World fellowship (IDRC, Canada). Prior to coming to York he was Assistant Professor, Global Studies at St Lawrence University, New York.

Ananya Mukherjee Reed is Associate Professor, Department of Political Science, York University, Toronto. She has published widely in a number of Indian and international journals and has recently guest-edited a thematic volume entitled *Corporate Capitalism in Contemporary South Asia*, for the journal *Contemporary South Asia*. She is also the author of *Perspectives on the Indian Corporate Economy: Exploring the Paradox of Profits* (Palgrave Macmillan, 2001).

Jayati Sarkar and Subrata Sarkar are Associate Professors, Indira Gandhi Institute of Development Research, Mumbai, India. They are highly reputed scholars of Indian corporate governance and economic reforms. They have published widely on Indian corporate governance in Indian and international journals and are regular contributors to the *India Development Report*. They are also visiting faculties at the Department of Economics, University of Southern California, USA.

1
Conceptualising Corporate Capitalism in Contemporary South Asia: Conventional Wisdoms and South Asian Realities

Ananya Mukherjee Reed

These are difficult times for South Asia. On the one hand there is the deepening spectre of 'terrorism', violence and the larger-than-life presence of the United States in the region. On the other, there is growing evidence of economic gloom as the twin experiments of globalisation and domestic economic reforms overwhelmingly fail to deliver on their promises. In the light of this, it is important to engage in an analysis as to why the experiments are failing, and how, if at all, a more stable trajectory of political and economic change can be identified. It is important perhaps to state at the outset that we do not embark on this task with an irrational nostalgia for all forms of state-led development, or more importantly, narrow economic nationalism. Our aim is to move beyond the false binary opposition between the borderless and the parochial; for, as the South Asian experience illustrates, both can be equally oppressive and inimical to the objectives of development, understood broadly as a progressive enhancement in the quality of life for the majority, through processes that are just, equitable and sustainable.

As is well known, the onset of globalisation, and the emergence of what some authors have called *global neo-classicism*, corporate capital has been designated as the primary agent of development. Our focus in this work derives from this unequivocal affirmation of the ability of corporate capital to solve the twin problems of equity and efficiency. However, our purpose is not to undertake yet another set of statistical analyses of performance indicators, which do not fully acknowledge the complexity of the underlying structures of accumulation. At the same time, we also wish to eschew overly deterministic structuralist analysis of

1

globalisation which minimises the role of internal social relations. What we aim at then, is a comparative and contextually specific analysis of the politics of accumulation in South Asia.

In addition to the hypotheses that emerge from our analysis here, I will conclude with the suggestion that a somewhat fundamental reconceptualisation of corporate economies has perhaps become necessary in the present situation, distinctive to which is the on-going *War on Terror*. In particular, it seems highly pertinent to explore the relationship between the corporate economy and the imperatives of the national security discourses that have emerged in South Asia since 11 September 2001. What kind of structures of accumulation can flourish in highly militaristic economies? What in fact are the structural affinities between firms geared towards profit and states geared towards defence, construed in conservative realist terms? In India for instance, the defence industry, India's hallmark of state power and sovereignty, has been opened up for 100 per cent private Indian ownership, along with a 26 per cent foreign participation. These new forms of enmeshment or 'coupling' between the state and the private sector need to be analysed with much more rigour.

One critical effect of the rise of militarism, is that political and economic decision-making becomes heavily contingent on the notion that the nation is perpetually in a 'state of war'. In South Asia today this certainly seems to be the case. There are two dimensions of the 'state of war': a political one and an economic one. The political dimension is associated directly with the threat of war, from external aggression as well as subversive anti-national acts by particular social groups; to protect citizens from this threat, the requirement is *a well-armed state*. The economic dimension invokes the need for a *strong economy, with high levels of macro-economic growth* and organised corporate power. The preoccupation with these two goals justifies a disproportionate allocation of resources towards national security and macro-economic growth – aggravating as a consequence the existing crises of development.[1] These crises are increasingly reflected in resistances, conflict, social unrest, activism, and so on, which threaten the legitimacy of the governments. Instead of responding to these resistances through strategies which can redress the underlying causes, these governments are increasingly showing a tendency to use them as justification for militarism and policies consonant with it. In this way, we see the conscious creation of a vicious circle: the deeper the crises in development, the greater the militaristic and economistic response, resulting in a further deepening of the crises.

Let us return to this point later – and proceed now to examine the problem I posed above.

The current context

As I noted at the outset, the economic and political situation in South Asia is a cause for grave concern. Beginning with Pakistan, we have the following grim picture from a noted commentator:

> Domestic and international debt of around $68 billion is today equivalent to 97 per cent of Pakistan's GDP; the economy continues to be in a recessionary state and investor and business confidence is still at a low level where it has been for at least the last two years; all governments since 1988, including the incumbent military one, have adhered to IMF structural adjustment programmes which have had very negative consequences on the economy; ironically, however, our dependence is so severe that Pakistan's economic machinery would come to a halt if it was not for multilateral and bilateral 'aid' and for bail-out packages, hence talk of 'self-reliance' is a rude joke; 36 per cent of Pakistan's population lives below the poverty line, and this trend has increased sharply in the last decade; many of our social indicators are amongst the worst in the world, with Pakistan located amongst the poorest 20 per cent of independent nations, both in terms of GDP per capita as well as human development.[2]

For Bangladesh, Quadir notes:

> Despite Bangladeshis apparent success in restoring macroeconomic balance in the last decade, the country continues to face major challenges to improve the nation's rather dismal record of human development. The impressive growth of the economy, which grew more than 5 percent a year throughout the 1990s, appears to have failed to create an opportunity for more than half of its 130 million population living below the poverty line. The country still has the highest incidence of poverty in the region, making it evident that Bangladesh is in need of adopting a pro-poor/pro-employment growth strategy.... What seems more disappointing is that the 'strong' growth of the economy proved to be unsustainable as enhanced economic vulnerability brought about mainly by external shocks in the new millennium negatively affected the performance of

the economy. In the financial year of 2001, consolidated fiscal deficits rose to 8 percent of GDP while domestic public debt increased to TK. 400 billion, which is equivalent to 15 percent of GDP. The country's foreign exchange reserves also hit the lowest level in ten years declining to $1.3 billion US in March 2002. Such deteriorating macroeconomic conditions already prompted the donor community to call for the implementation of a more aggressive stabilization and economic reform program.[3]

A similar malaise, not surprisingly, persists in Sri Lanka. As Embuldeniya notes, while profits of companies listed in the Colombo Stock Exchange 'have increased by 86 per cent from Rs 2.1 billion in the last quarter of 2001 to Rs 3.9 billion in the first quarter of 2002', the 'diversification of the economy away from its traditional reliance on commodity exports and low-value products remains too slow to generate a significant increase in incomes.'[4] In India, by many indicators, corporate profits are at a record low, aggregate demand is sluggish, and growth rates are repeatedly being projected downwards. In part, of course, this is a reflection of the global trends; however, it is also increasingly being acknowledged that the reforms are not able to take the South Asian economies into a path of steady growth. There are two critical aspects of the problem. The first is a continuing crisis of governance within the leading economic institutions. The second involves the continuing insufficiencies in consumer and industrial demand. In India, for instance, large lending institutions – especially public sector banks are reportedly finding it difficult to identify feasible outlets for investment. Similarly, the stock market, allegedly the fulcrum of the new economy, has been unable to provide the expected stimulus to small savers/investors. As a recent study has revealed, the average middle-class Indian is not looking to invest his/her money in the stock market. In India, the collapse of the major savings institutions such as the Unit Trust of India (UTI) is symptomatic of the problematic consequences of economic liberalisation.

Broadly speaking, the economic reforms were expected to solve precisely these two problems of governance and lack of economic stimulus. So what went wrong? There are two dominant hypotheses in this regard. The first suggests that these are short-term problems of adjustment which will disappear over time. The second suggests that there may be inherent problems in the way the reforms have been designed and implemented. Both these lines of analysis devote more attention to the macro-level than the micro-level, and even fewer consider the two in tandem. In particular, scant attention is given to the underlying processes through which corporate profits are generated and distributed. This is precisely where the focus of this work lies: in delineating the practices of profit generation and the underlying structures of accumulation, with a view to examining their potential impact on development. It is critical for such an exercise to posit at the outset what is meant by development. While a full debate on the normative justifications of underlying models of development is outside the scope of this chapter, we can proceed with a few observations. The *mixed economy* framework that characterised South Asia over the last five decades, had as its premise the following elements of development:

- a strategic emphasis on developing a modern corporate sector;
- a sustained increase in assets, incomes and skills of workers, through direct intervention and participation of the state in the economy;
- a gradual democratisation of the realm of production, again through an active intervention of the state in promoting rights of workers and citizens.

According to this model, the state was to undertake two somewhat contradictory tasks. On the one hand, it was to actively aid, promote and subsidise the accumulation of private capital. On the other hand, the state was to legitimise such accumulation by ensuring that it did not jeopardise certain minimal requirements of social equity. Most importantly, it was to contain untrammelled growth of private accumulation by retaining control over the general direction of the economy. Second, the state was to directly own, control and operate large-scale enterprises in some key sectors of the industrial economy. Third, to whatever extent possible, the state was to provide some basic elements of social welfare to its citizens. Of foremost importance, however, was the attempt to develop a modernised corporate sector with active state intervention.[5]

The effects of the model were, of course, different in different South Asian economies. By most counts, however, the experiment failed to deliver on its promises and came to be seriously criticised from both sides of the political spectrum. Those on the left saw the *mixed economy* as having failed to deliver even the minimal requirements of human development, because of the state's primary allegiance to capitalist accumulation; those on the right argued that the cumbersome mechanisms of state intervention have been singularly responsible for the absence of economic growth.[6] Since the late eighties, this government failure thesis inspired a different model of development, that is, one compatible with neo-liberalism. There is little need to re-state here the presuppositions of a neo-liberal model of development: it should suffice to note that with neo-liberalism, development is largely treated as a 'residual' – determined by a minimally regulated market system of prices and incentives. The assumption is that under such a system markets would clear, generating as a 'natural' consequence optimal outcomes with respect to growth and employment (barring, of course, institutional rigidities, imperfections and information asymmetries). A central factor in the success of this process will be the degree to which domestic economies are globally integrated.

The contrast between these two models of development will inform our analysis, in particular by helping us to assess whether the underlying strategies of accumulation in each of the models are actually able to fulfill the developmental aspirations. While it is already known that such success has been limited, the interconnections between the failures and the underlying institutional dynamics of the corporate economy are relatively less frequently explored. Further, putting them in a comparative context, as we have attempted to do here, should help us in answering a question that has become popular these days, viz., whether there exists a regional model of capitalism in the developing world – similar to the Anglo-American, European and Japanese models of the advanced capitalism.

In order to explore the issues raised above, we proceed as follows. First, we need to examine the relationship between corporate capitalism and economic growth as explicated in the relevant literature on corporate capitalism. Next, we will examine whether these theoretical premises hold in the context of capitalism in developing economies, in particular those where the genesis of corporate capitalism has occurred in the context of colonialism. In what follows, I will first discuss the theoretical premises and then go on to discuss the question of context, drawing upon the various contributions in this volume. The effects of context and specificity are themes which have been explored in different ways by the authors here. Cheema, for example, in his study of the relationship between accumulation and corruption in Pakistan argues that 'achieving zero-corruption is akin to the zero-transaction cost market-efficiency benchmark in economics, which we all know is unattainable; nonetheless, economists continue to use it as a benchmark. What this does is strengthen the neo-liberal position as it justifies recommendations for liberalisation even though it is quite likely that in certain economies liberalisation may well be inefficient.' For India, Basil and Harris-White show how the corporate economy functions through a much more complex structure of accumulation than is suggested by the standard literature. In order to appreciate the full import of these divergent approaches, I begin with a discussion of the standard literature.

Corporations and economic growth: the arguments

There are several strands of literature I wish to consider, each of which offers explanations as to how modern corporations may contribute to development. In what follows, I will discuss five approaches to the question:

(a) the organisational learning argument (as advanced by Chandler, Amsden *et al.*);
(b) the aggregate demand argument (of Boyer and the Regulationists);
(c) the transaction cost argument (as developed by Coase and Williamson);
(d) the classic finance-theoretic arguments about the centrality of shareholder value maximisation (Friedman, Miller and other Chicago economists);
(e) the corporate strategy-centred argument that critiques the finance-theoretic model (Porter and Prahalad).

Consider first the Chandler-Amsden theses that emphasise the following aspects of the corporate form:

• its ability to exploit economies of scale;
• its ability to recruit and develop the kind of human capital necessary for using and commercialising new technologies as soon as they come into existence;
• its ability to become the primary driver of technological advances and the seat of continuous learning (Chandler and Daems, 1980; Chandler *et al.*, 1997).

As is well known, Chandler emphasises the superiority of the corporate form with respect to its ability to learn and commercialise technology, and argues that despite the fact that the rise of the large corporation led to the early emergence of distorted market structures, such distortion aided – rather than hindered – overall industrial growth rates in the US. A similar argument about the efficacy of oligopolistic capitalism to engender technology-driven economic growth has been made more recently by Baumol (Baumol, 2002).[7] Baumol points out the many interesting ways in which oligopolistic markets manage to fare much better at generating and managing innovation than other economic regimes. The commodification of knowledge that occurs under oligopolistic capitalism creates, according to Baumol, the appropriate set of incentives and price structures that produce a continuous stream of innovations. In a true Schumpeterian fashion, Baumol sees these innovations as the major driver of capitalist expansion, and, as some have already noted, conspicuous by absence is any regard to the role of the state in fostering these processes. Neither does one see any critical appraisal of the problem of commodification of knowledge.

With regard to the institutional dynamics underlying oligopolistic capitalism, Amsden makes an essentially similar argument (in my view, even more powerfully) in the context of ('late') development; she demonstrates exactly how the South Korean state harnessed the organisational strengths of oligopolistic enterprises, while at the same time *being able to deter typical profit strategies associated with oligopolistic behaviour from dampening the speed of growth.* This point is absolutely critical in understanding the dynamics of growth through big business in East Asia. It provides not only an explanation of East Asian growth, but can also give us important pointers as to why such growth was also conducive to increasing material well-being of East Asian workers, as well as a continuous enhancement of their skills and abilities. This could explain in turn, why East Asia's record of income distribution has been much better than that of the US. However, none of these East Asian successes can take away from the essentially undemocratic political structures to which East Asian workers (and civil societies) were subjected, especially during the miracle years (although assessing them simply by contrasting them to the structures of formal democracy in the West is not likely to be useful).

Why, then was it the case in East Asia that growth-dampening oligopolistic behaviour could be contained? Several answers are available in the literature. Amsden, for instance, argues that the answer lies in the particular abilities and visions of the East Asian bureaucracy. Others draw upon the uniqueness of Confucian ethics. Business historians and corporate strategists offer yet a third explanation: namely, that East Asian companies place little value on market profits relative to the expansion of size, assets and 'corporate honour'. As McCraw (1997: 543) points out:

> If there is any one key to the Japanese economic miracle, it lies in the maintenance of a fever pitch of inter-firm competition that by the 1990s had persisted without abatement into its fourth decade. This

remarkable aspect of Japanese capitalism is insufficiently understood in the West, and its importance is often underestimated even by Japanese scholars. It is a competition that emphasises market shares as much as profit, if not more. It is a ceaseless, almost obsessive drive to uphold the status of the company – not for the purpose or with the aim of driving domestic competitors out of business, but of maintaining position and corporate honour, and of avoiding shame.

Adherents of this latter view attempt to break with the strong statist interpretation of East Asian success, which portrays business as a passive partner in the process of development (Johnson, 1982; Evans *et al.*, 1985; Amsden, 1989; Haggard, 1990). Not surprisingly, business historians often reject this passive image, as they salvage from the archive of corporate histories the various corporate strategies, decision-making processes and value systems that contributed to the growth process (McCraw, 1997). In any case, the fact remains that the East Asian economies were able to prevent some of the common growth-retarding effects of oligopolistic behaviour (the most important of which was to retain price-based competition), which in turn was predicated on continuous 'learning'. This ability, it may be argued, also accounts for the more egalitarian distribution of income that it produced (at least), relative to the US and other parts of the developing world – despite the absence of any state-administered redistributive measures.

As has often been argued, this technology-centred argument is necessarily incomplete in that it ignores the other side of the equation, that is, the problem of demand. What made this continuous learning, expansion and commercialisation feasible? What guaranteed the requisite increases in the size of the market? The answer to this question is fairly straightforward in the East Asian case: markets were found abroad. As is well known, a number of scholars have identified this outward-orientation of the East Asian regimes as their primary source of growth, and the inward-orientation of countries like India as the primary reason for their stagnation (Krueger, 1974; Bhagwati, 1988; Bhagwati and Srinivasan, 1999).

In the case of the West, however, it is not enough to point to the importance of exports; the dynamics of the domestic market also must be explained. Neither Chandler nor the other growth theorists of his genre address this issue in a fully satisfactory way. Was there anything particular to classic Fordist capitalism that ensured the expansion of aggregate demand? As Boyer (1996) argues, the fact that in the Fordist model productivity gains were directly translated into wage increases led in turn to a synchronisation of productivity increases and aggregate demand. In addition to Continental Europe where this certainly was the case, Boyer argues that this held true even in the US until the seventies when US Fordism allegedly entered its process of structural decline; the 'golden phase' in the US was also marked by an unprecedented reduction of wage differentials which resulted in a similar synergy between growth of productive capacity and aggregate demand (Boyer, 1996: 51). Boyer then goes on to make an even stronger argument. Contrary to the neo-liberal assertion that the redistributive elements of Fordism are responsible for its decline, the truth may in fact be the reverse: it is exactly those elements of redistribution, rather than technological learning, that accounts for the 'golden age', both in the US and the Continent.

While I accept the general thrust of Boyer's theses, it is important to add to it the economic relationships between the developing world and the West that also contributed to the rising aggregate demand during the golden age. The relationship between the two worlds which occurred in the period immediately following decolonisation and under the aegis of the World Bank formed a central pillar of growth under the Fordist regime. Let us return to the question of aggregate demand at a later point, and for now, go on to consider several other strands of relevant literature. I wish to consider next, the Coase-Williamson type of argument that corporations create wealth by minimising transaction costs. Despite the growing popularity of this literature, transaction cost economics can have only limited relevance to the problem of development, even when 'development' is conceptualised in a narrow sense (Bardhan, 1989, 1998). For this approach, because of its normative and epistemological commitment to neo-classical economics, does not provide us with a theory as to why particular transaction costs evolve in particular economies – or more generally why particular institutions emerge in particular contexts. Neither can it explain why 'inefficient' institutions persist over long periods of time. As Bardhan (1989) argues, these 'non-explanations' reflect a fundamental problem with the approach, that is, its total disregard for the issues of power and inequity.

Next, consider the classic shareholder value maximisation (SVM) argument put forward by Friedman, Miller and their cohorts from the Chicago School. The essence of the argument is, of course, as old as corporate capitalism itself, namely, businesses create value by maximising wealth for their shareholders. In this model, there is no possibility of a shortage of aggregate demand; according to a tenet that economists call Say's Law, in this model an increase in supply automatically creates an increase in demand.

This model has been further developed by finance theorists to argue that as providers of equity capital, shareholders are the *residual claimants* who bear most of the risk, and they accordingly should receive the lion's share of the rewards. Other corporate stakeholders – customers, employees and local communities – should be *adequately* compensated and no more. Implicit in this view is a clear hierarchy of corporate objectives – in which the maximisation of shareholder value reigns supreme, and 'the ultimate scorecard for managers becomes the current stock price – or more precisely, stockholder returns over a definite time horizon' (Prahalad, 1997: 51).

This orthodox finance-theoretic model has been strongly criticised by corporate strategists like Porter, and more recently by Prahalad (1997). Porter's argument is that in order to contribute to economic growth, companies must remain globally competitive. Global or macro-competitiveness in turn, depends on how well companies invest in *intangibles* like the building of strong networks, process improvements, employee training and so on. In Porter's view, the US system – with its focus of near-term profitability and shareholder value – discourages investment in intangibles and hence undermines the prospects for the long-term growth of the economy. Porter (1997) and Prahalad (1997) puts forward an even stronger argument: that no significant change in corporate behaviour can be brought about unless we acknowledge that corporations must add value in a way that all its stakeholders' interests are ascribed equal primacy. This would imply eschewing the hierarchy of stakeholders in which shareowners reign supreme, and corporate goals are oriented towards the maximisation of shareholder value. The obvious problems of the value maximisation approach are apparent to us at this moment perhaps as never before.

Both Porter and Prahalad note that the East Asian and European systems of corporate governance are better equipped to discourage short-termism and allocate investment in favour of intangibles. This is so because both these systems are able to control the extent to which the capital market is able to shape corporate – and even some social objectives. However, they also acknowledge, particularly in the wake of Euro-sclerosis and the Asian crisis, that those systems are also flawed in that there is too little external disciplining (this in fact is the immensely popular thesis advanced by Paul Krueger). What they propose, therefore, is an amalgamation of the two models; their suggested model, however, is quite different from the one that seems to be evolving in Europe, East

Asia and in other parts of the developing world. While they suggest designing governance mechanisms that combine the interests of the various stakeholders – with a clear reduction in the importance of the *stockholder* – what is occurring in reality is quite the opposite. As the Indian case clearly demonstrates, the *maximisation of shareholder value* is clearly the shared objective of all the critical actors: the state, business, international donors, foreign institutional investors as well as a fairly large and influential community of scholars associated with many leading institutions in India and abroad. Echoes of a similar commitment to shareholder value can be heard in Mexico, Brazil, South Africa and in much of the developing world, as well as in the transitional economies of Europe. Of crucial importance here is also the global emergence of mechanisms that seek to *legitimate* the concern for shareholder value, especially in the developing world – through the creation of codes, norms of governance and the various schemes intended to demonstrate corporate social responsibility.

The somewhat obvious, yet critical, point about SVM which is largely ignored in the corporate strategy is that profit strategies which maximise shareholder value often inhibit development; in other words, there may be a fundamental and systematic incompatibility between an SVM-driven strategy and macro-economic growth. The incompatibility is obviously likely to be stronger if we look for redistributive growth; the important point, however, is that the possibilities of expansion may be severely limited even without the criterion of redistribution. To state the point in strongest terms, the claim that SVM drives growth is hardly sustainable: what SVM does drive is corporate growth in the (very) short term. Theories which claim a positive relationship between the SVM model and the macro-economic growth are premised on a false equation between corporate growth and macro-economic growth.

Furthermore, SVM has the potential of pitting the interest of the shareholder against that of the worker. Consider, for instance, the famous Yorkshire businessmen, James Hanson and George White who, during Margaret Thatcher's regime, were held as paragons of British business and awarded peerages for their performance as wealth-creators. Hanson became particularly noted for 'commitment to his shareholders' and his ability to acquire companies that continuously maximise share-holder value. The strategy to accomplish this did not, however, come from the growth and expansion of the businesses acquired. Rather it came 'from closing factories, from shedding labour, from pension holiday's and appropriating surpluses in pension funds, from avoiding stamp duty on purchases by shuffling assets internationally, by tax evasion through the use of 26 Panamanian companies, etc.' (Hampden-Turner and Trompenaars, 1993: 314). The more recent experience with employee stock option schemes (ESOPs) offered by companies such as Enron confirms our suspicions to an even greater degree.

In contrast to these Anglo-American approaches to wealth creation, consider the Japanese/East Asian strategy:

> One key factor in Japanese growth was the willingness to invest heavily in both product development and process development for more than two decades while cash returns were low and growing too slowly... Over the same period many American firms were actually ceding products and functions to foreign competitors and diversifying into less risky and more profitable areas such as car rentals and financial services, unrelated to their original lines of work.[8]

Given the turmoil that occurred in Asian corporate economies, we are now legitimately more wary of the East Asian model. However, the debate on the Asian crisis is fairly divided as to whether the crisis was caused by the Asian model or by the incoherent super-imposition of the Anglo-American model on the Asian context. As Bardhan has argued,

> .... Many of the institutional and governance structures that have delivered growth with equity in East Asia over a reasonably large period are not replicable in other societies... and may not deliver as well even in East Asia in the future, since these structures have a particular history and a particular context. But by the same logic, the Anglo-Saxon super model that the market missionaries push with tireless evangelical zeal is also not easily replicable in other societies where the process of social, political, and economic history has been singularly different.[9]

Two major observations emerge from the above. First, the claim that a neo-liberal macro-economic model premised on the supremacy of SVM can lead to a self-sustaining growth path is not borne out by history. There is even less evidence that such a model can work in the context of less developed economies. Second, and more critical perhaps is the concern that the model has been imposed in political–economic contexts where they are ill suited. In other words, models of corporate governance must be considered within the broader political–economic framework. Table 1.1 below presents the three models of corporate

Table 1.1 Models of corporate capitalism

	Anglo-American	Continental	East Asian
Primary economic objective	Micro-economic, private accumulation	Growth with redistribution	Macro-economic growth
Nature of the state	Liberal	Corporatist	Developmental
Nature of markets			
Labour markets			
Inducement to high effort	High unemployment and efficiency wage	High involvement induces effort even with low unemployment	Combination of flexible employment strategies and life-time employment
Compensation	Contractual wages	Wages plus profit sharing	Wages plus bonus
Wage differentials	High differential as incentive for individual advancement	Low differential for increased group solidarity and cohesiveness	Low differential for increased group solidarity and cohesiveness
Employment security	Low: dismissal is credible threat for discipline	High security to promote identification with enterprise	Combination of low and high security
Training costs	Paid by individual to increase marketability	Paid by firm and state as long-term human capital investment	Paid by firm and state as long-term human capital investment
Other benefits to workers	Determined and paid at employer's discretion, with input from trade unions which have relatively low bargaining power	Determined by trade unions and the state	Determined and paid at employer's discretion, with input from trade unions which have relatively low bargaining power

Macro-environment	Can adjust to and contribute to larger recessions with layoffs	Works better with and contributes to fewer and smaller recessions by avoiding layoffs	Can adjust to and contribute to larger recessions with layoffs because of flexible employment
Product & factor markets			
Relationship	Arm's-length, market-oriented and competitive	Long-term relation based on commitment, trust and loyalty	Long-term, state-mediated relationship between economic agents
Product	Standardised (to foster competition)	Customised to buyer or seller	Customised to the export market
Curb to opportunism	Exit and competition	Voice, commitment, and trust, state regulations	State regulations
Capital markets			
Relationship	Arm's-length and market-oriented finance, with the capital market as the central allocating agent	Long-term relational finance, with banks as the central allocating agent	Long-term relational finance, with banks as the central allocating agent
Time perspective	Short-term	Long-term	Long-term
Costs of equity	Low costs since no sharing of income or control rights with workers	Lower costs for internal equity since workers already share some income and control rights	Equity has much less importance than debt

Source: Adapted from Stiglitz (1999).

governance which show how they are embedded and their different dimensions.

Such a framework allows us to assess more fully the nature and impact of the reforms, and the conventional wisdoms about the nature of peripheral capitalisms which seem to drive the reforms. At the present conjuncture, there are four such wisdoms that seem to have become hegemonic:

(1) Path dependency of peripheral capitalisms, to the extent that they exist, can be overcome through appropriate changes in corporate governance;
(2) Corruption and rent-seeking are the primary causes of inefficiency of accumulation in the periphery;
(3) These inefficiencies can be corrected by reducing state intervention through the introduction of economic reforms and globalisation;
(4) Globalisation and economic reforms, in conjunction with an Anglo-Saxon model of corporate governance have the potential to fundamentally alter corporate behaviour.

Conventional wisdoms and South Asian realities

Path dependency of peripheral capitalisms, to the extent that they exist, can be overcome through appropriate changes in corporate governance

Let us begin with the question of path dependency. There is now a voluminous literature on path dependency especially in the context of globalisation. The debate here is well known. As against the popular thesis that globalisation is bringing about convergence in the structures of production and accumulation, some authors have argued that such change is less evident. In the context of advanced industrial economies, Hollingsworth argues that a society's system of production is path dependent and very specific. Drawing upon a comparative study of the manufacturing sectors in Japan, the US and Germany, Hollingsworth shows that the adoption of certain common management practices does not in any way indicate a fundamental transformation of the underlying structures of production (Hollingsworth and Boyer, 1997). The notion of convergence, that Hollingsworth critiques here, is even more readily hypothesised in the context of developing countries; in fact in the case of the latter, convergence is posited as an unmitigated 'good' which should be engineered in order to improve economic performance. This view of the convergence reflects yet another problematic notion that the obstacles to convergence emanate from elements of 'tradition', viz., caste, religion, ethnicity and so on.

As Basile and Harris-White demonstrate in this volume, the convergence/path dependence debate needs to be more cognisant of the dynamic nature of the *path* itself. In particular, this chapter illustrates how a static reading of 'tradition' and its associated elements leads to an erroneous understanding of peripheral capitalisms. Using the analytical framework of *social structure of accumulation* (SSA), the authors show how the elements of tradition such as caste, patriarchy and religion work in unison to strengthen the hegemonic position of the capitalist class. They identify this structure of accumulation as *social corporatist* – and one which is structured through many dimensions, such as occupation, commodity, party politics, religion, gender and locality. However, the most prominent single category, according to the authors, comprises caste – and similar occupational associations. Set in the context of a small town in Southern India, the authors write with respect to the role of caste:

> The interplay between caste and the economy may be differentiated but it is consistent with corporatism. Corporatism, let us recapitulate, limits class conflict inter alia by involving both capital and labour in the 'self government' of the economy. It rests on two pillars, one institutional and one ideological. Together they impregnate production relations to generate the overlap between economy and society that is the distinctive feature of corporatism. In this we think caste plays a triple role. First, it provides an ideological backcloth for the corporatist 'project'. At the same time it generates (and is consistent with the formalisation of) the institutional structure on the back of which corporatist organisations have evolved. In this urban society, caste **still** supplies the hierarchical order.[10] Through caste, the link between ideology and institutions is particularly strong. The ideology itself (in distinguishing castes) is the source of the institutions (caste and closely-related, finely-defined occupational associations). Furthermore, caste helps in the creation of the conditions for the overlap between economy and society that is necessary to the working of the corporatist project. The corporatist ideological and institutional framework imprints production relations, the main features of which can be distinguished according to: (1) class relations; (2) gender; (3) the local territorial organisation of the urban economy and (4) relations between the urban economy and the state.

Basile and Harris-White's discussion on caste as well as the respective roles of gender, locality and the state in the SSA reveals the extremely complex dimensions of peripheral capitalisms that the simplistic framework of convergence cannot accommodate. Similarly, the notions such as the Hindu Rate of growth are unable to capture the flexibility with which caste and religion may accommodate the ideological bases of the existing structures of accumulation.

While Basile and Harris-White focus on the ideological aspects, a historical anaylsis of the material dimensions of structures of accumulation also show high degrees of path dependency. As I have discussed elsewhere, the model of accumulation that emerged in South Asia during the colonial period has proved to be remarkably resilient to different policy regimes, including the recent changes since 1991. The central feature of this pattern of accumulation was that it enabled firms to generate and sustain high profits without expanding output (as characteristic of an oligopolistic rather than a competitive economy), or undertaking product and process innovations. Accumulation in this model became a direct outcome of concentration, non-competitive pricing policies, and political patronage, circumscribed by an extreme skewness of assets and incomes that is characteristic of an underdeveloped economy. In the context of the First World War, a well-known Indian historian writes:

> While the war meant misery ... for the majority ... it also contributed to fabulous profits by business groups taking advantage of the War demand, the decline in foreign competition, the price differential between agricultural raw materials ... and industrial goods, and the stagnation or decline in real wages (Sarkar, 1983: 171–2).

Similarly, in the context of the disastrous famines in 1943, which killed three million people, the same author writes:

> Yet war and famine also meant super profits for some, and as in 1914–18, a major step forward for the Indian bourgeoisie. ... The really fantastic increase was not in production but in profits, particularly speculative gains through profiteering in food, share market operations and the black market in general. The Indian bourgeoisie was a specific kind of bourgeoisie, characterised by a 'ravening greed', and a mania for speculation rather than initiative or efficiency in production (Sarkar, 1983: 406–7).

The primary structure of governance which enabled this pattern of accumulation in colonial India was the *managing agency system*. The terms *managing agents* and *managing agencies* were used to designate individuals or business firms (partnerships or private companies) that entered into a legal contract with joint stock companies to manage the corporate affairs of the latter. Initially, managing agencies were predominantly established by merchant families. These merchant families were attracted to the managing agency system primarily because of two reasons:

(1) it allowed for a quick turnover of capital; and
(2) it also allowed a small quantity of capital to be spread over a relatively large number of ventures.

These two features permeated the rubric of the Indian corporate system in a very fundamental way.

The managing agency was a novel development in that it shifted the locus of corporate power and corporate control from the level of the individual joint-stock company to what was, in effect, a parent or apex company, viz., the managing agency. (In this regard, the managing agency system was a precursor of the industrial conglomerate, as we know it today.) Another characteristic of the system was that most Indian managing agencies were founded as partnerships among members of a single family. This nexus between the managing agency and the business family established the structural basis for the family-controlled conglomerates that have dominated the Indian economy since independence.

The developmental implications of these profit strategies are several. At one level, it allowed for an accelerated pace of accumulation of capital which aided the process of industrialisation. However, the process did not encompass systematic backward and forward linkages but developed out of the *ad hoc* profit-seeking tendencies of businesses. In other words, the logic of laissez-faire capitalism, while succeeding somewhat in bringing about industrial development in the West, failed to produce the same in South Asia's colonial context. Specifically, being circumscribed by the managing agency model, this process failed to generate social wealth either in the form of wages or shareholder incomes. Managing agents blatantly violated the basic rights of shareholders, and sought consciously to exclude them from having any effective voice in the manner in which firms were run (Rungta, 1970).

Quite predictably, the monopolistic character of accumulation also characterised other South Asian economies. As Cheema argues in the case of Pakistan, until the early eighties the capitalist class in Pakistan was largely organised around the monopoly houses which belonged to migrant trading communities, which settled and conducted business in the urban areas of United India, outside the areas which came to constitute Pakistan (Papaneck, 1962; Amjad, 1983; Cheema, 1999). These houses are characterised by family ownership under a centralised decision-making authority, usually the patriarch of the family, and consist of several legally separate companies engaged in highly diversified activities. Furthermore, there is no separation of ownership from control in the case of these houses.

In Bangladesh and Sri Lanka, the degree of state involvement was somewhat higher in the period following decolonisation. In Bangladesh, the public sector was in total control of the country's manufacturing sector until the beginning of the 1990s. State-owned enterprises (SOEs) represented some 92 per cent of the entire manufacturing sector in the mid-1970s. The state also had a monopoly in the commercial sector. Most banks and insurance companies were under the direct control of the state; the dominance of the public sector over the flow of international trade was also overwhelming. In Sri Lanka, a very similar situation prevailed until 1977, albeit with a stronger emphasis on social development. As is well known, Sri Lanka was able to achieve much higher levels of human development than other developing countries, although many of these gains were reversed once economic reforms were attempted to correct the contradictions of its inward-looking state-led model of capitalism. What exactly were these contradictions? As we pointed out above, one major tenet of the conventional wisdom in this regard is about the role of corruption. This is what we turn to now.

Corruption, governance and intervention

The conventional wisdom about corruption and misgovernance is the central focus of Chapter 6.[11] He provides a critique of the neo-liberal approach to corruption by exploring the problem of *inefficient accumulation* in Pakistan over the recent decades. Examining the case of Pakistan's key manufacturing sector, 'spinning', Cheema finds that 'the standard explanation, based on poor policy choice, cannot explain why state policy was consistent with both high rates of accumulation and productivity during the sixties'. In fact, Cheema demonstrates that there was not much change in either the magnitude or the nature of policy transfers for the spinning sector between the sixties and the eighties. In spite of this, productivity growth plummeted in the latter period.

The explanations based on looting, corruption and rent-seeking are equally lacking. These explanations encounter two problems. Firstly, again, they cannot explain why processes of rent-seeking and corruption resulted in efficient accumulation during the sixties. Secondly, they cannot explain the manner in which these processes lowered the efficiency of accumulation during the eighties and nineties. To be useful, explanations based on rent-seeking and corruption must reveal the manner in which these processes inhibited efficient accumulation during the eighties and nineties. In order to understand the role of these processes as constraints on efficient accumulation, the changing context of political power and state organisation during the eighties and nineties must be mapped out. Such a mapping out of the context of political power reveals a critical difference, Cheema suggests, between *efficient* and *inefficient* accumulation.

As Cheema demonstrates, during the sixties the structure of corruption was consolidated and centralised. It set incentives for a centralised bureaucracy to reward capitalists offering the highest economic spending power in an inter-temporal context. This structure was sustainable as it was based on repeat play between a small bureaucracy and a numerically small, and politically weak, capitalist class. The *de facto* outcome of this structure was that it promoted efficient accumulation. However, Cheema points to two reasons as to why this structure unravelled during the seventies. Firstly, the civil service reforms of the seventies weakened and fragmented the state. Secondly, there was a fragmented growth of 'transfer-seeking' coalitions that were bidding for state 'transfers'. Zia-ul-Haq, by incorporating these fragmented factions into the state structure, produced the phenomenon of *decentralised corruption*. The distinctive feature of *decentralised corruption*, in Cheema's view, is that it ended up shortening the time horizons of both state officials and the new 'transfer-seekers'. This created incentives for both sides to maximise short-term payoffs, even if they came at the expense of long-term efficiency.

One consequence of this structure was that state allocation of credit to industry no longer necessarily benefited the efficient firms. As a result there was significant entry of low productivity firms in the sector, which reduced sectoral efficiency. Matters were made worse by loss-making firms' ability to negotiate political bailouts. In short, by the eighties-nineties the structure of rent-seeking and corruption had become inconsistent with efficient state-led accumulation.

Some analysts argue that the only way in which the 'new' structure of corruption can be addressed is by minimising the state. While the role of the state has to be clearly reduced in certain areas, Cheema expresses serious reservations about a complete withdrawal of the state, given the current predicament of Pakistan. Cheema's observations, read in conjunction with the current political turmoil in Pakistan with respect to the process of democratisation, set the context for examining the claims as to whether reforms can correct the kind of inefficiencies in accumulation that occur in peripheral capitalisms. Here, the contributions on Bangladesh and Sri Lanka by Quadir and Embuldeniya respectively give us important insights. As both these chapters indicate, the issue is not simply that reforms are unable to correct inefficiencies; it is rather that the reforms were neither designed nor implemented with the intent of correction. So what in fact was the underlying intention? While the answers are somewhat obvious, it is important to engage briefly with the context in which the reforms were motivated.

Economic reforms as a corrective to inefficient accumulation

As Quadir concludes from his discussion of the reform process in Bangladesh:

> Successive regimes treated market reforms as an instrument to build and maintain political coalitions – in particular with traders and industrialists. In exchange for political support, they allowed business elites to use market liberalization programs as the primary tool to attain their financial and economic objectives. As a consequence, economic liberalization programs hardly contributed to the improvement in the macroeconomic management of the economy. Nor did they succeed in achieving the goals of human development.

Quadir goes on to show that the two military regimes of Zia and Ershad in Bangladesh used economic reform programmes largely as a tool to both legitimise and consolidate their unconstitutional power base. They allowed big business to emerge as a major player in national decision-making, which in turn adversely affected the state's ability to either enforce contracts or to develop a mechanism for redistributing assets. Both the Generals also encouraged, albeit indirectly, the country's financial and economic elites to accumulate huge wealth through the abuse of scarce public resources. In return, not only did big business lend its political support to the legitimisation of the military regimes; perhaps more importantly, businessmen and industrialists also contributed generously to the coffers of the ruling parties, helping them to expand their political support base. Quadir goes on to observe that a similar trait characterised the democratically elected regimes of both Mrs Zia and Sheikh Hasina: economic reforms did not appear to be a means of improving either the performance of the economy or the living standards for the majority. Here too, economic reform programmes substantially increased the power of the business elites and further reduced the state's ability to develop an effective regulatory framework for efficient accumulation.

This particular pattern of motivation of the economic reforms goes directly to explain why reforms do not result in overall stimulation of the economy. As I have argued elsewhere, the primary contradiction, which characterised the context in which the reforms were undertaken, was manifest in the fact that despite considerable growth in accumulation, and fairly high levels of profitability, the effects of this growth were hardly evident on the rest of the economy. It is this contradiction that we should take as the starting point for our assessment of the post-interventionist model. While the post-interventionist model encompasses several fairly far-reaching institutional changes, the model is potentially highly capable of deepening the existing hiatus between the corporate sector and the rest of the economy. The potential is rooted in the particular assumption on which the post-interventionist model is premised; that is, the key to unleashing the growth dynamics in peripheral economies lies in increasing levels of corporate profitability. As in the interventionist era, there is little focus on the *content* of corporate profits; that is, the various strategies that firms are likely to employ in order to realise increased profits. Will these profit strategies be based on increased innovation or, as in the previous era, on price and output manoeuvres? Will they increase employment and incomes? Will they involve patterns of corporate financing that free up scarce state resources for deployment elsewhere?

In my recent work on India, I have found that the theoretical answers that are available – from either the neo-classical or the institutionalist perspective – seem to be somewhat simplistic. The institutionalist assumption – that certain market logic can be set in motion by simply establishing an ensemble of legal/institutional mechanisms – is fraught with great contradictions. Most fundamentally, by assuming the problematic nature of the state, and the complex of motivations behind its attempts at institutional change, institutionalists provide us with few analytical categories with which to understand the specificities of the reforms as they unfold in each different context. The fallacy of the neo-classical assumption is also equally apparent. Contrary to the principal neo-liberal claim that reforms bring about a separation between state and business, what emerges as a critical structural characteristic of the post-interventionist era in India is the positive association between corporate growth and increased state support.[12] This continuity with the interventionist era is rather striking. Indeed, it is manifest in the way public resources continue to be deployed in an otherwise 'liberalised' regime: through state-led demand management programmes, through increased disbursement from financial institutions, through increased state spending on infrastructure, through sacrifices in the state's revenue incomes as a result of tax concessions and so on. The distributional (and political) implications of this are obviously complex and far-reaching. But leaving that aside for a moment, let us focus attention on how such a continuing relationship between corporate growth and state support disrupts the logic of the post-interventionist model. The premise of this model is that, by reducing direct economic participation of the state, the distortions of the incentive mechanisms that occurred under the interventionist regime can be corrected. Such a corrected, 'marketised' incentive mechanism will then generate growth. However, the incentive mechanisms produced by the reforms do not reflect any substantial increase in the degree of marketisation; there is no clear evidence of increased competitive pressures on firms; further, there is no evidence at all that state involvement now is any less unidirectional than in the previous regime.[13] In fact, the reverse may be true (Mukherjee Reed, 2001).

Quadir's analysis also raises some doubts about the globalisation thesis popular both amongst the left and the right, namely that economic reforms are an inevitability that has been imposed externally on the developing world. While there is little doubt that globalisation has imposed some major constraints with respect to macro-economic policy, domestic responses to the demands of globalisation were not necessarily pre-ordained. In that sense, the responses to globalisation from South Asia reflect particular choices of the ruling elites in South Asia, and could have been different had a different set of social relations existed in South Asia. Embuldeniya finds the same for Sri Lanka. In Sri Lanka economic reforms began in 1977, under the aegis of the newly elected United National Party government. The impetus for this reform programme was multi-fold: growing internal and external financial imbalances, increasing rates of unemployment and so on. In this context, reforms were seen as a major stimulus to strengthening the balance of payments, improving industrial production, increasing employment, and expanding private sector-led economic activities. The reforms, aimed at transforming the highly state-controlled economy to a more liberalised one, resulted in the rapid growth of large-scale firms and a relative diversification of industry. Not surprisingly, the results with respect to income and employment growth have been less than satisfactory; but more importantly, the reforms remain unable to solve the structural crisis of the Sri Lankan economy.

Let us proceed now from the macro- to the micro-aspects of the reforms. As we stated above, these changes constitute a critical element of the conventional wisdom about peripheral capitalisms.

> Globalization and economic reforms, in conjunction with an Anglo-American model of corporate governance have the potential to fundamentally alter corporate behaviour.

Table 1.2 represents the firm-level or corporate governance reforms that South Asian countries have embraced between the later eighties and now.

What has been the actual impact of these changes on the corporate sector? Chapter 3 specifically explores this issue in the context of India, but with a focus that is different from existing studies. Unlike existing studies which focus on the corporate sector as a whole, Sarkar and

Table 1.2 Changes sought in the post-interventionist model

Changes in corporate governance, structure and ownership	Changes in the macro-economy
• Free pricing of shares	• Deregulation of the capital market
• Buyback of shares	• Deregulation of the banking sector
• Foreign ownership of corporate equities	• Deregulation of trade policy
• Reduction of capital controls	• Convertibility of the current and the capital account
• Relaxation of controls on inter-corporate investments	• Repeal of the Foreign Exchange Regulation Act (FERA)
• Relaxation on limits to expansion and diversification of corporations	• Liberalisation of foreign investment and technology regimes

Sarkar analyse the impact of liberalisation at the disaggregated level of distinct ownership groups that have historically co-existed in Indian manufacturing. The objectives of their study are two-fold. The first is to describe how the process of economic liberalisation, through the implementation of the various trade and industrial policy measures, is expected to change the institutional environment of the different ownership groups. The second is to empirically analyse the impact of liberalisation on the performance of companies in the various ownership groups against the background of the institutional changes noted above.

As the authors explain, the motivation for studying institutional changes and performance impacts by ownership groups comes from two sources, each having policy implications in the context of an emerging economy like India. The first is the literature on ownership and corporate governance which analyses why potential differences in performance may exist between public and private companies as well as among companies under different forms of private ownership, and how changes in competitive market conditions may iron out the existing ownership differentials. This debate has implications for the policy issue as to whether privatisation is necessary in an increasingly liberalised environment, and in the event it is deemed so, what forms of private ownership are likely to be optimal.

The second is the literature on the political economy of structural reforms which argues that policy reforms like trade and industrial liberalisation could render losses to the status quo and create new constituencies that gain from the reforms, thereby leading to a new set of 'gainers' and 'losers' (Rodrik, 1994). While the exact distributional consequences cannot be predicted with certainty as reforms may have 'unanticipated' effects on constituencies, be these on the supporters or on the opponents (Krueger, 1993), there is little disagreement in the literature that the sustainability of reforms depends on their impact on powerful pressure groups, especially in developing countries. In many such countries, dissatisfaction among such groups has threatened the political stability, brought down governments and reversed the reforms process (Rodrik, 1994; Martinelli and Tommasi, 1997).

In India, companies with different ownership status have co-existed in the corporate sector, with public sector companies playing a relatively dominant role since the country's independence in 1947. Within the private sector, there are both domestic and foreign companies, and within each, companies belonging to business groups co-exist with standalone companies. With the recent reforms transformation, the relative importance as well as the fortunes of these different groups is likely to be affected so as to throw up 'gainers' and 'losers' on the way.

With respect to the level of performance, the study found significant and persistent profitability and efficiency differentials between private and public companies. Private companies, as a group, perform significantly better than public companies throughout the entire period of nine years in the study. Regarding performance differentials *within* private ownership groups, the finding is that while there are some differences in performance between domestic and foreign companies, and within each group, between standalone and group companies, these differences are not statistically significant. These results thus suggest that ownership effects within the private sector do not exist at the broad group level. *Ownership effects, if any, must be related to the level, and possibly to the composition, of equity ownership.*

Coming to the response of the different ownership groups to the liberalisation process – the main focus of the chapter – the authors find that the liberalisation process has thrown up 'gainers' and 'losers' from each of the ownership groups.

Strikingly, it is observed that those who gained were in fact the under performers of the pre-reform period while those whose performance declined were the performers of the earlier period. This is true for all ownership groups. This result indicates that the lifting of regulations has enabled under-performing companies to achieve their potential whereas companies which were well tuned to the license-raj and protected markets and earning profits are the ones which are finding it difficult to cope with market pressures. Among the "gainers", we find competitive pressures to have somewhat narrowed down the performance differentials across the various ownership groups. However, we do not find similar effect for the "losers". For the losing companies we find significant performance differentials to persist among the various ownership groups.

In an indirect way, this analysis also points in the direction of path dependency, a point that emerges even more clearly in Chapter 5. D'Costa examines with great rigour three leading sectors in India – steel, auto and software – and comes to the conclusion that:

The evolution of these sectors reveals a changing face of Indian corporate capitalism. However, it is not a break with the past. The growth of Indian trade-based capital under the British was consolidated and differentiated under the protective umbrella of the state in the pre-reform period. New capitalists emerged in the continuing redistribution of state largesse within the dominant coalition. Family firms remained important and political/personal connections were crucial in their expansion under a regulatory regime. Monopoly control of markets remained the principal strategy of most firms, which also dictated their diversification strategies. However, the gradual professionalization of management, including family members, fostered industrial learning and sharpened modern commercial knowledge. With changes in the regulatory regime, Indian capitalists were well-positioned to respond to new opportunities and constraints thrown open by reforms. The backlog of Indian technology and increased competition prompted Indian firms to seek foreign technology (steel, auto), foreign equity (auto, software), and foreign markets (software). Liberalization has also allowed Indian capitalists to venture abroad, not only deepening sectoral integration but also contributing to an increasingly mature and differentiated capitalist class.

How are these new profit strategies affecting the overall dynamics of the economy? Interestingly, contrary to the general perception that the software industry has been the driving force behind the structural change in the nineties, D'Costa's finding is that software actually shows the least change in terms of innovations. In his view, 'the work carried out has involved low-value, mostly non-innovative tedious tasks, such as coding and testing. Thus far, India's exports of on-site services have not been on the cutting edge.[14] Similarly, off-shore services, such as multinationals setting up subsidiaries in India, have taken advantage of low-cost, skilled workers for exporting services to their parent company.' This observation, quite similar to the one made by Peter Evans in his comparative work on India, South Korea and Brazil, goes to validate our concerns about the reform process. The concern, once more, is about the ability of the reforms to alter the underlying structures of accumulation in a manner that unleashes the productive capacities of the economy. With respect to this question, the evidence is largely negative, although not without some positive indications. Sarkar and Sarkar's study does demonstrate that some underperformers under the previous regime had improved performance in the new regime. This indicates that it is necessary to undertake much more systematic research as to the underlying causes of performance differences; as well it is necessary to map out whether these performances reflect the dependence on short-term strategies or they reflect more substantive correction of inefficiencies.

Towards a conclusion

We examined above, through a variety of approaches, those conventional wisdoms about South Asian economies which have inspired the on-going economic reforms and the changes in corporate governance. The debate about the efficacy of these reforms also continue to be dominated by these conventional wisdoms, often resulting in a polarised opposition between advocates of economic reforms and its opponents. As many have stated, however, that the choice between the reforms as they have been instituted so far and the pre-reform scenario is a false one.

Rather than reiterating this debate here, I would like to conclude by raising some of the issues I raised at the outset, in particular, the issue of rising militarism in South Asia. There are two important features of this phenomenon. The first is the international linkages, in particular the deepening ties with Israel and the US.[15] The second is the growing participation of the private sector in defence. Recently the Confederation of Indian Industries (CII) – the largest business association in India – collaborated with the Ministry of Defence to organise an international event to showcase India's military capabilities. As emphasised by India's Minister of Defence at the event, India will be concentrating all its efforts in developing the capacity of the corporate sector to produce military equipment to take advantage of the huge markets globally, within India, and its 'neighbourhood'. Viewed in the context of heightening tensions in South Asia, these developments indeed are a cause for concern. It is in this context that need to identify the structural affinity between corporate sectors geared towards profit and states geared towards defence, construed in such conservative realist terms.

Some pointers are available from the US, noted historically for its military-industrial complex – which signifies a highly symbiotic relationship between the defence industry and the state. The symbiosis was at its height during the Cold War. Since the end of the Cold War, there has been significant consolidation in the US defence industry. Many of the mergers and buyouts that have occurred in the last decade are the result of the *Last Supper* which took place in 1993, when the then Secretary of Defense Les Aspin urged top industry officials to consolidate or go out of business. Aspin correctly noted that the dissolution of the Soviet Union would mean lower defence budgets and fewer contracts, resulting in surplus production capacity in the industry. This situation has changed considerably since 11 September. On 26 October 2001, amidst deep recesssion in most sectors of the US economy, the Pentagon awarded $300 billion contract to Lockheed-Martin – the largest single defence contract issued by any state in history, which is estimated to mature into a $1 trillion a year business for the company.

Is such a military-industrial complex likely to emerge in South Asia? In Pakistan, which one author recently described as an 'army with a state', the conditions may well be ripe. Some seminal research in these areas point us towards some interesting hypotheses. As Agha suggests in her analysis of Pakistan, the military has a huge commercial empire, involving the airlines, banking, real estate, production, oil and gas, education, security services and other industries. The financial worth of this empire would be around $50 billion. As Agha points out,

> ... with an absolute lack of transparency of military's business, it is difficult to conclude that the military controlled business foundations have contributed towards economic well being. The study found no evidence that these businesses were making a profit. Unlike Indonesia, where such activities are used to carry out off-budget financing, Pakistan's military foundations were found to be diverting resources from the annual defense budget for their survival. This fact alone has negative repercussions for economic planning.[16]

The critical point in this context is that the military has historically played a proactive role in business. This was particularly true of the military government of Ayub Khan which had the specific intention of improving the revenue generation capacity of the state and the economy. This was the only way that the military could benefit in terms of getting resources for its institutional infrastructure and major weapons procurements.

In India, where traditionally the military has had a limited role to play and the private sector barred from participation in defence, the situations seemed to have changed dramatically in that direction. Bangladesh, Nepal and Sri Lanka are caught in cycles of violence where the governments respond determinedly through military means.

Obviously, a very active research agenda is required in order to capture these developments, central to which must be an effort to reconceptualise the state and its relationship to other institutions, most notably organised corporate capital and the military. In this context, it is necessary, first and foremost, to discard the popular view that the nation-state is moving inextricably towards its demise during the present era of globalisation. It is our hope that the chapters in this volume offer some pointers in this direction, and helps to focus our attention on the nature of the state in all its complexity and contradictions.

Notes

1 Mia, Z. 'The Poverty of Security', in *Rethinking Development, Rethinking Security*, Sustainable Development Policy Institute, Islamabad, Pakistan, 1996.
2 Zaidi, A. 'Pakistan: Political Economy of Peace', *Economic & Political Weekly*, 12–18 February 2000.
3 See contribution in this volume.
4 See contribution in this volume.
5 However, as I have argued elsewhere, there is a need to break with the liberal/interventionist dichotomy that has been so central to the understanding of the state in traditional social science. As I hope this discussion will reveal, this dichotomy does not take us very far in comprehending the complexity of the state's role in developing capitalism in much of the developing world. On the one hand, the state remained quintessentially committed to a model of liberal capitalism. This was reflected, amongst other things, in the body of corporate law fashioned after the British model. On the other hand, the state sought to regulate capital in a somewhat substantive way, often exceeding the requirements of liberal regulation. Some elements of this regulation, however, often pertained to fairly routine or trivial aspects of corporate management; while these might have imposed certain restrictions on the powers of management, they were unlikely to have radically altered the nature of the capitalism that emerged.
6 For views from the left, see Bagchi, A.K. *The Political Economy of Underdevelopment* (Cambridge: Cambridge University Press, 1992); Kurien, C.T. *Global Capitalism and the Indian Economy* (New Delhi: Orient Longman, 1994). For views from the right, see Ahluwahlia, I.J. *Industrial Growth in India: Stagnation Since the Mid-Sixties* (New Delhi: Oxford University Press, 1985). Bhagwati, J. and P. Desai, *India: Planning & Industrialization* (New Delhi: Oxford University Press, 1970).
7 Baumol, W.J. *The Free-Market Innovation Machine: Analyzing the Growth Miracle of Capitalism* (Princeton, NJ: Princeton University Press, 2002).
8 Excerpted from *Made in America: Regaining the Productive Edge*, The Massachusetts Institute of Technology Commission on Industrial Productivity, 1989, cited in (Hanmpden-Turner & Tompernas, 1993: 184).
9 Bardhan (1997).
10 An order entrusted to the state in the Italian case (Mancini *et al.*, 1983).
11 For a general review of the issues see Bardhan, P. 'Corruption and Development', *Journal of Economic Literature*, September 1997.
12 For instance, with respect to the deceleration in GDP in 1997–98, the *Economic Survey* states that 'the deterioration of growth is perhaps even worse, if

one takes into account the fact that fully one percentage point of growth is attributed to the 20 per cent increase in real value added in the "public administration and defence sub sector" arising chiefly from pay increases to government servants' (*Economic Survey 1999*, Ministry of Finance, Govt of India, Chapter 1, p. 1).

13 Following Alice Amsden I distinguish between reciprocal and unidirectional intervention. 'The premise of late industrialization is a reciprocal relationship between the state and the firm.... It [reciprocity] means that in direct exchange for subsidies the state exacts certain performance standards from firms' (Amsden, 1989: 146). By contrast, *unidirectional* intervention occurs where the state continues to augment accumulation even when capital consistently defies standards of behaviour or performance set by the state. It also implies intervention where the state may choose to augment accumulation without requiring or specifying a priori, anything in return.

14 Heeks, R. *India's Software Industry: State Policy, Liberalisation and Industrial Development* (New Delhi: Sage, 1996).

15 Bedi, R. 'The Tel Aviv connection grows', New Delhi: Indian Press Service, 26 July 2002; Swami, P. 'A deal and some posers', *Frontline*, Volume 19, Issue 10, 11–24 May 2002.

16 Siddiqa-Agha, A. *Power, Perks, Prestige and Privileges: Military's Economic Activities in Pakistan*, Jakarta, 16–19 October 2000.

References

Ahluwahlia, I.J. *Industrial Growth in India: Stagnation Since the Mid-Sixties* (New Delhi: Oxford University Press, 1985).

Amjad, R. 'Industrial Concentration and Economic Power in Pakistan', in H. Gardezi and J. Rashid (eds), *Pakistan: The Unstable State* (London: Zed Press, 1983).

Amsden, A.H. *Asia's Next Giant* (Oxford: Oxford University Press, 1989).

Bagchi, A.K. *The Political Economy of Underdevelopment* (Cambridge: Cambridge University Press, 1992).

Bardhan, P. 'The New Institutional Economics and Development Theory: A Brief Critical Assessment', *World Development v*, 17 September 1989, pp. 1389–95.

Bardhan, P. 'Corruption and Development', *Journal of Economic Literature*, September 1997.

Bardhan, P. 'Development Thinking Today in an Asian Perspective', in L. Emmerij (ed.), *Economic and Social Development into the 21st Century* (Baltimore: Johns Hopkins University Press, 1997).

Baumol, J. *The Free-Market Innovation Machine: Analyzing the Growth Miracle of Capitalism* (Princeton, NJ: Princeton University Press, 2002).

Bedi, R. 'The Tel Aviv Connection Grows' (New Delhi: Indian Press Service, 26 July 2002).

Bhagwati, J. and P. Desai. *India: Planning & Industrialization* (New Delhi: Oxford University Press, 1970).

Bhagwati, J.N. 'Export-Promoting Trade Strategy: Issues and Evidence', *World Bank Research Observer*, 3(1), pp. 27–57, 1988.

Bhagwati, J.N. and T.N. Srinivasan. 'Outward Orientation and Development: Are the Revisionists Right?' (New Haven: Yale University, Economic Growth Center, 17 September 1999).

Boyer, R. 'The Seven Paradoxes of Capitalism. Or is a Theory of Modern Economies Still Possible?', CEPREMAP, Paper no. 9620, October 1996.

Chandler, A.D. Jr and H. Daems (eds). *Managerial Hierarchies: Comparative Perspectives on the Rise of the Modern Industrial Enterprise* (Cambridge Mass. and London: Harvard University Press, 1980).

Chandler, A.D., F. Amatori and T. Hikino (eds). *Big Business and the Wealth of Nations* (Cambridge: Cambridge University Press, 1997).

Cheema, A. 'Rent-Seeking, Institutional Change and Industrial Performance: The Effect of Regulation on the Productivity Growth Performance of Pakistan's Spinning Sector 1981–1994', PhD Dissertation submitted to The University of Cambridge, Sidney Sussex College, Cambridge, 1999.

Evans, P.B., D. Reuschemeyer and T. Skocpol (eds). *Bringing the State Back In* (Cambridge: Cambridge University Press, 1985).

Government of India, *Economic Survey 1999* (New Delhi: Ministry of Finance, 1999).

Haggard, S. *Pathways from the Periphery: The Politics of Growth in Newly Industrializing Countries* (Ithaca, NY: Cornell University Press, 1990).

Hampden-Turner, C. and A. Trompenaars. *The Seven Cultures of Capitalism: Value Systems for Creating Wealth in the United States, Japan, Germany, France, Britain, Sweden, and the Netherlands* (New York: Currency Doubleday, 1993).

Heeks, R. *India's Software Industry: State Policy, Liberalisation and Industrial Development* (New Delhi: Sage, 1996).

Hollingsworth, J.R. and R. Boyer (eds). *Contemporary Capitalism: The Embeddedness of Institutions* (Cambridge, New York: Cambridge University Press, 1997).

Johnson, C. *MITI and the Japanese Miracle: The Growth of Industrial Policy, 1925–1975* (Stanford, California: Stanford University Press, 1982).

Krueger, A.O. 'The Political Economy of the Rent-Seeking Society', *American Economic Review*, 64(3), pp. 291–303, 1974.

Krueger, A. 'Virtuous and Vicious Circles in Economic Development', *American Economic Review*, 83, pp. 351–5, 1993.

Kurien, C.T. *Global Capitalism and the Indian Economy* (New Delhi: Orient Longman, 1994).

Mancini, O., F. Perrillo and E. Zagari (eds). *La Teoria Economica del Corporativismo*, Volumes 1 and 2 (Napoli: ESI, 1983).

Martinelli, C. and M. Tommasi. 'Sequencing of Economic Reforms in the Presence of Political Constraints', *Economics and Politics*, 9, pp. 115–31, 1997. Reprinted in Sturzenegger, F. and M. Tommasi (eds), *The Political Economy of Reform* (Cambridge, Massachusetts: The MIT Press, 1998), pp. 285–304.

McCraw, T. 'Government, Big Business, and the Wealth of Nations', in A.D. Chandler, F. Amatori and T. Hikino (eds), *Big Business and the Wealth of Nations*.

Mia, Z. 'The Poverty of Security', in *Rethinking Development, Rethinking Security*, (Islamabad, Pakistan: Sustainable Development Policy Institute, 1996).

Mukherjee Reed, A. *Perspectives on the Indian Corporate Economy* (Basingstoke: Palgrave, 2001).

Papaneck, G. 'The Development of Entrepreneurship', *Economic Review*, 52(2), pp. 46–66, 1962.

Porter, M.E. 'Capital Choices: Changing the Way America Invests in Industry', in Donald H. Chew (ed.), *Studies in International Corporate Finance and Governance Systems* (New York: Oxford University Press, 1997).

Prahalad, C.K. 'Corporate Governance or Corporate Value Added: Rethinking the Primacy of Shareholder Value', in Donald H. Chew (ed.), *Studies in International Corporate Finance and Governance System* (New York: Oxford University Press, 1997).

Rodrik, D. 'The Rush to Free Trade in the Developing World: Why so Late? Why Now? Will it Last?', in Stephen Haggard and Steven B. Webb (eds), *Voting for Reform: Democracy, Political Liberalization, and Economic Adjustment* (New York: Oxford University Press, 1994), pp. 61–88. Reprinted in Sturzenegger, F. and M. Tommasi (eds), *The Political Economy of Reform* (Cambridge, Massachusetts: The MIT Press, 1998), pp. 209–40.

Rungta, R.S. *The Rise of Business Corporations in India: 1851–1900* (Cambridge: Cambridge University Press, 1970).

Sarkar, S. *Modern India* (Delhi: Macmillan, 1983).

Siddiqa-Agha, A. *Power, Perks, Prestige and Privileges: Military's Economic Activities in Pakistan*, Jakarta, 16–19 October 2000.

Stiglitz, J. *Labor Participation and The East Asian Crisis* (Washington: World Bank, 1999), Accessed online.

Swami, P. 'A Deal and Some Posers', *Frontline*, **19**(10), 11–24 May 2002.

Zaidi, A. 'Pakistan: Political Economy of Peace', *Economic & Political Weekly*, 12–18 February 2000.

2
Legitimization, Patrimonialism, and Regime Consolidation: The Myth of Market Reform in Bangladesh

Fahimul Quadir

Bangladesh's search for a free market economy began in the mid-1970s, long before structural economic reform had appeared on the agenda of the International Financial Institutions (IFIs) such as the World Bank and the International Monetary Fund (IMF). Over the last 27 years, successive regimes, both military and civilian, undertook wide-ranging reform policies that led to the creation of what is often called a market-friendly framework for economic governance. Their policies focused primarily on restructuring the public sector, adopting an export oriented growth strategy, strengthening the private sector, liberalizing the trade and exchange regimes, and establishing an enabling environment for economic growth.

Most studies claim that after more than a quarter century of experiments with market reform, Bangladesh's economy is still struggling to both sustain macro-economic stability and develop a framework for rapid economic growth. Despite some progress in stabilizing the economy in the early 1990s, the sudden increase in fiscal deficit, record low foreign exchange reserves, weak balance of payment situation, a revenue short-fall, and the crash of capital markets have already called into question the ability of Bangladesh to restore the fiscal health of its economy through liberalization programs. What concerns policy-makers and development practitioners most, however, is the slow progress that Bangladesh has made in improving its dismal human development record. The performance of the economy, which grew 5 per cent a year during the 1990s, proved to be inadequate to alleviate the country's poverty conditions. Bangladesh still has the highest incidence of poverty in the region. Some 45 million people, in other words, half of its 89 million rural population live below the poverty line. The deteriorating poverty situation in urban areas is making things even worse. A vast majority of the poor have little or no access to education, health care, safe drinking water, and other essential services.

The World Bank blames 'the unfinished reform program' for the failure of the country to bring the poor out of poverty. It therefore focuses on the need for further accelerating reforms, 'choosing the high road of faster policy and institutional reforms' (World Bank, 1995: xvii). In contrast, a number of authors have criticized the international creditor community for imposing inappropriate reform policies that failed miserably to address the unique socio-economic reality of Bangladesh (Sobhan, 1993).

This study, however, questions both of these analyses. By comparing and contrasting major interpretations of why and how market reforms failed to bring about desired socio-economic results, it argues that economic reforms were used primarily to consolidate the power of the ruling elites. Successive regimes treated market reforms as an instrument to build and maintain political coalitions, in particular, with traders and industrialists. In exchange for political support, they allowed business elites to use market liberalization programs as the primary tool to attain their financial and economic objectives. As a consequence, economic liberalization programs hardly contributed to the improvement in the macro-economic management of the economy. Nor did they succeed in achieving the goals of human development.

This chapter is comprised of four main sections. It first looks critically at the liberalization measures undertaken by General Ziaur Rahman (1975–81). Section two presents an explanation for the political use of pro-market reforms by General Hussain M. Ershad's (1982–90) military regime. In particular, it analyzes why a military general focused more on the ways of developing a political coalition with key socio-political actors for his contested regime, than developing a healthy market mechanism. The third section provides an account of the failure of the two democratically elected regimes of Khaleda Zia (1991–96) and Sheikh Hasina (1996–2001) to both enact and enforce laws necessary to improve governance in the financial sector. By identifying the main constituencies of Mrs Zia and Sheikh Hasina, it examines the growing role of big business in the country's decision-making. The last section offers some concluding remarks based on its main findings.

General Zia: legitimization and regime consolidation through economic liberalization

The severe financial and economic crisis that General Zia had inherited from the Awami League (AL) regime created the ground for his neo-liberal regime to initiate a formal search, for a better alternative to the excessively interventionist development model adopted by the Mujib government that came into power after the inception of Bangladesh in 1971. Zia's desire to move away from the state-led development approach was clearly manifested in December 1975, when his military regime announced its first major economic policy which came to be known as the Revised Investment Policy (RIP). One of the major objectives of this RIP was to allow the private sector to play a major role in national economic development. It emphasized the need for transferring State Owned Enterprises (SOEs) to the private sector and encouraged private entrepreneurs to invest in all but 8 strategically important sectors. The RIP significantly increased the ceiling of private investment to Tk 100 million and announced that the state would never nationalize any private enterprises.[1] It offered compensation to those Bengali and non-Bengali owners who had suffered financial losses due to the Mujib regime's nationalization program. The RIP also opened up new opportunities for foreign investors and facilitated the formation of the country's first Export Processing Zone (EPZ) in the port-city of Chittagong (Government of Bangladesh, 1976: 228–9).

Central to Zia's pro-market reforms was a comprehensive disinvestment program that allowed private investors to become the engine of Bangladesh's economic growth. A series of actions, including the creation of a Disinvestment Board, were undertaken simply to facilitate the role of the private sector in both industrialization and capital mobilization. The Disinvestment Board, for instance, was given the responsibility of implementing the regime's just announced privatization policies. Efforts were made to foster private investment, largely through the reactivation of the Dhaka Stock Exchange and the establishment of an Investment Promotion Center in Dhaka. Zia's military regime also directed Development Finance Institutions (DFIs) to provide massive financial support to private entrepreneurs leading to the emergence of the DFIs as the major financial source of private investment in Bangladesh (Sobhan and Mahmood, 1991: 158).

Restoring macro-economic balance also appeared to be a priority of the government. Complying with the conditionalities set out in the IMF/World Bank sponsored adjustment and/or Extended Fund Facility

(EEF) programs, the military regime undertook measures to reduce budget deficits, reform the public sector, restructure the tax system, lower inflation, withdraw subsidies on items such as food, fertilizer, and petroleum, increase exports, improve the country's foreign currency reserves, and liberalize the trade regime. The government also announced different policy measures designed to develop a competitive exchange rate policy for the Bangladeshi currency (Rahman, 1994: 13–14).

While it appeared that Zia's major concern was to ensure a rapid recovery of the collapsing economy, empirical evidence suggests that his market-oriented reforms were driven primarily by his political goals. He was indeed smart enough to realize that his military regime suffered from a severe crisis of legitimacy as its rule was based on military might rather than the consent of the electorate. The need for him to stay in power thus demanded that his 'unconstitutional government' make efforts to both develop a popular support base and generate a new political coalition.

As a pragmatic politician, he clearly understood the inability of any interventionist development strategy to keep him in power for a longer period of time, let alone expand his support-base. From mid-1974, the pressure for liberalizing the economy was gradually mounting. The World Bank had already begun to push the Mujib government to embark upon a denationalization program so that the private sector could come to play a key role in the economy (Islam, 1977: 246). The assassination of Mujib in August 1975 added a new dimension to the growing power of such external actors. Both the IMF and the World Bank saw the demise of Mujib's center-off left political regime as an opportunity to pursue their market-driven economic policies. They did not hesitate to use Zia's political vulnerability to the advantage of the global forces of production and finance. The IMF and the World Bank increased their pressure upon Zia's military regime for immediately abandoning the statist approach adopted by the Mujib regime.

The pressure from key domestic actors, namely the emerging Bengali entrepreneurs, and high-level bureaucrats and technocrats, was also increasing as they began to demand an immediate improvement in the business environment. Importantly, while most of these actors never lent their support to the AL's interventionist development strategy, they kept their silence until the weakening of Muzib's popular support. Given the extremely disappointing economic results of Muzib's so-called socialist policies, these traditionally powerful actors start to exert their political influence for opening up the economy in general, and for stimulating private investment, in particular.

Zia grabbed this rare conjuncture to form an anti-Awami League and anti-socialist political coalition designed to allow him to both stay in power and mobilize popular support in favor of his military government (Franda, 1982: 223). His target was to develop tactical alliances with such dominant politico-economic groups as civil–military bureaucratic elites, businessmen, and industrialists. His initial focus, however, was limited to the creation of a political coalition comprised mainly with Western-educated senior civil and military officials, and professionals. Considering them as his strategic allies, he decided to heavily rely upon senior civil–military bureaucrats, which was clearly reflected in the formation of his first Council of Advisors. The 17-member Council was composed of 7 senior civil bureaucrats/technocrats, 5 professionals, 3 former chiefs of the armed forces, and 2 politicians (Alam, 1993: 313). As part of his attempt to make such groups his coalition partners, he continued to focus on the appointment of bureaucrats, military officials, and technocrats as his advisors and/or cabinet ministers throughout his rule (Islam, 1988: 122). Such a trend remained largely unchanged even after the completion of both the presidential and parliamentary elections. In 1981, for instance, senior civil bureaucrats and high level military officials dominated his so-called civilian cabinet. Of the 24 members, civil–military bureaucrats occupied a total of 17 positions, accounting for some 70 per cent of the total (Islam, 1988: 123).

Apart from the bureaucrats and professionals, Zia's military regime drew its support from both established and emerging industrial and business elites of Bangladesh.[2] As Zia began to legitimize his 'unconstitutional power-base' through a program of what is known as 'civilianization of military regimes', he went on to expand his coalition mainly by incorporating traders and industrialists.[3] After becoming his key partners, these influential business and industrial groups offered financial and political support to Zia's legitimization initiative. Both in the presidential elections of 1978 and in the *Jaitya Sangsad* (parliamentary) elections of 1979, Zia and his newly formed political platform 'the Bangladesh Nationalist Party' (BNP) received huge funds from businessmen and industrialists, which greatly helped Zia and his party candidates meet their massive election expenses. Much of these funds were spent lavishly on pleasing and entertaining the voters. What is more interesting to mention is that the candidates never bothered to report their actual campaign costs as the Election Commission did very little to either monitor or audit their election expenditures (Kochaneck, 1993: 226).

Zia's attempt to make big business his coalition partner became more evident in the *Jaitya Sangsad* elections of 1979. About 28 per cent of the newly elected BNP members of the *Jaitya Sangsad* were traders and industrialists, thus emerging as the largest occupational group in the parliament. By contrast, the professionals and bureaucrats/technocrats accounted for 26 and 13.4 per cent of the BNP members of the *Jaitya Sangsad* respectively. Zia's effort to find a commanding position for the newly become 'millionaires' was also reflected in the composition of the BNP Executive Committee in 1981. The businessmen and industrialists constituted 33.5 per cent of the BNP Executive Committee, which allowed them to come out as a dominant actor in the Party's decision-making process. Following the *Jaitya Sangsad* elections of 1979, Zia also appointed four businessmen as cabinet ministers. Such a move was a clear indication of his desire to share state power with the large trading families of Bangladesh (Islam, 1988: 123).

It was no wonder that the business–industrialist group used Zia's political weakness to its own politico-economic benefit. Knowing that Zia would always turn to them for political and financial support, they were able to develop a true patrimonial state structure in Bangladesh. This is, however, not to say that, without Zia's tacit consent and involvement, the state took a 'patrimonial' shape. On the contrary, General Zia deliberately offered legal and illegal, formal and informal, economic and political concessions to business and industrialist groups. In return for donations and political support by business to his legitimization process, Zia indeed allowed them to use public resources to enhance their personal and organizational goals. The government, for instance, showed its reluctance to instruct relevant financial institutions, including Bangladesh Bank, to design and implement a tighter credit policy. It overlooked large-sale tax evasion and made little efforts to enforce legal provisions.

In particular, the use of economic reform programs to benefit a small group of traders and industrialists was reflected quite clearly in the privatization of SOEs, which was the major component of his market liberalization program. His military regime seemed to have done nothing to identify the broad objectives of the privatization program. Nor did it make any meaningful attempts to justify the government's decision of embarking on its program of transferring SOEs. What is even more important is that, unlike most adjusting nations, Zia and his policy advisors did not seek to generate revenues from the sale of public enterprises. Although it is a common practice that the market should determine the value of an SOE and the unit should be sold for cash, most

SOEs were virtually sold for what Palmer calls 'give-away prices' (Palmer, 1994: 31). The buyers did not have to invest their money to purchase a public enterprise. Subsidized credits from public funds were made readily available to them. Furthermore, the entire process of transferring SOEs to the private sector lacked transparency. The government hardly bothered to keep the people informed about the process of valuation and formal negotiations that took place between the state and interested buyers behind close doors. Nor did it consult with the labor unions to address their concerns. The government overlooked the need for launching a public awareness campaign as to the goals of privatization, which eventually contributed to the development of political opposition to economic reforms. Almost all trade union federations demanded the scrapping of the government's privatization program.

The government–business relationship also reduced the military regime's ability to develop an appropriate legal and regulatory framework essential to enhance competition and efficiency of the private sector as well as to protect public interests. This in effect encouraged private entrepreneurs to quickly become rich by misusing public resources. A considerable number of buyers of SOEs and private investors, who borrowed money from different DFIs, emerged as 'willful defaulters' as they refused to service their debts. Most of them invested money in non-productive and even illegal areas of business, thus making huge unreported profits (Maniruzzaman, 1992: 219). Virtually no legal action was taken against them as they continued to enjoy political patronage from General Zia's regime. In other words, corruption began to find institutional foundations during the rule of Zia, who himself admitted that 'corruption and misuse of power have led to the wasting of almost 40 per cent of the total resources set apart for development' (Puchkov, 1989: 171–4). Despite his awareness of such a deplorable situation, he did not take any initiatives to either develop a well-defined legal framework or to enforce existing laws in order to prevent what Tat Yan Kong calls the 'private misappropriation and abuse of public funds' (Kong, 1996: 49).

While such a mutually dependent relationship between the government and big business severely undermined the ability of the government's economic reform programs to live up to its expectations, it indeed enabled Zia to legitimize his unconstitutional regime. The political and financial support he received from big business gave him a great deal of confidence in successfully carrying out the so-called civilianization programs. He registered a landslide victory, for instance, in the presidential elections of 1978, receiving 76 per cent of the total votes cast.

Likewise, the voters responded positively to his 19-point program in the *Jatiya Sangsad* elections in 1979. His BNP had no difficulty whatsoever in securing a two-thirds majority in the parliament (Khan, 1984: 179–80). By contrast, during his five-year rule, the opposition remained highly fragmented and therefore failed to build a momentum in its fight against military authoritarianism.[4] Part of the reason for their inability to mobilize popular support in general, and to draw support from the business community in particular, was that, unlike the ruling party, they did not have any control over the established post-independence 'patronage' system (Kochaneck, 1993: 229).

General Ershad: market reform and the emergence of a patrimonial state

General Hussain M. Ershad's military takeover in March 1982 dramatically changed the pace of market-oriented economic reforms in Bangladesh. Soon after the seizure of power, General Ershad introduced his reform package through the declaration of his New Industrial Policy of 1982 (NIP). Drawing upon Zia's pro-market reform strategy, this economic restructuring program aimed to accelerate the process of privatization and improve the policy framework mainly to institutionalize the role of the private sector in economic development. Such a program further limited the scope of the public sector and focused on the urgent need to ensure macro-economic stability (Government of Bangladesh, 1983: 87–8).

Hoping to speed up the process of both economic and financial liberalizations, the military regime announced its second reform package in 1986, which was popularly known as the Revised Industrial Policy of 1986 (RIP). This reform package was designed primarily to further expand the role of the private sector in general, and to stimulate private investment – both local and foreign – in particular. It was aimed also to strengthen the on-going processes of adjustment and stabilization. The RIP sought to accelerate the process of privatizing SOEs through a number of measures, notably the return of industrial units to their original owners, disinvestment of industries that were left abandoned by their Pakistani owners, and the conversion of SOEs into public limited holding companies largely through selling off the shares to ordinary people and employees. As part of its goal of achieving higher levels of efficiency, this reform program promoted the idea that the management of public sector corporations might be handed over to interested private management companies (Government of Bangladesh,

1988: 70). Ershad's military regime expected that such a provision would eventually stop the drain on the national budget. Apart from these, it also undertook quite a few important measures to deregulate the financial sector and to liberalize the trade, particularly the import regime.

In brief, unlike Zia's hesitant approach, Ershad adopted a more focused and aggressive path to the market. His privatization program, for instance, was not limited to the transfer of either loss-making SOEs or strategically insignificant, small-scale industries. It aimed to transfer all sorts of industrial and commercial enterprises, including a number of key industries in the jute and textile sectors, to the private sector. Within a year of the announcement of the NIP, Ershad's military regime transferred the ownership of 60 large jute and textile industries to private investors (Humphrey, 1990: 60). In addition to this, the government continued to hand over the ownership of 'profit-making' public enterprises. The number of such profit-making units transferred to the private sector rose from 32 per cent in 1981 to 78 per cent in 1985 (Sobhan and Ahsan, 1984: 47).

This raises an inevitable question: Why did Ershad adopt such a radical approach to the market? While most studies blame the international donor community for pressurizing the military regime to speed up the country's on-going market reform programs, this study looks at the internal politico-economic dynamics to identify the factors that led Ershad to undertake a relatively aggressive path to the market. After his ascension to power, General Ershad dealt with a rather complex political situation that Zia never confronted during his entire tenure. Despite Ershad's promise of quickly restoring democracy, eliminating corruption, bringing back people's confidence in the deteriorating law and order situation, and rebuilding the economy, he found himself in a position that was less than welcoming (Hakim, 1993: 11). The country seemed to have been surprised by the military takeover of General Ershad that took place only five months after the presidential election through which the country was slowly returning to civilian rule. Justice Sattar's democratically elected government was enjoying a high level of approval rate when Ershad seized power. Thus, it was no surprise that the coup drew widespread condemnation from all major socio-political groups, including students, workers, journalists, and university professors. These civil society groups wasted very little time to launch a massive resistance movement against Ershad's military dictatorial regime – a situation that General Zia did not witness.

The rational choice for General Ershad, therefore, was to rely on key domestic and external actors for consolidating his position. He knew that the donor community, especially the World Bank and the IMF, was dissatisfied with the slow pace of reforms. Both the World Bank and the IMF made it distinct to him that, without a clear commitment from his government to restructuring the economy, they would stop pumping any aid money into Bangladesh's troubled economy. The IMF, for instance, suspended its EFF program for the apparent failure of the country to conform to all the adjustment-related conditionalities (Rahman, 1994: 14). However, the military regime's quick decision to pursue greater liberalization programs in general, and to meet the terms set out in the articles of agreement of the IMF in particular, restored the confidence of the donor community. Pressure for economic and financial liberalization also came from local actors. The business community was particularly anxious to see the immediate removal of all kinds of ambiguity from the private sector-led development strategy adopted by Zia. Senior military and civil bureaucrats, most of them are western-educated and/or -trained, were as well calling for the adoption of a more focused approach to the market.

As a survival strategy, thus, Ershad sought to build political coalitions with these powerful external and internal actors. Having subscribed to a structural reform package sponsored by the World Bank and IMF, he went on to build alliances with major local players. Like General Zia, he also found a great deal of support for his regime among the bureaucratic elites. Although he looked for ways of drawing support from what is known as the 'civil–military bureaucratic oligarchy', he chose to rely more on the military than its civilian counterpart (Alam, 1993: 317). This was done largely to keep the military, as his primary constituency, fully satisfied. Military officials, for instance, dominated his first Council of Advisors. Out of the total of 17, the military alone occupied 8 positions, followed by bureaucrats and technocrats with 7 spots. As Ershad moved to the phase of legitimization and/or civilianization, he expanded his coalition by adding a significant number of businessmen, industrialists, and politicians to his decision-making structures, including the cabinet.

But in the face of growing resistance to his military authoritarian regime, Ershad found it increasingly difficult to both expand and legitimize his political support base. Unlike Zia, he clearly failed to keep ordinary citizens calm about and supportive of his regime. Realizing that he would probably never be able to draw widespread support from key civil society actors, such as the students, the poor, public sector employees, workers, and intellectuals, General Ershad went on to strengthen his ties with the business community, particularly with trading and industrial giants. In order to give his legitimization programs a chance to survive, he opened the floodgate to political donations from the business community. This proved to be an important survival strategy for his military authoritarian regime as 'business donations' contributed to the thriving of his own political platform known as the *Jatiya Party*. Generous donations from big business, also allowed him to silence some key opposition political parties that threatened the very survival of his unconstitutional government. As Kochanek noted, it was believed that, General Ershad bribed the agitating opposition, which had initially refused to participate in any elections under his military regime. The immediate success of his buy-off strategy was reflected in the suddenly changed mood of a number of major opposition parties that stunned the country by announcing their decision to take part in the parliamentary elections of 1986 and 1988, giving his legitimization process some sort of credibility (Kochaneck, 1993: 226–7).

In exchange for their generous contributions to the party funds as well as their support for military rule, General Ershad allowed the business elites to further their material interests largely through the misappropriation of public resources. His economic liberalization programs became the means by which private entrepreneurs continued to enrich themselves. The massive transfer of SOEs to the private sector, for instance, was done basically without putting an appropriate mechanism in place. There was no standard basis for the valuation of public enterprises. As in Zia's time, no clear step was taken either to generate revenues for the state through the sale of public enterprises or to even make the deals transparent. Such a relaxed environment proved to be extremely beneficial for the buyers as it offered them an excellent opportunity to increase their wealth by manifolds at a relatively shorter period of time.

By contrast, the liberalization of the import regime suddenly created a huge demand for foreign goods, ranging from trivial cosmetic items to electronic appliances and luxury automobiles. This increasing demand helped the traders multiply their profits in two specific ways. First of all, taking advantage of an undervalued foreign exchange rate, they simply flooded the local markets with imported goods and sold them at relatively higher prices. And secondly, with the help of senior government officials, they widely used the under-invoicing technique mainly to evade appropriate customs duties and sales tax, therefore lowering the cost of imported goods and significantly increasing their profits (Maniruzzaman, 1992: 218–19). Unofficial imports, in particular smuggling, also became a common practice during this period. According to one estimate, illegal imports have come to constitute about 18 per cent of the total imports into Bangladesh, owing to loose enforcement of legal provisions (World Bank, 1996: 7).

Such an absence and/or weak enforcement of legal terms was also reflected in the financial sector, where the problems of loan default reached a dangerous level. Despite his promise to decisively act against the loan defaulters, General Ershad did virtually nothing to check this problem. A number of studies suggest that he actually encouraged the DFIs to make loans that were highly unlikely to be recovered (Sobhan, 1991: 10). The World Bank also criticized the government for politically using the DFIs' lending operations. According to a World Bank report,

The high default rate among Nationalized Commercial Bank (NCB) borrowers has occurred because these banks have been poorly managed and have had little incentive to make good loans. . . . NCBs have had to make high-risk loans to priority sectors, new entrepreneurs, public corporations, 'sick' industries and borrowers with political influence. They have also had to endure loan forgiveness programs by the government (World Bank, 1995: 138).

DFIs' loan defaults doubled in the 1980s, increasing from Tk 5.2 billion in 1982 to Tk 10.5 in 1990 (Sobhan, 1991: 5). It was no wonder that the private sector accounted for 96.5 per cent of the total bad lending. Of particular importance is that the debt equity ratio reached 90:10 during General Ershad's nine-year rule (Humphrey, 1990: 75).

In addition to the weak implementation of existing rules, Ershad's increasing political dependence on big business also enabled the defaulters to evade legal actions. With the intensification of an anti-military movement led by key civil society groups, Ershad began to focus on the inclusion of large business and industrial houses in his coalition. Like Zia, he encouraged them to maintain their dominance in the country's economic and political decision-making process. In his 1988 cabinet, for example, he appointed six businessmen as ministers (Kochaneck, 1993: 223). While the unavailability of any reliable data makes it difficult to provide a clear picture of business representation in decision-making, according to one estimate, some 40 per cent of Jatiya Party (JP) members elected to the 1986 *Jaitiya Sangsad* were big businessmen. Representation of big business in the decision-making process continued to increase during the next few years of his rule.

Despite such growing partnerships with big business, the military, and senior civil bureaucrats, General Ershad was not able to resolve the severe legitimacy crisis that he confronted from the very beginning of his tenure. Failing to overcome growing political opposition to his military authoritarian regime, he had to step down in December 1990, paving the way for the country's transition to democracy. Yet the fact cannot be denied that, without a solid political support base, he remained in office for full nine years largely with the help of his coalition partners that benefited greatly from the World Bank–IMF sponsored market adjustment programs.

Democracy and fast track market reform: the cases of Mrs Zia and Sheikh Hasina

Although Ershad made a departure from his predecessor's gradual approach to economic reform, it was not until the assumption of power by the democratically elected regime of Mrs Khaleda Zia in 1991 that the country actually witnessed the implementation of a radical liberalization program. Under the leadership of Finance Minister M. Saifur Rahman, the regime outlined its reform priorities through the announcement of the National Industrial Policy (NIP). At the heart of this policy was an attempt to change the traditional role of the state in development. By both simplifying the investment procedures and eliminating the regulatory role of key governmental agencies, Mrs Zia's democratically elected regime formally expressed its desire to assume a 'promotional', rather than a 'regulatory', role in facilitating the development of what it called a healthy private sector. The NIP also emphasized the need for implementing a comprehensive privatization program with a focus on the jute sector that continued to operate in the red (Bangladesh Bank, 1992: 7).

The creation of a solid export base appeared to be a priority of the BNP regime. It undertook measures to diversify the country's export base, encouraging both local and foreign investors to set up export-oriented enterprises. The government offered the foreign investors tax exemptions on the interest of foreign loans, royalty, and technical assistance fees. It allowed them to freely import machinery and receive long-term credit facilities from national financial institutions (World Bank, 1992: 82). Local investors were also given incentives for undertaking similar export-oriented industrial and commercial schemes (DCCI, 1997: 20). As part of its plan to create a competitive export-oriented economic structure for the country, the government further accelerated the process of freeing up import regulations and removing non-tariff barriers. It announced a relatively low tariff regime, speed up the process of rationalizing the tariff structure, and replaced the import sales tax, domestic excise duty, and development surcharge with the Value Added Taxation (VAT).

What, thus, comes into sight is that the pace of economic reforms reached a new height under the democratically elected regime of Mrs Zia. What explains Mrs Zia's adoption of such a faster path to the market? Popular assumptions often refer to the growing external pressure for liberalization as the primary cause of the introduction of a massive liberalization program by the BNP regime. There is absolutely no doubt that the international actors, especially the World Bank and the IMF, were not happy with the slow progress of Bangladesh's attempt to make a transition to the market. On numerous occasions, they expressed, along with other key bilateral donor countries and/or organizations, their serious concerns about the inability of the country to adopt a more defined approach to reforms. They were particularly critical of the failure of Ershad's military regime to develop an appropriate legal and regulatory framework for ensuring a better performance of structural economic reforms. Their frustration was clearly manifested in the reduced aid commitment in the Aid Group meeting in 1990 (Kabir, 1995: 565). Thus the collapse of the military regime in December 1990 appeared to have made the donors feel relieved as they hoped to use the newly created democratic space to the pursuit of a more aggressive reform agenda. Considering market reform as the only means to achieve broader goals of economic development, poverty alleviation, and employment generation, they began to push the BNP government to speed up its economic restructuring programs (UNB, 1994).

This external pressure helps to explain the shift, but only in part. The government's inability to neutralize and/or resist donor pressure resulted from two major factors. First, Bangladesh's historical reliance upon foreign aid virtually made it impossible for the BNP regime to ignore donor advice. Despite a decline in the flow of foreign aid into the country, between 1990 and 1995 Bangladesh received a total of $7564 million USD, which constituted some 48 per cent of the country's development expenditure (Government of Bangladesh, 1997: 8). There exist hardly any doubt that without such a massive volume of external aid, the BNP would find it almost impossible to keep the wheels of the economy moving.

Second, and perhaps more importantly, the growing government–big business nexus either pushed or encouraged Mrs Zia's government to accelerate market reform programs. Like the donor community, key business actors believed that neither Zia's nor Ershad's regimes did enough to ensure private participation in Bangladesh's economic development. They were particularly critical of successive military governments' reluctance to allow the private sector to get involved in improving infrastructure facilities and activities. They also were disappointed with what they called 'the slow pace of trade reforms', especially the liberalization of the import regime.[5] Thus, they demanded that the BNP government must take concrete steps to further deregulate the economy and promote greater competition. These key business actors also asked the government for making some 'actual progress' in privatizing SOEs (Kabir, 1998).

Mrs Zia's regime could not do much to neutralize these pressures due to her party's traditional reliance upon big business. Instead of acting independently of the business community, the BNP indeed showed its willingness to establish even closer ties with big trading and industrial houses which became crystal clear in the *Jatiya Sangsad* elections of 1991, when the party deliberately picked up almost half of its candidates from the big business category (MRCB, 1991: 6). This was done partly in response to the rapidly changing nature of electoral politics in Bangladesh. From the mid-1980s, it increasingly became evident that the chance of winning would no longer depend upon the candidate's credentials or the party's election manifesto. The candidate needs to spend millions of Tk simply to ensure his/her victory in any elections. Without a lavish display of wealth one can now hardly imagine getting people's endorsement for holding a public office in Bangladesh (Kibria, 1994).

The staggering campaign costs encouraged the BNP leadership to nominate the 'millionaires' in the crucial *Jatiya Sangsad* (national parliament) elections of 1991, therefore further strengthening its formal relations with big business. This is not to say, however, that such a practice was only limited to the BNP. All other major political parties that participated in the elections of 1991 also adopted a similar policy when choosing party candidates. Almost 33 per cent of AL candidates and 33.3 per cent of Jatiya Party (JP) candidates, for example, were from the big business category (MRCB, 1991: 6). High campaign costs, as Hakim noted, 'discouraged many formidable aspirants of low financial ability to contest the parliamentary elections' (Hakim, 1993: 48).

It was no wonder that not only did the BNP emerge as the single largest party in the *Jatiya Sangsad*, but also traders and industrialists came out as the dominant group in the parliament. The business–industrialist group constituted some 59 per cent of the newly elected members of the *Jatiya Sangsad*, reflecting an increase of about 95 per cent over a period of just twelve years.[6] The number of business representatives in the *Jatiya Sangsad* increased from 67 in 1973 to 91 in 1979 and 177 in 1991. Out of the 141 BNP members elected to the parliament of 1991, 94 of them were businessmen and industrialists (Maniruzzaman, 1992: 216). While businessmen and industrialists constituted 28 per cent of the elected BNP members in the 1979 *Jatiya Sangsad*, the same group comprised some 67 per cent of the BNP legislators in the parliament of 1991.[7] The dominance of big business in decision-making was also reflected in the composition of Prime Minister Mrs Zia's ministry. Big business accounted for some 58 per cent of the 1991 ministry, which was formed following the country's return to parliamentary democracy. Such overwhelming majority of business legislators and ministers made it evident that big business had emerged as the dominant political force in Bangladesh.

During Mrs Zia's five-year rule, the business community therefore played a central role in implementing a rapid liberalization program. While the adoption of a fast-track liberalization program enabled the country to achieve some sort of macro-economic stability, it sparked off popular opposition to reforms, which was manifested in the BNPs' failure in the mayoral elections in Dhaka and Chittagong in 1994. Both of the party candidates lost miserably in the election. By choosing opposition candidates, the people of Dhaka and Chittagong indicated a strong desire for the development of a safety net for those who were badly hit by the government's fast-track market reform programs. They expected that such a signal would create the ground for the BNP regime to manage distributive conflicts generated by its massive reform programs. However the government was not even able to address the distribution issue, partly because of the resistance that it faced from big business.

What is perhaps more important to mention is that, business legislators and ministers were able to use the liberalization program to ensure their personal gains in both economic and political terms. The increasing presence of big business in decision-making put formidable obstacles to the creation of an appropriate legal and regulatory framework necessary to ensure that private entrepreneurs comply with the rules of the game. Using their growing political power, businessmen–industrialists prevented the government from constructing a well-functioning legal system that would protect consumer rights, make contracts enforceable, and stop inappropriate/illegal business practices. Although, under donor and public pressure, the democratically elected regime of Mrs Zia made some attempts to improve the regulatory framework, the lack of enforcement continued to help big business to abuse public resources for private gains. The newly established Financial Loan Courts, for instance, made little progress in either recovering overdue loans from the defaulters or in ensuring an improved performance of the lending institutions. Apart from making the legal provisions for setting up these courts, the government hardly did anything to enhance the ability of these courts to act decisively against the politically influential defaulters (World Bank, 1997: 17).

The absence of a minimum consensus on economic reforms under a democratic regime also contributed to the apparent failure of adjustment policies to bring about sustained politico-economic results. Like Generals Zia and Ershad, the BNP regime evidently neglected the importance of generating popular support in favor of its liberalization program. It made very little efforts to hold dialogs with relevant actors, including the trade unions and student groups, thus failing to develop a broad-based consensus on market reforms.[8] Of particular importance is that, despite widespread expectations, Mrs Zia's democratically elected regime did not undertake any programs to educate the people as to the costs and benefits of market reforms. Nor did the government make, as mentioned above, any meaningful attempts to resolve the distributive conflicts associated with market-oriented reform programs. Since her market reform programs were not accompanied by any satisfactory mechanisms designed to compensate the losers/sufferers, these liberalization initiatives continued to generate political resistance.

Considering the government's privatization program as a direct threat to the livelihoods of public sector employees, the *Sramik Karmachari Oikka Parishad* (SKOP) – an alliance of some fifteen national trade union federations – launched a massive anti-reform movement. Although it was widely hoped that a democratic government would pay more attention to the welfare of the workers, like Zia and Ershad, Mrs Zia's regime failed to overcome the workers' opposition to the on-going liberalization program. This was due largely to the inability of the government to implement an acceptable compensation package that would ensure the protection of the interests of the workers (World Bank, 1994: 49–50). Also, in the absence of an effective reconciliation mechanism, the government could not act appropriately and rapidly to resolve labor disputes, further contributing to the development of a highly confrontational labor–government relationship in the country, which eventually prompted the fall of the BNP regime.

The coming into power in 1996 by the AL that once refused to let the private sector become a partner of the country's social and economic progress appeared to have made no negative impact on Bangladesh's pursuit of a free market economy. Structural economic reform remained a top priority for Sheikh Hasina's regime that registered a convincing victory in the parliamentary elections of 1996 held under the supervision of a neutral, caretaker government. Most civil society groups, including the SKOP, that lent their unequivocal support to the AL's election campaign hoped that the AL's return to power would provide them with the political space essential for the initiation of a meaningful search for alternative policy agendas. To the surprise of many activists, Sheikh Hasina's democratically elected government refused to even consider the adoption of a strategy designed to strike a balance between the private and public sectors. In the Fifth Five Year Plan, which was introduced in 1997, the AL government assured the donors that it has no plans whatsoever to abandon the export-oriented growth strategy originally introduced by General Zia in the late 1970s.[9] Her government promised to continue to implement a fast track liberalization program in order to accelerate economic growth (Government of Bangladesh, 1997).

Improving the country's macro-economic structure remained a major focus of the AL's reform package. Policies were directed to contain the fiscal deficit, maintain a competitive real exchange rate, build a strong foreign exchange reserve, reduce public expenditures, and increase government revenues. The government announced various policies to ensure that the private sector continued to play a crucial role in the country's economic and social development. It also emphasized the need for transferring SOEs to the private sector. Between June 1996 and May 1998, for instance, the Privatization Board finalized the selling and/or transfer of 32 public enterprises (World Bank, 1998: 13). As part of its plan to facilitate export, the government continued to liberalize the trade regime mainly by removing both non-tariff barriers and quantitative restrictions. It undertook various measures designed to both reduce tariffs and streamline import procedures.

The results of such liberalization programs were somewhat encouraging at least in the beginning. For much of the 1990s, the economy grew at 5 per cent a year mainly due to the expansion of the agriculture sector. The country became almost self-sufficient in food production as agriculture continued to show a relatively strong performance in the late 1990s. The stable macro-economic environment, coupled with the liberalization of the trade regime attracted foreign investment in areas such as energy, infrastructure, and export-oriented manufacturing. Inflows of foreign direct investment (FDI) increased from US$83 million in

1994/95 to US$630 million in 1997/98. If the current trend continues, the country is expected to receive an average of US$800 million of FDI each year (World Bank, 1999: 32–4).

Such relative macro-economic stability, however, proved to be unsustainable as the economy plunged into a crisis situation in the beginning of the new millennium. The growth of the economy dropped from 5.9 per cent in 2000 to almost 5 per cent in 2001. Per capita GDP growth fell from 4.9 per cent in 2000 to 3.8 per cent in 2001. Growth rates in all the three sectors, namely industry, agriculture and service, also dropped. Consolidated fiscal deficits rose to 8 per cent of GDP in fiscal year 2001, while domestic public debt increased to Tk 400 billion, which is equivalent to 15 per cent of GDP. Bangladesh's foreign exchange reserves also hit the lowest level in ten years declining to US$1.3 billion in March 2002 (Government of Bangladesh, 2002). The performance of the financial sector also remained extremely disappointing as the crisis of debt default reached a precarious level. According to an estimate, the non-performing loans constituted some '33 per cent of the combined portfolio of the Nationalized Commercial Banks and domestic private banks' (World Bank, 1998: 15). A major weakness of the financial system also came into light when the capital market crashed in 1996, making millions of investors virtually penniless.

Although the volatility in the external environment was in part responsible for the weakening of Bangladesh's macro-economic structure during the late 1990s, the inability of Sheikh Hasina's democratically elected regime to regulate the market properly also contributed to the apparent failure of her government to stabilize the economy. Her regime found it particularly difficult to put the country's financial sector in order, because of its growing ties with big business and industrialists. The new realities of the post-Cold War coupled with its desire to come to power largely through the creation of a broad-based political coalition seemed to have created the basis for the AL leadership in the 1990s to abandon its center-off left political identity. Not only did it adopt a neo-liberal approach to economic development, the party, under the leadership of Sheikh Hasina, also began to incorporate traders and/or industrialists into the heart of its decision-making process.

The payoffs of such transformations of the AL were indeed huge, especially in the parliamentary elections of 1996 when it emerged as the majority party with some 155 seats in the 300-member *Jatiya Sangshad*. After 21 years of failed attempts, the AL finally formed the government that heavily relied upon its new coalition partner big business and industrialists. Out of the 155 MPs elected to the 1996 parliament,

87 of them represented the interests of business and/or industries. This growing bondage with business, in effect, constrained the government's ability to maintain its autonomy vis-à-vis traders and industrialists. Despite its promise of taking actions against the debt defaulters, for instance, Sheikh Hasina's democratically elected regime was not able to reform the legal framework necessary to take punitive measures against both the defaulters and the banks. Nor was it able to strengthen the regulatory and supervisory capacity of Bangladesh Bank. The capital markets also suffered from a major crisis of governance owing to the inability of the government to enforce laws. No meaningful efforts were made to ensure the accountability of the stock exchanges.

The AL's newly developed tie with big business also caused enormous tensions in its traditional friendly relationship with labors and public sector employees. These two groups were hoping that the return to power by the AL would allow them to play a role in the country's economic policy-making. They soon felt alienated as the priorities of Prime Minister Sheikh Hasina shifted from responding to popular demands to the maintenance of its strategic relations with both big business and donors. It, therefore, didn't take long before a sense of frustration returned to civil society, leading to the shocking defeat of the AL in the parliamentary elections of 2001.

Conclusions: the myth of structural economic reforms

This study finds little empirical evidence to support the widely held assumption that pro-market reforms were undertaken in Bangladesh in order to improve either its macro-economic performance or its poverty conditions. Successive regimes, both civilian and military, implemented various types of economic liberalization programs, including the transfer of SOEs to the private sector, reforming the financial sector, and liberalizing the trade and import regimes primarily to develop political coalitions with both external and internal key actors. In particular, the two military regimes of Zia and Ershad used economic reform programs largely as a tool to both legitimize and consolidate their unconstitutional power base. Both of them sought to develop political alliances with senior bureaucrats, businessmen, and industrialists mainly through their reform measures.

This research discovers that Generals Zia and Ershad allowed big business to emerge as a major player in national decision-making, which in turn adversely affected the state's ability to either enforce contracts or to develop a mechanism for redistributing assets. Both Generals also encouraged, albeit indirectly, the country's financial and economic elites to accumulate huge wealth through the abuse of scarce public resources. In return, not only did big business lend its political support to the military authoritarian regimes' legitimization programs, perhaps more importantly, businessmen and industrialists also contributed generously to the coffers of the ruling BNP and JP, helping them to expand their political support base.

Even under the democratically elected regimes of both Mrs Zia and Sheikh Hasina, economic reforms did not appear to be a means of improving either the performance of the economy or the living standards for the majority. Instead, economic liberalization programs were used primarily to protect and promote the goals of big business during their rules. Despite widespread optimism, these two democratically elected regimes did not even succeed in winning popular support in favor of their fast-track reform programs. This research also finds that economic reform programs undertaken by both Mrs Zia and Sheikh Hasina substantially increased the power of businessmen and industrialists, and subsequently further reduced the state's ability to develop an effective regulatory framework required to stop the abuse of public resources by business elites.

It concludes that big business emerged as the dominant political force in Bangladesh, preventing the state from carrying out various redistribution programs designed to reduce the sufferings of those who are badly affected by the country's transition to the market. Economic liberalization thus continued to frustrate the hopes of its advocates and ordinary citizens of Bangladesh.

Notes

1 However, in a later decision the government abolished the so-called investment ceiling.
2 It is important to mention that traders and industrialists have always relied upon the state for financial and technical support required to operate business and industrial enterprises in Bangladesh. This is due largely to the failure of the local bourgeoisie to emerge as a dominant economic force during the periods of British and Pakistani colonial rules. Unlike the Indian case, at independence Bangladesh lacked a strong entrepreneurial class that could maintain its autonomy vis-à-vis the state. Such a situation in turn contributed to the emergence of a mutually dependent relationship between the state and big business (Sobhan, 1979: 23–40).
3 Zia became quite aware that without developing a political system based on popular support, his military regime might not be able to survive. He therefore sought to initiate a process of giving his military regime a civilian

character, which is known as 'civilianization of military regimes' (Maniruzzaman, 1980: 214–28).

4   The successful use of a 'carrot and stick' policy by General Zia significantly reduced the ability of the opposition to emerge as an effective challenge to his military regime. Such a policy enabled Zia to co-opt a number of important opposition leaders, which in effect frustrated the hope of launching a nation-wide anti-military movement in the late 1970s. Despite several attempts, the mainstream opposition led by the AL failed to generate adequate popular support needed for the restoration of democracy.

5   Interviews with a representative of the Metropolitan Chamber of Commerce and Industry, Dhaka, who wanted to remain anonymous, June 1998.

6   It is worthwhile to note that all major socio-political groups in Bangladesh tend to view parliamentary membership as a key to success in both economic and political terms. This is simply because of the fact that, while the *Jatiya Sangsad* does not always play a crucial role in decision-making, parliamentary members can use their position as a bargaining tool. In other words, parliamentary membership is often used to advance individual and/or group interests.

7   Similarly, businessmen and industrialists emerged as the dominant force among the legislators of the two major opposition parties, namely the AL and the JP, in the *Jatiya Sangsad* elections of 1991. About 63 per cent of the JP members of parliament were businessmen, while big business constituted some 51 per cent of the AL legislators (Maniruzzaman, 1992: 216).

8   This was due primarily to the government's inability to act independently of the business community. The increasing reliance of the BNP government upon big business prevented the state from undertaking programs designed to promote and protect the interests of vulnerable groups.

9   While most external actors were initially uncertain as to the commitment of the AL to pro-market reform programs when the party signaled that it might undertake a 'go slow' approach, different policy statements issued later by both Prime Minister Hasina and Finance Minister ASM Kibria confirmed the government's determination of embracing the market.

References

Alam, A.M. Quamrul (1993) 'The Nature of the Bangladesh State in the Post-1975 Period', *Contemporary South Asia*, 2(3): 311–25.

Bangladesh Bank (1992) *Annual Report: 1991–92*, Dhaka: Ministry of Finance, Government of Bangladesh.

DCCI (1997) *A Guide to Investment and Business in Bangladesh*, Dhaka: Dhaka Chamber of Commerce and Industry.

Franda, Marcus (1982) *Bangladesh: the first decade*, New Delhi: South Asian Publishers.

Government of Bangladesh (1976) *Bangladesh Economic Survey: 1975–76*, Dhaka: Ministry of Finance, Government of Bangladesh.

Government of Bangladesh (1983) *Bangladesh Arthonoytik Jarip [Bangladesh Economic Survey]: 1982–83*, Dhaka: Ministry of Finance, Government of Bangladesh.

Government of Bangladesh (1988) *Bangladesh Arthonoytik Jarip [Bangladesh Economic Survey]: 1986–87*, Dhaka: Ministry of Finance, Government of Bangladesh.

Government of Bangladesh (1997) *The Fifth Five Year Plan: 1997–2002*, Dhaka: Ministry of Planning, Government of Bangladesh.

Government of Bangladesh (2002) *Memorandum for Bangladesh Development Forum: 2002–2003*, Dhaka: Ministry of Finance, Government of Bangladesh.

Hakim, Muhammad A. (1993) *Bangladesh Politics: the Shahabuddin interregnum*, Dhaka: University Press.

Humphrey, Clare E. (1990) *Privatization in Bangladesh: economic transitions in a poor country*, Boulder, CO: Westview Press.

Islam, Nurul (1977) *Development Planning in Bangladesh: a study in political economy*, London: C. Hurst & Company.

Islam, Syed Serajul (1988) *Bangladesh: state and economic strategy*, Dhaka: University Press.

Kabir, Bhuian Monoar (1995) 'Politico-Economic Limitations and the Fall of the Military Authoritarian Government in Bangladesh', *Armed Forces & Society*, 21(4): 553–72.

Kabir, Laila R. (1998) 'Privatization Policy in Bangladesh and Options', Commentary prepared by President of the Metropolitan Chamber of Commerce and Industry at a seminar on Privatization, Dhaka, 18 June.

Khan, Zillur R. (1984) *Martial Law to Martial Law: leadership crisis in Bangladesh*, Dhaka: University Press.

Kibria, Shah A.M.S. (1994) 'A House of Millionaires: is this the kind of Parliament we fought for?', *The Daily Star*, 27 February.

Kochanek, Stanley A. (1993) *Patron-Client Politics and Business in Bangladesh*, Dhaka: University Press.

Kong, Tat Yan (1996) 'Corruption and its Institutional Foundations: the experience of South Korea', *IDS Bulletin*, 27(2): 48–55.

Maniruzzaman, Talukder (1980) *The Bangladesh Revolution and its Aftermath*, Dhaka: Bangladesh Books International.

Maniruzzaman, Talukder (1992) 'The Fall of the Military Dictator: 1991 elections and the prospect of civilian rule in Bangladesh', *Pacific Affairs*, 65(2): 203–24.

MRCB (1991) *Nirbachan 1991 [Election 1991]*, Dhaka: MRCB.

Palmer, George F. (1994) *The EIU Global Privatisation Manual: a practical guide to the process and practitioners*, London: The Economist Intelligence Unit.

Puchkov, V.P. (1989) *Political Development of Bangladesh: 1971–85*, New Delhi: Patriot Publishers.

Rahman, Mashiur (1994) *Structural Adjustment, Employment and Workers: public policy issues and choices for Bangladesh*, Dhaka: University Press.

Sobhan, Rehman (1979) 'Public Enterprises and the Nature of the State', *Development and Change*, 10(1): 23–40.

Sobhan, Rehman (1991) 'National Sovereignty, External Dependence and Government of Bangladesh', National Professor Anwar Hossain Memorial Lecture, Dhaka.

Sobhan, Rehman (ed.) (1991) *Debt Default to the Development Finance Institutions: the crisis of state sponsor entrepreneurship in Bangladesh*, Dhaka: University Press.

Sobhan, Rehman (1993) 'Structural Maladjustment: Bangladesh's experience with market reforms', *Economic and Political Weekly*, 28(19): 925–31.

Sobhan, Rehman and Ahsan, Ahmed (1984) *Disinvestment and Denationalization: profile and performance*, mimeo, Dhaka: Bangladesh Institute of Development Studies.

Sobhan, Rehman and Mahmood, Syed Akhter (1991) 'Trends in Repayment Performance to the DFIs: 1971–72 to 1981–82', in Sobhan (ed.), *Debt Default to the Development Finance Institutions: the crisis of state sponsored entrepreneurship in Bangladesh*, Dhaka: University Press: 142–96.

UNB (1994) 'Donors for Pushing Thru' Reforms', *The Daily Star*, 11 February.

World Bank (1992) *Bangladesh: selected issues in external competitiveness and economic efficiency*, Washington, DC: South Asia Country Department, World Bank.

World Bank (1994) *Bangladesh: privatization and adjustment*, Washington, DC: South Asia Country Department, World Bank.

World Bank (1995) *Bangladesh: from stabilization to growth*, Washington, DC: World Bank.

World Bank (1996) *Bangladesh Trade Policy Reform for Improving the Incentive Regime*, Washington, DC: Public Sector Development and Finance Division, World Bank.

World Bank (1997) *Bangladesh: annual economic update – economic performance, policy issues and priority reforms*, Washington, DC: South Asia Region, World Bank.

World Bank (1998) *Bangladesh: economic trends and policy agenda*, Dhaka, the World Bank Group in Bangladesh.

World Bank (1999) *Bangladesh: key challenges for the next millennium*, Washington, DC: World Bank.

World Bank (2002) *Country Brief: South Asia Region – Bangladesh*, Dhaka, the World Bank Group in Bangladesh.

3
Liberalization, Corporate Ownership and Performance: The Indian Experience

Jayati Sarkar and Subrata Sarkar

Introduction

Industrial and trade policy liberalization has been an integral part of the overall structural reforms program initiated in India since July 1991 and has entailed a radical change in the institutional and regulatory environment for the Indian corporate sector. Such liberalization has involved removal of restrictions on industrial capacity expansion and adoption of measures to facilitate foreign trade and foreign capital investment.[1] The primary objective has been to bring the performance of the hitherto protected Indian companies in line with international best practices by subjecting these companies to increasing domestic and international competition. While explicit policy commitments towards industrial deregulation and trade liberalization can be traced back to the mid-eighties, it is only since the inception of the "New Industrial Policy" of 1991 that reform measures became part of a long-term development strategy.

Nine years into the reforms, some studies regarding the success of deregulation and liberalization in improving the performance of the Indian corporate sector have started emerging. The evidence to date is mixed, notwithstanding the fact that the periods of analyses in these studies are somewhat non-overlapping in their coverage of the post-reform years. While some studies have found evidence of improvements in profitability and efficiency in the post-reform period (see for example, Joseph *et al.*, 1998; Krishna and Mitra, 1998; Mitra, 1999), others have not found any noticeable change (for example, Mani, 1999; Neogi and Ghosh, 1998).

The present chapter seeks to contribute to this growing volume of literature on the impact of economic liberalization in India, but with a focus that is different from those of the earlier studies. Unlike existing studies which focus on the corporate sector as a whole, the present study analyzes the impact of liberalization at the disaggregated level of distinct ownership groups that have historically co-existed in Indian manufacturing. The objectives of the study are two-fold. The first is to describe how the process of economic liberalization, through the implementation of the various trade and industrial policy measures, is expected to change the institutional environment of the different ownership groups. The second is to analyze empirically the impact of liberalization on the performance of companies in the various ownership groups keeping in background the above institutional changes.

The motivation for studying institutional changes and performance impacts by ownership groups comes from two sources, each having policy implications in the context of an emerging economy like India. The first is the literature on ownership and corporate governance which analyzes why potential differences in performance may exist between public and private companies[2] as well as among companies under different forms of private ownership,[3] and how changes in competitive market conditions may iron out existing ownership differentials.[4] This debate has implications for the contentious policy issue of whether privatization is necessary in an increasingly liberalized environment, and in the event it is deemed so, what forms of private ownership forms are likely to be optimal.

The second is the literature on the political economy of structural reforms which argues that policy reforms like trade and industrial liberalization could render losses to the status quo and create new constituencies that gain from the reforms, thereby leading to a new set of "gainers" and "losers" (Rodrik, 1994). While the exact distributional consequences cannot be predicted with certainty as reforms may have "unanticipated" effects on constituencies, be these on the supporters or on the the opponents (Krueger, 1993), there is little disagreement in the literature that the sustainability of reforms depends on their impact on powerful pressure groups especially in developing countries. In many such countries, dissatisfaction among such groups has threatened the political stability, brought down governments and reversed the reforms process (Rodrik, 1994; Martinelli and Tommasi, 1997).

In India, companies with different ownership status have co-existed in the corporate sector, with public sector companies playing a relatively dominant role since the country's independence in 1947. Within the private sector, both domestic and foreign companies have operated, and within each, companies belonging to business groups have co-existed with standalone companies. With the transformation of the industrial and trade policy regime from a stringently regulated one of the sixties to a more market oriented one of the nineties, the relative importance as well as the fortunes of these different groups is likely to be affected so as to throw up "gainers" and "losers" on the way.

Empirical work on the effect of liberalization on companies belonging to different ownership groups is limited with respect to India. Studies using data pertaining mostly to the early years of liberalization and confined to a comparison of public and private companies, reveal a mixed picture. While the studies by Bhaya (1990), Jha and Sahni (1992) and Ramaswamy and Renforth (1994) reveal no significant differences in performance between private and public sector companies, the study by Majumdar (1998) does find such differences existing over a fifteen-year period when the policy regime was being gradually liberalized. Other cross-sectional studies confined to the private sector and not particularly focused on the effect of liberalization, find that the performance of domestic private companies is significantly inferior to that of foreign companies (Chhibber and Majumdar, 1999) and that the performance of privately owned companies depends critically on the structure of equity ownership and corporate financing pattern (Khanna and Palepu, 1997, 1998, 2000; Sarkar and Sarkar, 1999, 2000). Our analysis of the relative performance of Indian corporates across the entire spectrum of ownership since liberalization can help identify the "gainers" and "losers" among the different ownership groups and at the same time provide some answers to the ownership versus competition debate, empirical evidence regarding which is still emerging and mixed.

The chapter is organized as follows. The second section "The road to economic liberalization" describes the important industrial and trade policy reforms initiated in the early nineties and discusses how these reforms have changed the institutional set-up and the incentives facing the private and public sector companies. The third section "Ownership effects" presents an empirical analysis of the pre- and post-reform performance of companies under different ownership groups based on a panel of 890 companies over a nine-year period, 1988–89 to 1996–97. Concluding remarks are made in Section 4.

The evolution of industrial policy: from regulation to market

The beginnings of industrial policy in independent India can be traced back to the formulation of the Industries (Development and Regulation)

Act, 1951 and the Industrial Policy Resolution (IPR), 1956. These blueprints of industrial policy accorded "commanding heights" to the public sector and emphasized extensive state regulation of private sector activity for it to "necessarily fit into the framework of the social and economic policy of the State". The private sector was expected to play only a residual role in the country's developmental process. Seventeen industries under Schedule A were reserved exclusively for state participation, while industries under Schedule B were to be progressively state-owned but private companies could be called upon to supplement the state efforts. The remaining ones were to be open to private sector participation. Consequently, several restrictions were placed on private sector activity, both domestic and foreign. These included industrial licensing to direct resources into priority areas, reservation of production activities to encourage the growth of the small-scale sector, location restrictions to promote the development of backward areas, size restrictions to prevent the concentration of economic power (Monopolies and Restrictive Trade Practices (MRTP) Act, 1969), and import licensing through import quotas and tariffs to create entry barriers for foreign investors (Foreign Exchange and Regulation (FERA) Act, 1973).

The road to economic liberalization

The first attempts to liberalize industrial and trade policies and make them more market-friendly were made in the seventies. By then, as Marathe (1989) notes, there was clear evidence and increasing realization that the complex web of regulations and controls was not effective in achieving the policy objective of "growth with social justice". Minor modifications in the industrial policy were attempted through the Industrial Policy Statement of December 23, 1977, to bring about "greater clarity in the investment climate" and to liberalize existing licensing requirements. However, the policy bias against the private sector, particularly against large business houses and foreign companies, continued. The regulatory framework did not essentially break away from its past and it was, therefore, not surprising that these modifications had limited impact on the performance of the corporate sector.

The first clear evidence of a new orientation in industrial policy came in the mid-eighties when Rajiv Gandhi became the Prime Minister after the assassination of the then Prime Minister Indira Gandhi in 1984. The new policy marked a clear ideological departure from the regime of licensing and control and signaled the "dawn of liberalization". It was under Rajiv Gandhi's regime that the need to attain industrial competitiveness,

higher productivity, and better quality became important policy objectives. Emphasis was placed on reducing the control of the state on private
sector activity. These decisions to clearly break away from the past and
introduce a new vision for modernizing India's industrial sector were
evident both in the rhetoric and in the economic and political actions
(Kohli, 1991).[5]

Policy statements increasingly emphasized external and internal
liberalization. This was to take the form of delicensing a large number
of industries, opening 40 industries in the core sector to private sector
participation, and allowing investment decisions of private companies
to be determined by the need of the market place. The regime also
sought to reduce the bias against private sector companies in general,
and big business and multinationals, in particular. Accordingly, restrictions
on size were considerably eased by recognizing the concept of minimum efficient scale of production, and changing the definition of
MRTP companies from the then existing asset limit of Rs 20 crores to
100 crores. The system of "broadbanding" was introduced under which
companies were free to diversify within a given range of industries.
Further, MRTP and FERA companies were exempted from licensing in
52 industries, provided such units were set up in backward areas. With
respect to public sector companies, the first conscious effort toward
structural reforms was made by giving them more autonomy, but at
the same time by creating competitive pressures through hardening of
their budget constraint and forcing them to raise investment capital on
their own.

Prior to the mid-eighties, an "uneasy triangle" prevailed between the
state, the private sector, and foreign capital (Kidron, 1965; cited in Shastri,
1999). The private sector, and especially the big business houses, while
lamenting the "license and permit raj", restrained from taking a strongly
adversarial role so as not to jeopardize their chances of getting industrial
approvals and clearances (Shastri, 1999). Attempts at liberalization,
however, brought forth a positive response from the private sector, and
it was perhaps for the first time that the government actively solicited
the support of businesses in policy formulation. The support from business
groups which was clearly articulated through the three apex chambers
of commerce, primarily stemmed from the new regime's emphasis on
technology and efficiency rather than on socialism (Kohli, 1991). Such
support was, however, somewhat muted regarding the desirability of
external liberalization and direct foreign investment because of the
concern that Indian corporates after years of protection would find it
difficult to compete internationally. The government paid heed to such

a concern and went back on its prior commitment of external liberalization and started emphasizing the need for domestic competition rather than international competition.

While the liberalization program in the mid- to late-eighties moved the industrial sector to a more market-oriented environment, its momentum started faltering as the parliamentary elections approached in 1989. Political resistance to the program started building up from the grass roots which included a section of the ruling party, moderate left opposition, and rural groups (Kohli, 1991, Chapter 11). The opposition centered on the argument that liberalization was anti-poor and represented a shift away from the long cherished Nehruvian goals of growth with social justice and elimination of poverty. Thus, with each successive Budget, especially from late 1986 when Rajiv Gandhi's overall popularity reportedly started declining, the policy rhetoric became rather "confused" with the pronouncements of liberalization and modernization gradually giving way to those emphasizing the need to remove social barriers for the weak, allocating resources to the benefit of the poor, and trying to impress that the modernization program was broad based (Kohli, 1991; Sengupta, 1996). Subsequently, the move towards economic liberalization and modernization slowed down and practically came to a halt by 1989 due to the combined effect of three factors – the fear of losing the elections, bureaucratic resistance, and lobbying by powerful vested interests within and outside the government that had stakes in the license-permit raj (Sengupta, 1996).

Liberalization in earnest: the "New Economic Policy" of 1991

Impressive rates of industrial growth coincided with the liberalization of industrial policy under the Rajiv Gandhi government, and was widely perceived to be the result of the process of "evolutionary reform" of the eighties (Ahluwalia, 1995). During the five-year period from 1984–85 to 1989–90, industrial output grew at the rate of 8.2 per cent which was substantially higher than the rate of 5.9 per cent that existed in the first half of the eighties (Srivastava, 1996). The growth of manufacturing output also followed a similar trend.

However, as the process of liberalization came to a halt, the economy began to slowdown and this state of affairs, accompanied by political instability at the Centre, continued until June 1991 when the Narasimha Rao led minority government came to power. Around that time, India faced a severe foreign exchange crisis, and the possibility of defaulting on payments arose for the first time. As a result, the Government had to turn to the IMF and the World Bank for financial assistance. The circumstances combined to compel the Government towards committing itself to a comprehensive and sustained structural reforms program that had as its core the liberalization of the industrial and trade policy regime. Apart from the economic crisis that triggered the liberalization process under the "New Economic Policy", there was also an overall change in the mood of political parties, with the exception of the left, away from the status quo and towards reforms (Bhagwati, 1993: 82–3). According to Bhagwati, the "ultimate compulsion" for reforms was provided by the "psychology of the leadership" that assumed power in 1991 for whom reforms seemed to be the only answer to strengthen India's voice in world economic affairs.

The "New Economic Policy" became formalized not only in the budget speeches of the Finance Minister, but also in the detailed Statement on Industrial Policy of 1991. Unlike the earlier policy initiatives, external liberalization was openly committed to by the Government and was an integral part of the agenda along with internal liberalization. Drastic changes, that were "sweeping by Indian standards" (Sengupta, 1996), followed. With respect to the private sector, licensing for all industries was abolished except for a short list of 18 industries with strategic and security concerns. The exceptions were gradually reduced over time to nine industries by 1997. With respect to big businesses, the concept of MRTP companies in terms of asset base was eliminated and the scope of the MRTP Act was completely changed from being concerned with the prevention of concentration of economic power to being concerned with unfair and restrictive trade practices. Thus, with the exception of a small set of industries and products, domestic private companies, particularly the large business houses, were free to invest, expand, and diversify consistent with their capabilities.

Along with the initiatives being taken through delicensing to increase competition in the domestic market, parallel initiatives were taken at encouraging international competition through a more liberalized policy toward foreign direct investment (FDI) and by reducing trade barriers and shifting away more decisively from the policy of import substitution. As Cable (1995) observes, the move towards encouraging greater foreign participation in domestic activity followed from several considerations, among which were the need (a) to provide increased competition to Indian private sector forcing it to "absorb international standards of business efficiency", (b) to augment capital formation, and (c) to benefit from an "integrated package of capital, management and technology" associated with FDI. Thus, the liberalization package that gradually evolved allowed majority foreign investment (upto 51 per cent) in most industries, foreign investment of upto 24 per cent equity in small scale industries, and foreign equity upto 100 per cent in export-oriented units and, based on merit, in other industries. Most importantly, the restrictive provisions under FERA for companies with more than 40 per cent foreign equity were abolished and no distinction remained between FERA and non-FERA companies.

With regard to external liberalization, there was clear evidence of a shift away from the import substitution regime. Import duties were reduced progressively for most commodities. As Misra (1998) notes, despite some liberalization of import controls over the eighties, at the time of the reforms in 1991, 20 per cent of India's total imports came through Open General License (OGL) and over 80 per cent of industry HS codes were subject to some form of licensing. Further, the tariff rates were among the highest in the world. The percentage of tradable GDP subject to quantitative restrictions in the manufacturing sector declined from 90 per cent at the end of 1990 to 36 per cent by 1995–96. This reduction was concentrated mainly with respect to intermediate and capital goods, in order to lower the existing costs of production; consumer goods continued to be subject to strict controls.[6] The rationalization of the tariff structure, along with a reduction in tariff rates, essentially followed the recommendations of the Chelliah Committee on Tax Reforms. Accordingly, the peak rate of customs duty declined from around 250 to 50 per cent in 1995–96, with across the board decline in import-weighted average tariff rates. Between 1990–91 and 1995–96, these rates declined from 164 per cent to 39 per cent for consumer goods, from 117 per cent to 24 per cent for intermediate goods, and from 97 per cent to 30 per cent in the case of capital goods.[7] Trade liberalization also took the form of a gradual removal of existing anti-export bias through tax exemptions on earnings from exports, provision of concessional finance, and the pruning of the negative list of exports.

In comparison to the growing resistance in the eighties to the reforms process, particularly with respect to external liberalization and foreign participation, there was much less resistance to such policies in the nineties. Shastri (1999), for instance, notes that although there were some divisions among the Indian business class on the issue of what would be the appropriate extent of foreign equity participation,[8] support for the 51 per cent foreign participation proposal came in from all apex business associations once the Government formally proposed it.

Also, while there were disagreements among different political parties as to the precise content and sequencing of the reforms, there was consensus among most major parties that the reforms process should continue and that the process was irreversible.[9] After the electoral defeat of the Narasimha Rao Government in 1996, there were three changes in the government with varying political ideologies between 1996 and 1999. The first was the center-left coalition government, the United Front, that lasted for only eighteen months with outside support from the Congress. The second was another coalition government of regional parties in 1998, but this time led by the right-wing Bharatiya Janata Party, that lasted for only thirteen months. The third, and still continuing (at the time of writing), was the twenty-two party coalition government, again led by the Bharatiya Janata Party, that came to power after the 1999 elections.

Amidst the political instability and the emergence of coalition politics, however, the process of liberalization continued, albeit at a slower pace, and again picked up after the 1999 elections. Thus, while there were changes in power at the Centre, there were (a) further liberalization of industrial licensing provisions and parameters for automatic approval in foreign collaboration in 1996, (b) expansion of the list of industries for automatic approval for foreign equity in 1997, (c) removal of restrictions to allow 100 per cent foreign participation in infrastructure projects such as electricity generation, transmission and distribution, and (d) further lowering and rationalization of import duty rates and other tax rates (like reduction of corporate taxes and abolition of surcharge) in 1998.

Notwithstanding the fact that divisions among most political parties and business classes regarding the desirability of the liberalization process were becoming less striking, some vocal opposition to the reforms still remained. For instance, a section of the Indian business class openly expressed reservation against the policy of encouraging foreign participation and reducing protection for domestic industries. This group, which came to be known as the "Bombay Club", argued that the reforms had created an uneven playing field between domestic and foreign companies with a bias built in favor of the latter. It demanded that prior to opening up the economy, the government should focus on internal reforms to make domestic producers more competitive. The "Club" argued that domestic producers were at a significant cost disadvantage vis-à-vis the multinationals because of high rates of domestic taxation, costly credit, fragmentation of market, and inadequate level of operating capital (Jansson *et al.*, 1995; Shastri, 1999). On the political front too, apart from opposition from the Left groups, there were still intra-party oppositions within members of the dominant right-wing member of the ruling coalition, the Bharatiya Janata Party. One can identify at least three types of economic thinking within this party (Jansson *et al.*, 1995). The first is the one that is in favor of all-out globalization; the second is the one with deep socialistic roots worried about market failure and economic inequality and is against privatization and entry of foreign investments; and the third is the one that is campaigning for the "swadeshi movement" where nationalistic ideologies are at the forefront.

Although pockets of resistance have remained and concerns continue to be expressed regarding an uneven playing field, the preceding description of the liberalization policies does indicate that there has been a considerable leveling of the institutional environment faced by the different ownership groups in the corporate sector. The bias against the private sector and, within the private sector, against big businesses and foreign companies have been gradually eliminated. Along with the reforms of industrial and trade policy, liberalization of the tax structure and financial sector liberalization have helped to create a more level playing field among different ownership groups. The rates of corporate taxes have not only declined over the years, but have also been rationalized. Thus, while widely held domestic companies were taxed at a lower rate than closely held private sector companies till 1993–94, their tax rates were equalized in 1994–95. The tax rate was lowered from 40 per cent to 35 per cent in 1997–98. Although foreign companies continue to be taxed at a higher rate than domestic companies, their rates have declined from 65 per cent in 1993–94 to 48 per cent in 1997–98. Financial sector reforms, particularly capital market liberalization, have made access to credit easier and cheaper for domestic companies, both in the domestic and international capital markets. Changes in takeover regulations have also been geared to create a more level playing field for domestic and foreign companies, and buy back of shares, one of the major concerns of the "Bombay Club", has been allowed since November 1998.

Some of the industrial and trade policy changes initiated in the nineties are summarized in Table 3.1. Along with the quantitative changes in some of development parameters there have been changes in the way the Indian corporate sector has been doing business. Apart from paying increasing interest to quality, marketing, and branding products, a growing number of companies are reportedly restructuring their operations through a variety of means which include changes in internal organization as well as consolidating their business activities through mergers, amalgamations, strategic alliances, takeovers, sales of assets/units, and so on. Such activities have led to a "corporate churning"

Table 3.1 Changes in selected indicators since the policy reforms

	Pre-reforms	Post-reforms
FDI flows (Rs Mn)	15,595 (1985–91)	1,500,440 (1992–97)
Foreign collaborations	5,981 (1985–91)	11,815 (1992–97)
Corporate acquisitions (no.)	121 (1988–92)	161 (1993–97)
Capital market indicators		
• No. of listed companies	6,229 (1991)	8,800 (1996)
• Market capitalization as percentage of GDP	20.6 (1990)	42.7 (1995)
Trade		
• Exports as percentage of GDP	4.9 (1985–90)	8.8 (1992–95)
• Imports as percentage of GDP	7.2 (1985–90)	10.05 (1985–90)
Trade regime		
Quantitative restrictions (QR)		
• percentage of tradable GDP s.t. QR	93 (end 1990)	66 (May 1995)
• percentage of tradable manufacturing sector GDP s.t. QR	90 (end 1990)	36 (May 1995)
Tariff rates		
• Maximum rate	400 (1990–91)	50 (1995–96)
• Average rates (import wtd)	87 (1990–91)	27 (1995–96)
Rate of protection in manufacturing (value added weights)		
• Effective rate	164 (1990–91)	72 (1994–95)
• Nominal rate	129 (1990–91)	55 (1994–95)

Source: Pursell and Sharma (1996) cited in Misra (1998), Ahluwalia (1999), *Emerging Markets Factbook* (1997), *Monthly Review of the Indian Economy*, CMIE, several issues, *Handbook of Industrial Statistics*, Government of India, several issues.

and have gathered steam since the mid-nineties. For instance, open offers/bids to take over companies were around 30 in 1996–97, and valued at Rs 166.9 crore, but increased to 66 by 1998–99, and were valued at around 10 times more, Rs 1606 crore.

Pre- and post-reform performance – an empirical analysis

Our analysis above of the evolution of the institutional environment points to the possibility that economic liberalization could have a different impact on the performance of the various ownership groups. Considering the public and private sectors, it can be expected that the private sector, particularly foreign and big businesses, would gain from the elimination of the significant supply-side bias that existed against it in the regulated regime. In the process, the private sector can be expected to create increased competitive pressures for the public sector that was hitherto protected from such competition besides being a beneficiary of subsidized inputs. Increased competition would in all likelihood put a downward pressure on prices and hence on profit margins, and which of the two ownership groups, public or private, would benefit relatively more remains an empirical question.

Within the private sector itself, relative positions may change as the hitherto protected domestic private companies start facing increased competition from their foreign counterparts due to liberalized direct foreign investment regulations that allow the latter to compete more effectively in the market place. Also, business groups, while benefiting from some policy initiatives, could be adversely affected by others. On the positive side, business groups that earlier had to go in for forced and unrelated diversification due to capacity restrictions and monopoly regulations, would have increased freedom to restructure their business operations in line with their comparative advantages and core competencies. On the negative side, business groups, being older entities than standalone companies, are likely to have more in-built organizational rigidity in the form of habits and structures setting in over time,[10] and could, therefore, be slow in responding to the new environment. However, their relative advantage in rent-seeking activities may still continue in spite of the lifting of industrial licensing and import liberalization. This could be because business groups, being by design "organizational device(s)" that facilitate rent seeking by a priviledged few, successfully redirect their efforts to have priviledged access to new opportunities (Ghemawat and Khanna, 1998).

Our empirical analysis of the impact of liberalization on different ownership groups is based on a balanced panel of companies and involves comparison of their pre- and post-reform performance. The balanced nature of the panel ensures that our inferences regarding changes in post-reform performances are not due to differences in company characteristics as could occur with an unbalanced panel. The panel includes 890 manufacturing companies each observed for nine years over the period 1988–89[11] to 1996–97. The data is sourced from the PROWESS database created by the Center for Monitoring Indian Economy (CMIE). The database contains detailed information on the financial performance of companies in India and is analogous to the Compustat database in the US. Our sample gives a good representation of the Indian manufacturing sector in that the sample companies accounted for nearly two-thirds of gross value added and over four-fifths of fixed capital employed in the manufacturing sector in 1991–92.

In our analysis, we consider five ownership groups as classified in the PROWESS database. These are public companies (PUBLIC), companies belonging to private Indian business groups (PIBG), private Indian standalones (PIALONE), private foreign business groups (PFBG) and private foreign standalones (PFALONE). The respective sample sizes of the ownership groups in our panel of 890 companies are 104, 450, 230, 38 and 68.

We use two performance measures namely Return on Assets (ROA) and Asset Turnover (AT) to analyze the performance of companies. ROA is defined as the ratio of net profit before depreciation, interest, and tax (PBDIT) to total assets, and AT is defined as the ratio of total sales to total assets. ROA has been widely used as a measure of company performance in the empirical literature. However, for an economy in transition, a decline in ROA may not necessarily signal a decline in company performance because such decline might be due to emerging competitive pressures which were either weak or absent in the regulated regime. It is for this reason that we also consider the measure AT; if greater competition leads to more rivalry between firms and hence encourages more efficient use of resources, one would expect AT[12] to increase. In general, ROA is interpreted as a measure of company profitability, and AT is interpreted as a measure of capacity utilization and hence of company efficiency, though ROA can be interpreted as a measure of efficiency as well.

Ownership effects

Our empirical analysis begins by looking at the time series performance of companies in the various ownership groups. Figures 3.1 and 3.2 give trends in the mean ROA and AT of companies over the nine years. As is evident from the figures, there exist significant cross-sectional performance differentials between public and private companies in terms of both ROA and AT. Performance differentials also exist among different types of private ownership, but these differentials are comparatively much narrower. Within private companies, foreign companies on the average have both higher ROA and higher AT than domestic private companies. Within each of these two broad ownership groups, there is not much difference in ROA between standalone and group companies. However, when we consider AT, we find foreign group companies performing better than standalone companies. The situation is reversed

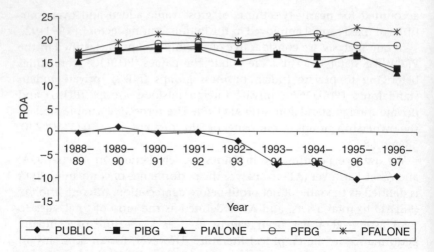

Figure 3.1   Trends in profitability (ROA) of different ownership groups: 1988–89 to 1996–97

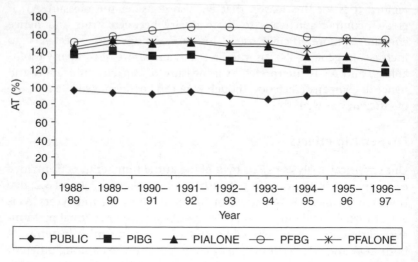

Figure 3.2   Trends in efficiency (AT) of different ownership groups: 1988–89 to 1996–97

for domestic private companies where standalone companies perform better than group companies. The last observation is consistent with the often cited phenomenon that group companies in the regulated regime tended to corner licenses and build excess capacity to pre-empt competition.

With regard to trends in ROA of different ownership groups, public companies have performed consistently poorly over the years, and this poor performance has aggravated sharply during the post-reform period (Figure 3.1). As far as domestic private companies are concerned, we observe a marginal fall in ROA during the post-reform period for both group and standalone companies. However, while the ROA of group companies has remained stable at the lower level except for the year 1996–97, the ROA of standalone companies has fluctuated periodically. Coming to foreign companies, we do not observe any noticeable change in the ROA of group companies during the post-reform period. For standalone companies, there is a slight positive trend in the initial years of the post-reform period which gets reversed in the later years. Thus, on the whole, we do not observe any sharp changes in the profitability of companies in the post-reform period. However, combining domestic private and foreign companies, we observe that the ROAs of standalone companies have tended to fluctuate more than those of group companies.

With respect to trends in AT, public companies do not exhibit any significant change over time (Figure 3.2). One noticeable point, however, is that the AT of public companies has been always below 100 unlike any other group, confirming that public companies are not only the least efficient of all companies, but that they also have sales which is lower than the value of assets owned. As far as domestic private companies are concerned, AT showed a declining trend over the post-reform period for both group companies as well as standalone companies suggesting a decline in their efficiency. However, the relative decline has been similar so that the ranking between these two groups of companies has been preserved, with standalone companies being more efficient than group companies. Coming to foreign companies, AT for group companies has increased consistently till 1992–93 and declined thereafter, whereas it has fluctuated for the foreign standalones with no discernible trend.

Are the trends in ROA and AT observed for each ownership group statistically significant, and how do these trends alter the relative rankings of the respective ownership groups in the post-reform period vis-à-vis the pre-reform period? Are the relative rankings in the pre- and post-reform period statistically significant? To answer these questions we selected the years 1991–92 and 1995–96 and did a means test by estimating for each performance measure, a regression using ownership dummies and interacting these ownership dummies with a time dummy. We took the year 1991–92 to represent the status of companies at the terminal year of the pre-reform period. This is probably justified given that the early liberalization measures were started to be introduced in the latter half of 1991. We used the year 1995–96 rather than the year 1996–97 to represent the status in the post-reform period because the former is more representative of the trend in the performance of companies in the post-reform period. In contrast, the year 1996–97 exhibited a sudden drop in the performance of the corporate sector and the economy in general, which is widely attributed to the political uncertainty that prevailed in India during this time. We chose foreign standalone companies as the reference group from which performance is measured in the base year. Thus, the coefficient of the ownership dummies indicates the difference in performance of the respective ownership group from foreign standalone companies in 1991–92, while the coefficient of the interaction terms represents the changes between 1991–92 and 1995–96 for each ownership group.

Table 3.2 represents the regression results. First concentrating on the profitability measure ROA, we find that all ownership dummies have negative sign suggesting that foreign standalone companies performed better in terms of profitability than any other group of companies. Also the magnitude of the coefficients suggests the following rankings of the various ownership groups. Foreign standalone companies performed the best followed by foreign group companies, domestic private group

Table 3.2 Ownership and time effects

Variable	Return on assets		Asset turnover	
	Estimate	t-statistics	Estimate	t-statistics
Intercept	20.57	7.67	151.43	18.96
Public	−20.68	−5.99	−56.77	−5.53
Private group	−2.12	−0.74	−15.58	−1.82
Private standalone	−2.56	−0.84	−1.58	−0.17
Foreign group	−1.36	−0.30	16.09	1.21
Time × public	−9.96	−3.25	−4.06	−0.44
Time × private group	−1.90	−1.29	−14.36	−3.27
Time × private standalone	−0.99	−0.48	−15.25	−2.48
Time × foreign group	−0.29	−0.06	−11.76	−0.78
Time × foreign standalone	2.10	0.55	1.26	0.11

companies, domestic private standalone companies and finally public companies. However, except for public companies, none of the coefficients are statistically significant suggesting that there are large *within-group* variations. Observe though that the t-statistics also follow the similar ranking as of the coefficients.

Coming to the interaction dummies, we observe that profitability has declined between 1991–92 and 1995–96 for all ownership groups, except for foreign standalone companies. The decline has been the highest for public companies. Within domestic private companies, profitability has declined much more for group companies than for standalone companies. Compared to these two ownership groups, the profitability of foreign group companies has fallen relatively less. However, as with the ownership dummies, none of the interaction dummies, except the one with respect to public companies, are statistically significant. This suggests that changes in profitability in the post-reform period have also varied significantly *within* each ownership group. Notice that the magnitudes of the time dummies imply that the ownership orderings in terms of profitability observed in the pre-reform year of 1991–92 has remained unaltered in the post-reform year of 1995–96, a fact that is highlighted in Figure 3.1.

Coming to the AT measure we observe that in the base year, the ownership effects as well as the time effects, are stronger compared with the profitability effect (Table 3.2). With respect to the year 1991–92, we observe that public companies performed significantly worse than foreign standalone companies, the coefficient of the public dummy being significantly larger than the corresponding coefficients of any other group. Within private companies, domestic companies belonging to business groups performed significantly worse, domestic private standalone companies performed similarly, while foreign companies belonging to business groups performed better than foreign standalone companies.

With respect to changes in AT between 1991–92 and 1995–96, the coefficient of the interaction dummies suggests time-effects that are different compared to those based on profitability. Public companies exhibit no significant change in efficiency in the post-reform period. In contrast, domestic private companies exhibit a significant decline in their efficiency; the coefficients are large with highly significant t-statistics. This suggests that the decline in efficiency as measured by AT has occurred consistently for most domestic private companies, whether belonging to business groups or standalone. Also the magnitude of the coefficients suggests that the extent of decline has been similar. Foreign companies belonging to business groups also exhibited a large

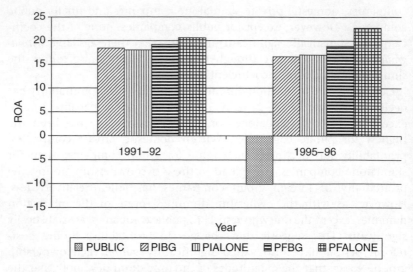

Figure 3.3   Ranking of ownership groups by profitability (ROA): 1991–92 and 1995–96

decline in their AT, but the interaction dummy is statistically insignificant, suggesting a large within-sample variation. Finally, foreign standalone companies did not exhibit any appreciable change in their asset utilization.

To summarize, our findings of the two performance indicators above suggest the following ordering of the ownership groups (see also Figures 3.3 and 3.4):

Profitability (pre-reform)   →   PFALONE, PFBG, PIBG, PIALONE, PUBLIC
Profitability (post-reform)   →   PFALONE, PFBG, PIALONE, PIBG, PUBLIC

Efficiency (pre-reform)   →   PFBG, PFALONE, PIALONE, PIBG, PUBLIC
Efficiency (post-reform)   →   PFBG, PFALONE, PIALONE, PIBG, PUBLIC

where PFALONE denotes private foreign standalone companies, PFBG, private foreign group companies; PIALONE, private Indian standalone companies; PIBG, private Indian group companies and PUBLIC, public companies.

"Gainers" and "Losers"

One noticeable point of our analysis is that, except for public companies, the time effects in profitability are statistically insignificant for

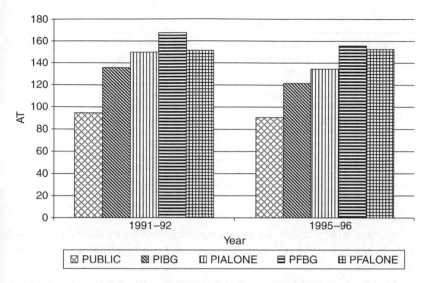

Figure 3.4 Ranking of ownership groups by efficiency (AT): 1991–92 and 1995–96

all ownership groups even though the magnitudes of the coefficients are quite large. This we said suggested that there were significant within-group variations in time performance, with some companies performing better and some worse from *each* ownership group, that is, there appears to be "gainers" and "losers" within each ownership group.

To pursue this point, we compared for each company its ROA in the years 1995–96 and 1991–92 and classified the company as a "gainer"/ "loser" if its 1995–96 return was higher/lower than its return in 1991–92. In other words, we classified a company to be "gainer"/"loser" if there was an improvement/worsening in its profitability in the post-reform period. We did a similar classification in terms of AT. Table 3.3 gives the percentage of "gainers" and "losers" for each ownership group based on each of the two performance indicators.

It can be seen from the table that there is a significant proportion of "gainers" and "losers" within each ownership in terms of both the performance measures. With respect to profitability, we observe that although the proportion of "gainers" within foreign companies is much higher than that within domestic private companies, nevertheless there is a significant proportion of foreign companies which exhibited a decline in their profitability in the post-reform period. Similarly, within domestic private companies too, there is a significant proportion of

Table 3.3   Proportion of gainers and losers

Ownership	Based on return on assets (%)		Based on asset turnover (%)		Sample size
	Gainers	Losers	Gainers	Losers	
Public	31.73	68.27	47.12	52.88	104
Private group	36.67	63.33	38.44	61.56	450
Private standalone	32.17	67.83	40.01	60.04	230
Foreign group	55.26	44.74	44.74	55.26	38
Foreign standalone	55.88	44.12	52.94	47.06	68

companies which registered an increase in their profitability perform-ance in the post-reform period. Similar conclusions follow if we use the AT measure.

What was the performance of the "gainers" and "losers", classified in terms of profitability, in the pre-reform period? Did the more profitable companies of the pre-reform period strengthen their performance in the post-reform period or did the less profitable companies perform better? Table 3.4 gives for "gainers" and "losers" the mean profitability in the years 1991–92 and 1995–96 and the difference between these two years. A few striking points emerge:

(a)   *The "gainers" are the less profitable companies of the pre-reform period.* This is true for all ownership groups. The less profitable companies of 1991–92 performed significantly better in the post-reform period. The mean ROA in 1991–92 of the companies that gained was substantially lower than the mean ROA in 1991–92 of the companies that lost out as of 1995–96.

(b)   *In 1995–96, the mean ROA of the "gainers" is substantially higher than the mean ROA of the "losers".* This suggests that not only did the less profitable companies of 1991–92 become more profitable in the post-reform period but they out-performed the more profitable companies of 1991–92. This suggests a "liberalization effect" which indicates that performers in a market-oriented regime, on the average, do better than the performers in a regulated regime. Figure 3.5(a–d) illustrates the four possibilities that could have arisen, given our definition of "gainers" and "losers", and the particular case, Figure 3.5(d), that obtains in our analysis. This complete reversal of fortunes is true for all ownership groups.

Table 3.4 Pre-reform and post-reform performance of gainers and losers – profitability

Ownership	Mean ROA (%) of gainers			Mean ROA (%) of losers			Mean ROA (%) of all		
	1995–96	1991–92	Change	1995–96	1991–92	Change	1995–96	1991–92	Change
Public	5.7	−4.4	10.1	−17.4	1.9	−19.3	−10.1	−0.1	−10.0
Private group	22.3	13.8	8.6	13.2	21.2	−8.1	16.6	18.4	−1.9
Private standalone	28.8	12.8	16.0	11.4	20.4	−9.1	17.0	18.0	−1.0
Foreign group	22.1	15.3	6.7	15.1	24.2	−9.0	18.9	19.2	−0.3
Foreign standalone	27.7	17.0	10.7	16.3	25.1	−8.8	22.7	20.6	2.1

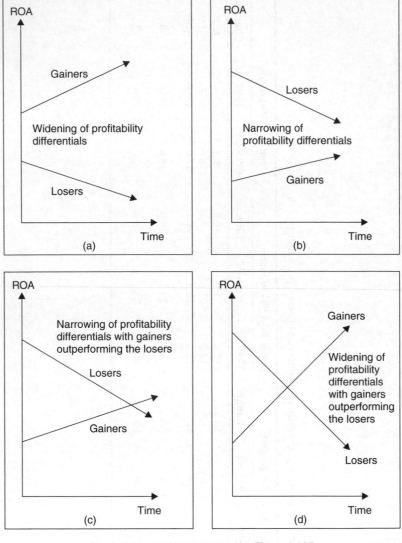

The Indian case is represented by Figure 3.5(d)

Figure 3.5   Possible configurations of gainers and losers in a liberalized environment

(c) For "gainers", the relatively large divergences in the mean ROA between foreign and domestic private companies in 1991–92 narrowed significantly in 1995–96. The "gainers" in these two broad ownership groups seemed to have moved closer to each other with not much cross-sectional differences in ownership. Thus, among the "gainers", the "competitive market effect" seems to have narrowed down the differences in performance across these two ownership groups. However, if we look at standalone companies and group companies separately within each ownership group, we find that standalone companies in each ownership group have done significantly better, both in terms of improvement and in terms of 1995–96 performance, than their group counterparts.

(d)   For "losers", the divergences in their mean ROA in 1991–92 continued to exist in 1995–96. Both the ownership effect and, within domestic companies, the group-affiliation effect, rather than the "competitive market effect", appear to be strong for "losers". Among the "losers", thus, domestic private companies continued to perform worse than the foreign companies, and within domestic companies, standalone companies performed relatively worse than group companies.

(e)   Almost identical conclusions follow if we consider the efficiency criterion of AT (Table 3.5). Companies which improved their asset utilization in the post-reform period were the less efficient companies of the 1991–92; their mean AT in 1995–96 was substantially higher than the mean AT of the "losers", and the heterogeneity in their asset utilization in 1995–96 was significantly lower compared to that of the "losers".

Our analysis points to some interesting differences in the response of companies to the reforms. First, companies that performed better or worse in terms of profitability or efficiency in the post-reform period do not overwhelmingly belong to any particular ownership group, foreign or domestic. Second, within the set of companies that performed better in the post-reform period, the response of standalone companies has been more compared to their group counterparts. This could be due to the fact that even well-performing companies belonging to business groups have more rigid organizational and decision-making structures that would stand in the way of making the most of new market opportunities relative to standalones. Third, within the set of companies which performed worse in 1995–96, group companies seemed to be affected less compared to their standalone counterparts. This may be due to the fact that the sheer size, scale of operations, and being part of a business group are likely to enable a group-affiliated company to be in a better position to absorb short-term losses and increased risk during the transition to a more market-oriented regime. Finally, in the set of

Table 3.5 Pre-reform and post-reform performance of gainers and losers – efficiency

Ownership	Mean AT (%) of gainers			Mean AT (%) of losers			Mean AT (%) of all		
	1995–96	1991–92	Change	1995–96	1991–92	Change	1995–96	1991–92	Change
Public	104.1	81.0	23.1	78.5	106.8	-28.3	90.6	94.7	-4.1
Private group	147.4	117.2	30.2	105.3	147.5	-42.2	121.5	135.8	-14.4
Private standalone	166.6	126.5	40.0	113.3	165.4	-52.1	134.6	149.8	-15.2
Foreign group	158.9	127.4	31.5	153.2	200.0	-46.8	155.8	167.5	-11.8
Foreign standalone	169.7	134.1	35.7	133.5	171.0	-37.4	152.7	151.4	1.3

those companies which have improved their performance in the course of liberalization, there is less heterogeneity in performance across the different ownership groups. Thus, our analysis suggests that in a liberalized environment, other company-specific characteristics apart from ownership are important in understanding the response to reforms of the Indian corporate sector. This provides some indirect evidence to the position that ownership is likely to matter less with increased competitive pressures.

In Table 3.6 we have computed for each ownership group the mean value of four structural characteristics namely, (i) size (as proxied by sales), (ii) age, (iii) export to sales, and (iv) import to sales ratio of the "gainers" and "losers". These structural characteristics pertain to the year 1991–92 and represent the initial conditions prevailing at the start of the reforms. The last column gives the Hotelling's F-statistics for the multivariate test of whether the characteristics of the "gainers" and the "losers" are statistically different. Table 3.6 relates to "gainers" and "losers" based on ROA while Table 3.7 is based on AT.

With respect to ROA, Table 3.6 shows size to be a discriminatory characteristic of "gainers" and "losers", with the nature of discrimination varying according to ownership groups. For all domestic companies, public and private, gaining companies appear to be the larger companies of 1991–92, and this size effect is particularly strong for private companies belonging to business groups. For foreign companies, the size effect is just reversed. Gaining companies appear to be the smaller companies of 1991–92, with again the size effect being very strong for companies belonging to business groups. Unlike size, age appears to be a discriminatory characteristic for only foreign companies. The gaining foreign companies appear to be much younger than the losing companies. When all the four characteristics are taken together, the Hotelling's F-statistics suggests that differences in characteristics of the "gainers" and "losers" are statistically significant for each ownership group. When we classify the "gainers" and "losers" based on the AT criterion (Table 3.7), the discriminatory characteristics of size and age are much sharper and uniform. Companies that improved their asset utilization in the post-reform period are the smaller and the younger companies of 1991–92 and this is true for all ownership groups other than publicly owned companies.

Concluding observations

This chapter discussed and analyzed the impact of industrial and trade liberalization initiated in India since the early nineties on the Indian

Table 3.6 Pre-reform characteristics of gainers and losers – based on ROA[a]

Ownership	Gainers				Losers				Hotelling's test – F-statistics
	Mean sales*	Mean age*	Mean export/sales	Mean import/sales	Mean sales	Mean age	Mean export/sales	Mean import/sales	
Public	12,150	29.3	3.1	12.3	5,519	28.8	0.9	9.4	21.99*
Private group	1,942	34.8	4.1	7.7	1,421	32.7	8.0	7.1	11.85*
Private standalone	3,970	32.9	3.8	8.1	3,760	30.0	10.6	7.4	14.98*
Foreign group	2,072	27.1	4.9	5.6	4,627	39.9	6.3	5.0	46.78*
Foreign standalone	1,357	31.7	8.4	13.7	1,355	38.8	7.5	11.5	11.02*

* Significant at 1 per cent level.
[a] Sales is in 1991–92 million Indian rupees (INR) and age is in years.

Table 3.7 Pre-reform characteristics of gainers and losers – based on AT[a]

Ownership	Gainers				Losers				Hotelling's test – F-statistics
	Mean sales*	Mean age*	Mean export/sales	Mean import/sales	Mean sales	Mean age	Mean export/sales	Mean import/sales	
Public	7634	25.9	2.1	11.5	7615	31.7	1.2	9.3	11.69*
Private group	1517	34.5	6.8	7.3	1671	32.8	6.4	7.3	0.85
Private standalone	328	26.8	4.1	8.3	419	33.7	11.4	7.2	27.58*
Foreign group	1386	29.1	5.2	6.4	4696	35.9	5.8	4.4	37.41*
Foreign standalone	832	32.3	8.2	14.0	1945	37.7	7.8	11.3	25.07*

* Significant at 1 per cent level.
[a] Sales is in 1991–92 million Indian rupees (INR) and age is in years.

corporate sector. Specifically, the analysis focused on tracking changes in performance across the different ownership groups, namely public and private, and within private, domestic and foreign companies. Further, within domestic and foreign companies, the analysis looked at possible differentials in response between group and standalone companies.

With respect to the level of performance, we find significant and persistent profitability and efficiency differentials between private and public companies. Private companies as a group perform significantly better than public companies throughout the entire period of nine years in the study. This result seems to tally with the result obtained by Majumdar (1998) in his study of Indian ownership groups for a period prior to the reforms. Regarding performance differentials within private ownership groups, we find that while there are some differences in performance between domestic and foreign companies, and within each group, between standalone and group companies, these differences are not statistically significant as revealed by the means test for two years 1991–92 and 1995–96. Our results thus suggest that ownership effects within the private sector do not exist at the broad group level. Ownership effects, if any, must be related to the level, and possibly to the composition, of equity ownership.

Coming to the response of the different ownership groups to the liberalization process – the main focus of this chapter – we find that the liberalization process has thrown up "gainers" and "losers" from each of the ownership groups. Strikingly, we find that those who gained were in fact the underperformers of the pre-reform period while those whose performance declined were the performers of the earlier period. This is true for all ownership groups. This result indicates that the lifting of regulations has enabled under-performing companies to achieve their potential whereas companies which were well tuned to the license-raj and protected markets and were earning profits are the ones which are finding it difficult to cope with market pressures. Among the "gainers", we find competitive pressures to have somewhat narrowed down the performance differentials across the various ownership groups. However, we do not find a similar effect for the "losers". For the losing companies, we find significant performance differentials persisting among the various ownership groups.

With respect to the response of group companies vis-à-vis standalone companies to the liberalization process, we find the response of group companies, among both the "gainers" and the "losers", to be much more muted compared to their standalone counterparts. For the "gainers", this result is consistent with our earlier argument that group companies may be slow to reorient themselves to the changing milieu given their larger size, scale of operations, and accumulated organizational rigidities. At the same time, some of these factors are likely to insure these companies against large downside risk that may follow from changes in the policy environment, a contention that is also borne by our result with respect to the "losers". Finally, with respect to the structural characteristics of the "gainers" and "losers", we find young and small companies to have gained relatively more than the older and the larger companies. As argued, the young and small companies are likely to have less baggage inherited from the regulated regime which make them relatively more flexible to adapt to a continually changing environment.

In conclusion, our results have been largely obtained within an univariate framework to get a preliminary idea of the response of the various ownership groups to the reform process. Our results suggest that the response to liberalization cannot be associated strongly with any particular ownership group and that there are "gainers" and "losers" within each group. Structural characteristics like size, age, and import and export intensity appear to influence the response of companies to liberalization. Further analysis within a multivariate framework that controls for the differences in these structural characteristics of companies as well as possible industry effects remains to be considered in the future.

Notes

1 See for example, Bhagwati (1993); Cable (1995); Ahluwalia (1995, 1999).
2 According to property rights theorists (for example, Alchian, 1965; de Alessi, 1980), superior performance of private companies stems from the presence of effective mechanisms in disciplining management and aligning shareholder and managerial interests in private companies, most of which are virtually absent in public companies. Complementing the property rights viewpoint, public choice theorists (for example, Niskanen, 1975; Levy, 1988) point to specific X-inefficiency factors that arise from government ownership *per se* irrespective of market conditions.
3 The corporate governance literature focuses on performance differentials among private companies that arise due to different mechanisms of corporate governance. For an excellent survey of this literature see Shleifer and Vishny, 1997 and the references therein. The literature focuses on issues like the differential impact of debt versus equity holding on corporate performance, on the differences in performance arising from block ownership as opposed to diffuse ownership, from insider ownership versus outside ownership, and the like.

4 According to this view (for example, Vickers and Yarrow, 1988; Allen and Gale, 1999), competitive environments make organizations, *irrespective* of their ownership characteristics, internally more X-efficient (Leibenstein, 1989) and hence ownership should not matter in such environments (Vickers and Yarrow, 1989). Market competition can also reduce agency problems by providing sufficient statistics, such as relative profits of a firm, to evaluate managerial performance (Holmstrom, 1982), as also in determining managerial remuneration in future (Fama, 1980).

5 For instance, as Sengupta (1996; p. 347) notes, the Finance Minister in his Budget Speech of 1985–86 highlighted the need to change the "thinking of the people of India to look ahead to the future and not keep on dwelling on the past...". Also, as Kohli (1991) observes, the word "socialism" was not mentioned even once in that budget speech.

6 These estimates are from Pursell and Sharma (1996), cited in Misra (1998).

7 These are Ministry of Finance and World Bank estimates presented in Ahluwalia (1999).

8 Shastri (1999) identifies three divisions. The first group, the "mature business groups" supporting the 51 per cent equity participation placing foreign companies on a level playing field vis-à-vis their domestic counterparts, another group maintaining that only 40 per cent equity participation should be allowed, and finally, a third group maintaining that even 40 per cent is high for certain sectors such as pharmaceuticals and that the limit should be 25 per cent.

9 Jansson *et al.* (1995) observe that the ideology of politicians with respect to liberalization somersaulted on many occassions; for instance, Chandra Shekhar who had publicly campaigned against the liberalization of industrial policy became a liberalizer himself when he became the Prime Minister.

10 These insights follow from the research on the evolution of optimal organizational forms (see for example, Williamson (1983); North (1990)).

11 The year 1988–89 represents the period from April 1988 to March 1989. Most companies in India adopt the period between April (of one year) and March (of the following year) as the financial year for accounting purpose.

12 See Glen *et al.* (1999) for a related discussion on performance measures in emerging markets.

References

Ahluwalia, I.J. (1995), "New economic policies, enterprises and privatization in India", in Robert Cassen and Vijay Joshi (eds), *India: The Future of Economic Reform*. New Delhi: Oxford University Press.

Ahluwalia, I.J. (1999), "Industrial and trade reforms in India", in Ric Shand (ed.), *Economic Liberalization in South Asia*, India: Macmillan.

Alchian, A.A. (1965), "Some economics of property rights", *Il Politico*, **30**, pp. 816–29, December.

de Alessi, L. (1980), "The economics of property rights: a review of the evidence", in Richard O. Zerbe (ed.), *Research in Law and Economics*, 2, pp. 1–47. Greenwich, Conn.: JAI.

Allen, F. and D. Gale (1999), Corporate Governance and Competition. Working Paper, Financial Institutions Center, Wharton School, University of Pennsylvania.

Bhagwati, J. (1993), "India's economy: the shackled giant in *The 1992 Radhakrishnan Lectures"*, Oxford: Clarendon Press.

Bhaya, H. (1990), "Management efficiency in the private and public sectors in India", in John Heath (ed.), *Public Enterprise at the Crossroads: Essays in Honour of V.V. Ramanadham,* London and New York: Routledge, pp. 228–40.

Cable, V. (1995), "Indian liberalization and the private sector in India", in Robert Cassen and Vijay Joshi (eds), *The Future of Economic Reforms.* New Delhi, Oxford and New York: Oxford University Press, pp. 209–31.

Chhibber, P.K. and S.K. Majumdar (1999), "Foreign ownership and profitability: property rights, control, and the performance of firms in Indian industry", *Journal of Law and Finance,* **42**(1), pp. 209–39.

Fama, E. (1980), "Agency problems and the theory of the firm", *Journal of Political Economy,* **88**, pp. 288–307.

Ghemawat, P. and T. Khanna (1998), "The nature of diversified business groups: a research design and two case studies", *Journal of Industrial Economics,* **46**(1), pp. 35–61.

Glen, J., Singh, A. and R. Matthias (1999), How Intensive is Competition in The Emerging Markets?: An Analysis of the Corporate Rates of Return from Nine Emerging Markets. IMF Working Paper 99/32, Washington.

Holmstrom, B. (1982), "Moral hazard in teams", *Bell Journal of Economics,* **13**(2), pp. 324–40.

Jansson, H., Saqib, M. and D. Deo Sharma (1995), *The State and Transnational Corporations: A Network Approach to Industrial Policy in India.* Edward Elgar: Aldershot, UK.

Jha, R. and B.S. Sahni (1992), "Measures of efficiency in private and public industries: the case of India", *Annals of Public and Cooperative Economics,* **63**, pp. 489–95.

Joseph, M., Sabnavis, M., Rege-Nitsure, R. and R. Bhagirathi (1998), "India's economic reforms: private corporate sector response", *International Journal of Development Banking,* **16**(2), pp. 43–64.

Khanna, T. and K. Palepu (1997), "Why focussed startegies for emerging markets?", *Harvard Business Review,* July–August.

Khanna, T. and K. Palepu (1998), "Emerging market business groups, foreign investors and corporate governance", forthcoming in Randall Morck (ed.), NBER volume on *Concentrated Ownership,* University of Chicago Press.

Khanna, T. and K. Palepu (2000), "Is group affiliation profitable in emerging markets? an analysis of diversified Indian business groups", *Journal of Finance,* **55**(2), pp. 867–91.

Kidron, M. (1965), *Foreign Investments in India.* London: Oxford University Press.

Kohli, A. (1991), *Democracy and Discontent: India's Growing Crisis of Governability.* Cambridge: Cambridge University Press.

Krishna, P. and D. Mitra (1998), "Trade liberalization, market discipline and productivity growth: new evidence from India", *Journal of Development Economics,* **56**, pp. 447–62.

Krueger, A. (1993), "Virtuous and vicious circles in economic development", *American Economic Review,* **83**, pp. 351–5.

Leibenstein, H. (1989), "Organizational economics and institutions as missing elements in economic development analysis", *World Development,* **17**(9), pp. 1333–47.

Levy, B. (1988), "A theory of public enterprise behavior". *Journal of Economic Behavior and Organization*, **8**, pp. 75–96.

Majumdar, S.-K. (1998), "Assessing comparative efficiency of the state-owned mixed and private sectors in Indian industry", *Public-Choice*, **96**(1–2), pp. 1–24.

Mani, S. (1999), "A survey of deregulation in Indian industry", in Mitsuhiro Kagami and Masatsugu Tsuji (eds), *Privatization, Deregulation and Institutional Framework*. Institute of Developing Economies, JETRO, pp. 197–221.

Marathe, S.S. (1989), *Regulation and Development: India's Policy Experience of Controls over Industry*, (second edition). New Delhi: Sage Publications.

Martinelli, C. and M. Tommasi (1997), "Sequencing of economic reforms in the presence of political constraints", *Economics and Politics*, **9**, pp. 115–31. Reprinted in Sturzenegger, F. and M. Tommasi (eds), *The Political Economy of Reform*. Cambridge, Massachusetts: The MIT Press, 1998, pp. 285–304.

Misra, V. (1998), India's Export Performance: 1950–1997, Report prepared for the Asian Development Bank.

Mitra, A. (1999), "Total factor productivity growth and technical efficiency in Indian industries", *Economic and Political Weekly*, July 31, pp. M98–113.

Neogi, C. and B. Ghosh (1998), "Impact of liberalization on performance of Indian industries: a firm level study", *Economic and Political Weekly*, 28 February, pp. M16–24.

Niskanen, W. (1975), "Bureaucrats and politicians", *Journal of Law and Economics*, **28**, pp. 617–43, December.

North, D.C. (1990), *Institutions, Institutional Change and Economic Performance*, Cambridge: Cambridge University Press.

Pursell, G. and A. Sharma (1996), "Indian Trade Policies Since the 1991/92 Reforms", *in process*, International Economics Division, World Bank: Washington, DC.

Ramaswamy, K. and W. Renforth (1994), "Evaluating the performance of state-owned enterprises and privately owned firms: the Indian experience", *Academy of Management Proceedings*, pp. 297–301.

Rodrik, D. (1994), "The rush to free trade in the developing world: why so late? why now? will it last?", in Stephen Haggard and Steven B. Webb (eds), *Voting for Reform: Democracy, Political Liberalization, and Economic Adjustment*, New York: Oxford University Press, pp. 61–88. Reprinted in Sturzenegger, F. and M. Tommasi (eds), *The Political Economy of Reform*, Cambridge, Massachusetts: The MIT Press, 1998, pp. 209–40.

Sarkar, J. and S. Sarkar (1999a), "The governance of Indian corporates", in Kirit S. Parikh (ed.), *India Development Report 1999–2000*, New Delhi: Oxford University Press, pp. 201–18.

Sarkar, J. and S. Sarkar (2000), "Large Shareholder Activism in Corporate Governance in Developing Countries: Evidence from India", *International Review of Finance*, **1**(3), pp. 161–94.

Sengupta, B. (1996), *India: Problems of Governance*. New Delhi: Konark Publishers.

Shastri, V. (1999), *State and Business in India: The New Mode of Collective Action*, ADB Project on the "Economic and Policy Reforms in India", National Council of Applied Economic Research, New Delhi.

Shleifer, A. and R.W. Vishny (1997), "A survey of corporate governance", *The Journal of Finance*, **LII**(2), pp. 737–83.

Srivastava, V. (1996), *Liberalization, Productivity and Competition: A Panel Study of Indian Manufacturing.* New Delhi: Oxford University Press.

Vickers, J. and G. Yarrow (1988), *Privatization: An Economic Analysis*, MIT Press Series on the Regulation of Economic Activity, no. 18. Cambridge, Mass. and London: MIT Press.

Vickers, J. and G. Yarrow (1989), "Privatization in Britain", in MacAvoy, Paul, W. *et al.* (eds), *Rochester Studies in Economics and Policy Issues series Privatization and state-owned enterprises: Lessons from the United States, Great Britain and Canada*, Norwell, Mass.: Dordrecht and Lancaster, U.K.: Kluwer Academic in cooperation with the University of Rochester, William E. Simon Graduate School of Business Administration, Bradley Policy Research Center, pp. 209–45.

Vickers, J. and G. Yarrow (1991), "Economic perspectives on privatization", *Journal of Economic Perspectives*, 5, pp. 111–32.

Williamson, O. (1983), *Markets and Hierarchies: Analysis and Antitrust Implications*, New York: The Free Press.

4

The Politics of Accumulation in Small Town India[1]

Elisabetta Basile and Barbara Harriss-White

Introduction: the social matrix of accumulation

In this chapter, we summarise the initial results of field research on one aspect of civil society which sprung from conversations about the politics of markets with Gordon White (White, 1993). The output of White's work on the politics of civil society in China ran rapidly to six papers and a substantial book (White *et al.*, 1996) and then flowed on into fertile intellectual distributaries: civil society and democratisation (Luckham and White, 1996; Robinson and White, 1998); the politics of social provision (Goodman *et al.*, 1998) and the political conditions for effective developmental states (Luckham and White, 1996). In comparison, our work in India was small in scope, proceeded comparatively at a snail's pace and has generated but one paper (Basile and Harriss-White, 1999)! Three strands of White's work have been indispensible to the framework we use to examine the impact of the politics of urban organisations on accumulation in South India: civil society, the politics of market organisation and corporatism. In this introduction, we will outline the framework of 'social structures of accumulation' (SSA) and weave in these strands.

While orthodox economics externalises the regulative environment, the school of SSA challenges the conventional double reductionism of capitalism to markets, and of markets to the economic domain. It seeks to examine growth and change in capitalist systems through the complex of social institutions that enable the collection of factors of production, the transformation of money into the means of production, the organisation of production and the reconversion of the product into money (Kotz *et al.*, 1994). Institutions and their interrelationships evolve as a period of accumulation comes into being and is sustained, but the consolidation of this institutional matrix has the capacity eventually to undermine the very system it has created. The motors of accumulation may include: institutions structuring labour and management and those managing demand and consumption; the character of industrial organisation; the institutions of finance; the role of the state and the political parties; social institutions of race and gender and the dominant culture or ideology. At the core of this ambitious intellectual agenda is a question about how this continually changing set of structures ensures or undermines stability, by reducing class conflict, conflict within capital and conflict between concentrations of capital.

In this chapter, we use this framework to help answer the question: within the set of institutions underpinning capitalist accumulation, what is the role played by organisations of civil society? In his political analysis of markets, White (1993: 7) grants civic organisations a prominent role as shapers of the politics of market organisation. Here competition is subordinated to collective action for the purposes of endogenous regulation, yet these conditions 'protect the market position' of participants, through unearned rents, to the detriment of those excluded. The balance between positive (regulatory) and negative (exclusionary) effects of such organisations, White concluded, needs more thought and investigation (ibid.). That is our purpose here. Beforehand, however, we have to briefly introduce and define other key analytical building blocks: civil society, caste and corporatism.

Civil society, caste and corporatism

White *et al.* define civil society as 'a sphere of free social interaction and organisation which is separate and independent of the State' (1996: 1). But the term is heavily contested, depending on the terms of the juxtaposition of state with civil society (Keane, 1988). To add relevance to our study of civic organisations and a new structure to the SSA, we need to draw from Gramsci (1975) the insight that civil society consists of the political, cultural and ideological hegemony which a social group exercises over society and by means of which the economy is regulated. The Gramscian concept of civil society combines two spheres of human life: economic interests and ideology. The institutions which result (including those crucial for accumulation) are the outcome not only of social contradictions and conflicts but also of the ideological factors by which consent is gained and personal interests are imposed. Ideology then becomes a major component of the institution-building process.

Two aspects of Indian development – rapid social and economic change and an increasing social complexity – reinforce the relevance of a Gramscian approach to SSA. Caste, in both its ideological and its politically organised forms, is central to both aspects.

Caste is 'a specifically Indian form of civil society', characterised by both 'continuity and change' (Fuller, 1996). The constraint of caste on Indian economic performance has long been debated. That economic liberalisation, and modernity more generally, will dissolve the caste system is now a common insight (Mendelsohn, 1993; Panini, 1996; Jayaram, 1996), seeding hypotheses about determinants and consequences. Caste, legitimated directly from, and 'inextricably intertwined with', Hindu religion remains a foundation of Indian society. While castes contribute to the architecture of Indian civil society, each individual caste is a 'dynamic force in interest articulation' (Jayaram, 1996). While 'modernisation' has undermined or transformed the organisation of caste, it has also revealed its 'tremendous flexibility' (Jayaram, 1996). Caste groups have shifted ritual position, due to the increasing contact of lower castes with the great Hindu tradition (Karanth, 1996). The process whereby 'a low caste takes over the customs, ritual, belief, ideology and style of life of a high caste' with the objective of improving 'the economic and political position of the group' is called 'Sanskritisation' (Srinivas, 1989: 56). Sanskritisation in turn accompanies 'modernisation' by which is meant – very specifically – an increasing dissociation of castes from their hereditary occupations. The combined effect of 'modernisation' and the contested implementation of positive discrimination via the Reservations policy of the Indian Government has been the emergence of a 'dual culture' (Karanth, 1996; Radhakrishnan, 1996), in which a caste attempts to claim a low or backward status in relation to the state, while claiming and protecting a high status in relation to society.

The secularisation of caste in India has involved a separation between the Hindu religious sphere and the social-economic sphere. As Béteille suggests (1996: 158), the caste system has been 'truncated': its future is 'not with religion but with politics'. If 'modernisation' has reworked caste, the question then is what kind of political society is currently being shaped by this transformed institution. The recent literature shows how caste plays a major continuity role as the economy diversifies. It is still possible to observe a caste-clustering in the contemporary distribution of occupations. But this clustering can be (and has been) explained by the distribution of skills and resources, by the imperfections of the labour markets affecting the control of individuals over information on economic opportunities, rather than with reference to the caste hierarchy per se (Panini, 1996). In addition, liberalisation has revealed a deeply segmented social structure in which caste is connected with networks of other civil organisations that comprehensively regulate economic and social life (Reiniche, 1996; Uphadya, 1997). Distinctions of status, even if they might still be expressed in the idiom of caste, are rooted neither in a caste system nor in a caste hierarchy, whose legitimacy has been eroded, but rather in social groups that are legitimated in economic terms (Fuller, 1996).

We can now turn to our hypothesis: *that the form of social regulation emerging from the secularisation of caste is corporatist.* Corporatism is a type of control over relations between labour, capital and the state, which is based on a specific economic order that is compatible with authoritarianism (O'Sullivan, 1988). The play between the interest groups defines the associative order that governs social interaction and shapes the SSA. The role of the state may vary, and a common distinction is made in literature between the state and societal corporatism (reviewed in White, 1996). In the first form, the state plays a 'directive' role and dominates its relationship with the associations and the relationships between associations. In the second form, theorised by Schmitter (1974) and Cawson (1985), associations are relatively independent from the state which performs the role of 'interest intermediation'. The relationships between state and corporatist associations are based on political exchange. The typical corporatist political exchange involves more than one organised interest, and the form of corporatism is tripartite, as state, capital and labour are involved simultaneously. The state is not a neutral arbiter, but instead the synthesiser of corporatist ideals and values, the repositary of a vision of society in which the power of capital and labour is asymmetrically distributed and biased towards the former. As a result, in corporatism, civil society, political society and economy overlap (Mancini *et al.*, 1983).

The neo-corporatist argument is highly relevant to our project on contemporary India. Organisations of economic interest may be created and/or controlled by the state for its own project of accumulation. Such institutions may not contribute to the democratisation of society. An alternative conception of the role of institutions of collective economic interest (business and trade associations) from that of narrow advancement to that of the mediation of potentially conflicting interest is opened up; and attention is drawn in the concrete circumstances of South India to the relationship between caste as a means of organising occupation and its evolving relation to the state.

The town

Our empirical material is of two types: a series of three field enquiries into the organisation of local urban capital, labour, commodities and into their politics by means of business histories got from a random 6 per cent samples of commercial enterprises in 1973–74, 1982–84 and 1993–94 (Harriss, 1991); and a systematic set of histories of almost all the groups and associations with which the business economy of a small town is linked and in which it is embedded: market and political institutions, civil society organisations and associations, gathered in 1997.

The market town is Arni, located in northern Tamil Nadu and acting as a central place for more than a hundred villages. It is 150 kms south west of Chennai with an economic base of administration, commerce (increasingly wholesale), paddy trading and milling, and silk saree weaving. Five per cent of its population is agricultural. Its population has grown from some 39,000 in 1971 to 49,000 in 1981 and 55,000 in 1991. The municipality, created in 1951 and converted to grade 2 status in 1971, has already engulfed 11 revenue villages. In fact the population directly associated with Arni's urban economy is likely to approach 100,000, the census population being inflated by transients and by regular commuting from its ring of satellite villages (which resist incorporation into the municipality, because of the increases this would make in local taxation – a situation which makes local urban government chronically relatively underfunded).

During the last twenty years, the number of businesses visible to our census record of businesses in Arni has trebled. By late 1993, the transformation in its economic base over the previous decade had been nothing short of astonishing. A number of agricultural and 'traditional' artisan activities had declined significantly or disappeared altogether. Agricultural inputs firms had stagnated (as had agricultural production). The activities comprising the economic base ten to twenty years ago had consolidated their position: rice mills had doubled in number, as had food wholesaling firms and durable consumer goods retail units. Urban silk manufacturing units had increased by 50 per cent and spilled massively into the countryside. Deregulation had led to a three-fold increase in fuel depots, and increased urban and rural incomes had generated demand for a thirty-fold increase in businesses dealing in non-food agricultural products.

New businesses attest not only to the metropolitanisation of economy and culture, but also to its rapid globalisation. Brand new telecommunications technologies have appeared; satellite and cable TV (and ways to poach it) and new telecommunications rental markets have spread throughout the urban area, along with courier services, xerox and video libraries. The town can now give up to 20,000 'doses' of cinema per day. The explosion of finance companies and chit funds, many not registered, many run with black money, the appearance of insurance, stocks and share dealing services, specialised commercial agencies for corporate industry, and architectural, accountancy and real estate professions attest to the emergence of sizeable elite markets. Tuition centres, typing and computing institutes and students' hostels indicate new patterns of skill acquisition and freedom for young people (although the town is extremely underdeveloped with respect to education). Automobile sales and rentals, tourist cars and vans businesses have responded to local piety, curiosity and incomes (for tourism is inextricably linked with pilgrimages and shrine-hopping). Prominent expansions of hotels, bakeries and sweets stalls and booths indicate new patterns of commensality. Modernisation has not simplified the institutional fabric. Quite the reverse. All these developments have added to the institutional complexity of the town. But while the town appears a model of growth centre in terms of number of enterprises, the prevalence and distribution of black finance capital suggest that there is a substantial element of accumulation which is non-productive. From field research we estimate that the output from trade and the income from finance equals or exceeds that from productive industry in Arni.

The vast mass of businesses are family firms with small labour forces. The average number of livelihoods (7–8 per firm) has not changed much over the period 1973–93. The proportion of purely family firms (petty commodity producers and traders) has risen from 28 to 35 per cent over the twenty year period, while the proportion of family labour in the entire labour force has remained static at around a quarter. The composition of this work force has changed with the entry of female family members of all castes. The mills, however, have become increasingly 'satanic' over time, through the casualisation of their labour force. Casual labour has increased from 23 per cent of jobs to 57 per cent between 1973 and 1993.

Forward Caste control over business is stable in absolute terms, and their apparent proportional decline masks the massive increase in concentration of their capital. Backward Castes (BCs) have gained ground as owners, while Most Backward Castes (MBCs) and Scheduled Castes (SCs) make up around 80 per cent of the casual labour force. Ten to fifteen per cent of firms still employ only labour of their own caste. In the great majority of firms, workers form an emulsion of caste. In the nineties, the town was swept by a new wave of 'primitive' accumulation in two senses of the term: though capitalist production relations have been long entrenched, each individual capitalist had to develop their own starting point for accumulation; and a significant element in these initial resources, even when acquired in the modern economy, is got in 'primitive' ways through economic crime, fraud and corruption (Harriss-White, 1996).

The politics of accumulation in Arni

Our empirical material shows that Arni's economy has lately been organised into a large number of private and state institutions (66), covering all aspects of social and economic life, and regulating it at the levels of the (male) individual, the household and the collective. The first to be created in the early part of the century were public service and public sector unions together with some of the politically militant but numerically small service castes. Over half have appeared since 1980 and 35 per cent in the nineties, based on new principles of organisation: new political parties, town level, cross-caste organisations, trade associations for new goods and services, organisations for scheduled castes and a handfull for women. Many associations have a cross-class nature and (male) individuals participate irrespective of their class position. This is most obvious in the caste-cum-occupational associations but holds for others, particularly welfare and charitable organisations. Most crucially, the interests of culture and religion come to be organised, in part, through caste associations. Then such organisations come not only to reflect culture and religion but also political and business objectives. Indeed the latter come to dominate the organisations, and the urban economy cannot operate without them.

There is a strong ideological element to these groups. Alongside a regulative economic agenda and claims from the state, practically every caste association aims to improve their own welfare and solidarity, reproducing within a caste an echo of the distributional rules that formerly operated between castes in this region. Groups representing more economically powerful interests also aim to improve (or to be seen to improve) the welfare of the town itself, albeit through small acts of redistributive charity which are also open to interpretation as legitimating accumulation. These attempts at self-regulation and economic governance are supported by a widespread ideology that conceals class interests under the veil of the wider interest of the 'community'. It is worth stressing that the strength of 'town-unity' extends across religions. Of some significance is the role of Muslim businessmen not only as Muslims but also as businessmen, as representatives of the town and as collective investors in (secular) educational infrastructure egregiously neglected by the state.

A very crucial pillar of the ideology in which the town is a 'unified body' – and part of the SSA fabric – is caste, which to date is showing no sign of the erosion foreseen by Panini and others. Instead caste is being selectively reworked to mean different things at different positions in the economic system of the town. Among SC and MBC,[2] caste remains a condition of hierarchy. Higher castes are repelled from low caste occupations. Access by low castes to higher caste occupations is prevented and, for the lowest castes, caste cannot even be used as an idiom in the organisations struggling for income and status. By contrast, among BCs, caste is more a matter of difference, economically competitive and increasingly internally differentiated. Here we see the contradictions of practices signifying a rise in status on the one hand, and pressure on the state to lower the status for the purposes of positive discrimination on the other. At the top, caste ceases to have a role to play in formal economic regulation, though it certainly does not cease to have a role in economic and social life outside that of the regulative group. So there is a distinct interplay between the economy and caste (and caste-based occupational) associations, which shows the flexibility of caste, the reworking and distancing between caste and religion, and the adding of economic regulative functions both to the institution of caste per se and particularly to its formal associations. For if castes are 'truncated and secularised' institutions which have lost their religious bearings, they are ineluctably vital as regulators of the economy. It seems that the sanskritising agenda of the caste associations has been sacrificed on the altar of the economy.

The interplay between caste and the economy may be differentiated but it is consistent with corporatism. Corporatism, let us recapitulate, limits class conflict inter alia by involving both capital and labour in the 'self government' of the economy. It rests on two pillars, one institutional and the other ideological. Together they impregnate production relations to generate the overlap between economy and society that is the distinctive feature of corporatism. In this we think caste plays a triple role. First, it provides an ideological backcloth for the corporatist 'project'. At the same time it generates (and is consistent with the formalisation of) the institutional structure on the back of which corporatist organisations have evolved. In this urban society, caste still supplies the hierarchical order.[3] Through caste, the link between ideology and institutions is particularly strong. The ideology itself (in distinguishing castes) is the source of the institutions (caste and closely related, finely defined occupational associations). Furthermore, caste helps in the creation of the conditions for the overlap between economy and society that is necessary to the working of the corporatist project. The corporatist ideological and institutional framework imprints production relations, the main features of which can be distinguished according to: (1) class relations; (2) gender; (3) the local territorial organisation of the urban economy; and (4) relations between the urban economy and the state.

Capital–labour relations

The town is organised according to the needs of local 'big' capital. However, 'big' local capital does not act in concert, but is divided by commodity and by caste. It is not weakened by such a political configuration. Rather, the latter may be seen as the hydraheaded alignments of a numerically small sector so as to maximise tactical advantages. Witness, for example, the ubiquitous attempts collectively to regulate and control (via the state where necessary) the matrices of market exchange in which these firms are embedded: those for raw materials, money, rates in derived markets and most particularly labour. The modalities of labour control include wage rates but also the means of increasing absolute surplus value (the terms and conditions of work, the length of the working day and week, the extent and periodicity of holidays, the use of female and child labour). Through this control, capital is able to transform labour productivity extensively and without a rise in mass consumption. In so doing capital frequently flouts the laws regulating and protecting labour (but most regulative law is flouted routinely). At the same time accumulation is permeated with petty crime and with widespread fraud, particularly with respect to every aspect of taxation.

Labour is weak and not organised. Independent trade unions are almost non-existent and party political support is opportunistic. Associations of low castes and workers' unions are no different from big commodity associations in this respect. There is no organised complaint or rebellion about working conditions, in spite of the fact that, as the major business associations reported, the town is close to full employment. A modern proverb has it that 'Caste is the strongest trade union', but even among low caste workers, caste is not organising 'labour' as opposed to 'capital'. In certain castes, occupations with a long history of caste-identification are vigorously defended for a mixture of purposes, such as social identity, insurance, trust and economic reputation, job security and credit, but extremely rarely for class identity. The commodity branding of many of the backward castes signals the relative status of the traders and the traded. But it carries no necessary implications for class position. Capital is blind to caste as it transforms the production and circulation of commodities. Caste has become an instrument to regulate workers' participation in the economy, rather than to legitimate caste/class opposition or to position people in a ranking of ritual status. There is then a sort of structural disequilibrium between capital and labour, as far as class consciousness is concerned: the capitalist class has a strong identity that is reinforced by convictions about the duties of the local elites in promoting urban welfare; while labour has a very weak perception of its class identity due to the absence of political representation and the pervasive presence of caste. But there are institutions other than caste which structure accumulation and with which caste is more or less entwined: gender, locality and the state.

Gender

While just under half the workforce is female, while a handfull of businesses are managed by women, practically no business is owned by women and corporate associational life is intensely male. Educated women (extremely few of whom are Scheduled Caste beneficiaries of christian educations and even fewer of whom are Backward Caste) have economic niches in clerical jobs in local government, medicine, teaching, and a toehold in the professions. It is very rare to find a woman lawyer or member of the police force. Those with other skills (such as computing), work in organised-sector firms outside the locality, on the outer periphery of Arni's collective life. Their role is confined to buttressing the ideological legitimation of the business/caste elite through cross-caste and class philanthropy. Women are but tiny minorities in a few caste and trade associations, and where they form an important proportion, their corporate affairs are managed by men, just as the interests of labour are frequently managed by capital. As labour, women are deliberately casualised and attempts to organise them are crushed. Urban civil society therefore tends towards the reinforcement of patriarchy in the market economy. By contrast, it is the Dravidian state which has provided opportunities for the relative empowerment of women, through education and through employment, though women are still conspicuous by their absence in the higher administrative echelons.

Locality

There are two aspects of locality which shape the organisation of the economy. First, since the tidal wave of commercial capitalist expansion in the sixties, the town has organised itself as a social unit across caste and to a lesser extent across class and gender. But the purposes of this unity have evolved from being socially redistributivist and legitimating via the accretion of enabling and claiming activity to substituting for the state. In its new, composite role, 'town unity' is pitted against the state as much as providing a crutch for it. The second aspect of the organisation of locality concerns its spatio-political dynamics. Those civil-social organisations which are not federated operate politically at the level of local municipal government, exerting pressure on the local state and demanding infrastructure. But the majority of civil-social organisations are components of hierarchical federations with their apexes in state or national capitals. This has two further consequences: local organisations have access to higher levels of skill and resources in their political and economic projects; and they may also be construed as conduits of information and instructions from headquarters and/or mobilised reactively in a competitive political arena located outside the town.

State

The economic role of civil-social organisations is partly self-regulative but for the most part directed towards the state. The state in the town is empowered to organise, mediate, protect, regulate and redistribute economic resources. In so doing it redistributes economic power between the genders, shapes the fortunes of castes, creates and regulates classes and formalises locality. If it ever was a secular institution, it is definitely being desecularised in the current era. Its efficacy is being shaped by the private social status of its officials (Harriss-White, forthcoming). At the same time, it is also riddled with incompetence, arbitrariness and oppressive practices. Private interest and private discretionary power generates corruption. So also does the party-political capture of bureaucratic allocative power in rivers of private tribute based upon departmental co-option. More quantitatively important than corruption is fraud, in which benefits are shared between individual politicians and the local business elite. Clearly, this is a collaborative state. But one thing its collaboration does not involve is control over the civil-social institutions described here.

Yet it is this state to which political appeal is made through caste and trade associations. Seven aspects to this set of claims appear from our empirical material: (i) prices and subsidies to combat the unruliness of market exchange; (ii) regulation (particularly of urban space while other aspects of the state's regulation of markets are energetically contested); (iii) direct commercial intervention (trading in raw materials or finished products, regulation of access, terms and conditions of finance and loans); (iv) infrastructure (not only physical infrastructure but also financial and social); (v) caste reservations and employment; (vi) collusion over control of labour; and (vii) taxation. The sites, scales and political outcomes of the seven fronts for civic contestation vary. But as long as the state is embroiled in these struggles (and from our evidence its role is intensifying, rather than declining, over the decade of liberalisation) there will persist not only the well chronicled tension between political inclusion and economic exclusion but also the less acknowledged tensions about the terms of political inclusion. These terms require the state to have an active redistributive role in the economy.

An increasingly restive political society with new, and newly assertive parties, with organisations representing lower castes and with the democratic formal structure of authority found in many organisations does not necessarily mean that civil society is democratising. Instead, as electoral democracy deepens, a politics other than party-electoral politics is emerging, in which caste rather than class plays the mobilising role. Electoral politics is suffused with caste competition and caste blocs. Party political alignment and caste compete as principles for votes. The town is at a stage in its political development when an increasingly caste-based electoral politics takes the shape of 'capitalist business', requiring private investment employing labour and yielding returns not simply through the crude and time-bound mechanism of votes but through the infinitely more subtle and enduring returns to corrupt intermediation, fraud, non-compliance and contractual allocations that are possible once in power.

Conclusion

So Arni's societal corporatist form of accumulation accords with Gramsci's concept of civil society. In Arni's civil society we have found the political, cultural and ideological hegemony of a single social group – the capitalist class – over the entire society. This class exerts its hegemony with the important support of a strong ideology based on transformations to the institution of caste. Due to the reinforcement of caste, patriarchy and the rhetoric of town unity, economic interests and ideological factors overlap in exactly the manner Gramsci thought the essence of civil society to be. In this sense, the institutional framework of civil society is the outcome of social contradictions and conflicts, which are resolved thanks to an ideological framework, the main role of which is to gain consent for the hegemonic project of the local capitalist class. Through the caste system and through patriarchy, ideology comes to form a significant component in the local SSA.

Acknowledgements

We are very grateful to Neil Armstrong, Chris Fuller, P.J. Krishnamurthy and M.S.S. Pandian for their swift and constructive comments on the first draft, to Paul Pandian, P.J. Krishnamurthy, M.V. Srinivasan and hundreds of citizens of Arni for their help with fieldwork over the period 1993–97, to Kaveri Harriss for tackling some of her parents' field-notes from 1983 and 1973, and to Maxine Molyneux and the editors for their comments at, and after, the Gordon White Memorial Conference, IDS, April, 1999. We take sole responsibility for the errors which remain.

Notes

1 A version of this piece was published in the Bulletin of the Institute of Development Studies, Special Issue "Politics in Development: Essays in Honour of Gordon White", 30(4): 31–8.
2 See Basile and Harriss-White (1999) footnote 19, p. 16 for a discussion of caste nomenclature.
3 An order entrusted to the state in the Italian case (Mancini *et al.*, 1983).

References

Basile, E. and Harriss-White, B. (1999) "Corporative Capitalism: Civil Society and the Politics of Accumulation in Small Town India", Paper to the Gordon White Memorial Conference, IDS Sussex (full version of current paper).
Béteille, A. (1996) "Caste in Contemporary India", in C. Fuller (ed.), *Caste Today* (Delhi: Oxford University Press).
Cawson, A. (1985) "Varieties of Corporatism: The Importance of the Meso-level of Interest Intermediation", in A. Cawson (ed.), *Organised Interests and the State* (London: Sage).
Fuller, C. (1996) "Introduction: Caste Today", in *Caste Today* (Delhi: Oxford University Press).
Goodman, R., White, G. and Kwon, H.-J. (1998) *The East Asian Welfare Model: Welfare Orientalism and the State* (London: Routledge).

Gramsci, A. (1975) *Quaderni del carcere* (Torino: Einaudi).

Harriss, B. (1991) "The Arni Studies: Changes in the Private Sector of a Market Town, 1971–83", in P. Hazell and C. Ramasamy (eds), *The Green Revolution Reconsidered: The Impact of High Yielding Varieties in South India* (Baltimore and London: Johns Hopkins University Press), pp. 181–212.

Harriss-White, B. (1996) "Liberalisation and Corruption: Resolving the Paradox", in B. Harriss-White and G. White (eds), *Liberalisation and the New Corruption*, IDS Bulletin, Brighton: IDS, 27(2): 31–40.

Harriss-White, B. (forthcoming) "The State and Informal Economic Order in S. Asia", in C. Fuller and J. Harriss (eds), *The Anthropology of the Indian State* (pub. unknown).

Jayaram, N. (1996) "Caste and Hinduism: Changing Protean Relationship", in M.N. Srinivas (ed.), *Caste: Its Twentieth Century Avatar* (Delhi: Viking).

Karanth, G.K. (1996) "Caste in Contemporary India", in M.N. Srinivas (ed.), *Caste: Its Twentieth Century Avatar* (Delhi: Viking).

Keane, J. (1988) "Introduction", in J. Keane (ed.), *Civil Society and the State* (London and New York: Verso).

Kotz, D.M., McDonough, T. and Reich, M. (1994) *Social Structures of Accumulation. The Political Economy of Growth and Crisis* (Cambridge: Cambridge University Press).

Luckham, R. and White, G. (eds) (1996) *Democratisation in the South: The Jagged Wave* (Manchester: Manchester University Press).

Mancini, O., Perrillo, F. and Zagari, E. (eds) (1983) *La teoria economica del corporativismo*, Volumes 1 and 2 (Napoli: ESI).

Mendelsohn, O. (1993) "The Transformation of Power in Rural India", *Modern Asian Studies*, 27: 805–42.

O'Sullivan, N. (1988) "The Political Theory of Neo-Corporatism", in A. Cox and N. O'Sullivan (eds), *The Corporate State. Corporatism and the State Tradition in Western Europe* (Aldershot: Edward Elgar).

Panini, M.N. (1996) "The Political Economy of Caste", in M.N. Srinivas (ed.), *Caste: Its Twentieth Century Avatar* (Delhi: Viking).

Radhakrishnan, P. (1996) "Mandal Commission Report: A Sociological Critique", in M.N. Srinivas (ed.), *Caste: Its Twentieth Century Avatar* (Delhi: Viking).

Reiniche, M.L. (1996) "The Urban Dynamics of Caste: A Case Study from Tamilnadu", in C. Fuller (ed.), *Caste Today* (Delhi: Oxford University Press).

Robinson, M. and White, G. (eds) (1998) *The Democratic Developmental State: Politics and Institutional Design* (Oxford: Oxford University Press).

Schmitter, P.C. (1974) "Still the Century of Corporatism?", in *Review of Politics*, 36.

Srinivas, M.N. (1989) *The Cohesive Role of Sanskritisation and Other Essays* (Delhi: Oxford University Press).

Uphadya, C. (1997) "Culture, Class and Entrepreneurship: A Case Study of Coastal Andhra Pradesh", in M. Rutten and C. Uphadya (eds), *Small Business Entrepreneurship in Asia and Europe* (Delhi: Sage).

White, G. (1993) "The Political Analysis of Markets", IDS Bulletin, 24(3).

White, G. (1996) "Chinese Trade Unions in the Transitions from Socialism: Towards Corporatism or Civil Society?", *British Journal of Industrial Relations*, 34(3).

White, G., Howell, J. and Shang Xiaoyuan (1996) *In Search of Civil Society in China* (Oxford: Clarendon Press).

5

Capitalist Maturity and Corporate Responses to Liberalization: The Steel, Automobile, and Software Sectors in India

Anthony P. D'Costa

Introduction

Throughout the 1980s, in a piecemeal fashion, and then boldly in 1991, the Indian government introduced reforms that purported to free the economy from government regulations. The rationale was that a more market-friendly environment would boost growth rates, foster economic development, and stabilize the economy from the ravages of balance of payments problems. It is not surprising that actual outcomes have fallen far short of expectations. Dynamic capitalist development requires appropriate institutional change and the elimination of structural impediments, both of which are challenging for post-colonial societies.[1,2] In India, entrenched state regulation and the domination of trade-oriented, family-owned conglomerates circumscribed competition. Both discouraged technologically driven competition. Hence we can anticipate that the mere withdrawal of the state from economic affairs will be insufficient for economic dynamism.[3] Private capital must also pursue an aggressive competitive strategy to realize the effects of liberalization. Whether corporations are actually doing this remains an empirical question. However, an understanding of the Indian political economy can provide the theoretical basis for anticipating broad corporate responses to reforms.

My expectation of Indian corporate responses to liberalization is different from the historically correct but static perception that family-owned conglomerates are non-innovative. Indian capitalists, having served British interests as junior partners and regulated by the post-independent state, devised accumulation strategies based on

106

non-technological resources. Relying on social and political contacts, administrative and accounting trickery, and short-term mercantile activity as opposed to production, the Indian conglomerates gained considerable notoriety. However, a cursory examination of the Indian economy shows that Indian corporations have responded to rising industrial and consumer demands, both at home and abroad. Some have been technologically and institutionally innovative, with a few securing an international presence.[4] The steel, auto, and software sectors, none of which revealed any competitive strength in the pre-reform period, are good examples of recent Indian success stories. A dynamic interpretation implies that Indian capitalists, even if family-controlled, have matured. The introduction of professional management, selective micro-economic deregulation and macro-economic liberalization has introduced greater corporate dynamism.

Even if counter-intuitive, Indian capitalists can be expected to respond competitively to economic reforms, notwithstanding the weight of structural barriers. The protective umbrella of the state preceding the reforms deepened capitalist relations, thereby contributing to the maturity and consolidation of Indian capitalists.[5] The increasing commercialization of agriculture, industrial diversification, and the creation of a large pool of technical talent are the very foundations of contemporary capital accumulation in India. While state domination restricted private capital operations, it also contributed to an increasing heterogeneity of the Indian capitalist class. New, dynamic corporations thrived under state tutelage, such as private-sector Reliance Corporation in the textile and petrochemicals sector and partially state-owned Maruti Udyog in automobiles. The more established conglomerates, such as the Birlas and Tatas, continued to diversify their portfolio. The proliferation of Indian alliances with foreign capital should not be interpreted outright as a sign of trading mentality. This strategy is in perfect consonance with the relative technological weakness of Indian firms. A charitable interpretation is that long-term technological savvyness does arise through learning. If it can be established that some firms have been technologically entrepreneurial before the reforms and others seized opportunities from internationalization after them, we can safely deduce the growing maturity and heterogeneity of the Indian capitalist class.[6]

This chapter demonstrates the creative adjustment of some segments of the Indian corporate sector to economic reforms. I explain corporate responses to liberalization as integral to their commercial maturity. I use the steel, auto, and software industries in India to outline some of the broader strategies of Indian firms. The diversity of strategies reflects the evolving institutional arrangements that continue to filter, regulate, and accommodate increased market pressures in contingent ways.[7] Theoretically, these arrangements contribute to "capitalist regulation", a system of rules and norms, formal and informal, tacit and otherwise, that purport to control, direct, promote, and sometimes thwart economic transactions. Institutionally based regulation, whether conducted by the state, private industry associations, or buyer–supplier networks, is necessary to stabilize capitalist development.[8] Thus recent economic reforms must be seen as changes in the *form* of national capitalist regulation rather than the wholesale dismantling of it. Consequently, the Indian corporate sector is likely to exhibit a wide range of responses to opportunities and constraints thrown open by changes in the state-led institutional foundation of capitalist regulation.

The chapter is divided into three parts. The first presents a brief discussion on the question of capitalist maturity and its differentiation. This is situated in the context of changing capitalist regulation in India and discusses the likely responses of the corporate sector to liberalization. The second part presents three industry case studies, steel, auto, and software, to show the varying profit-making strategies in the changing national and global contexts. The industry analyses suggest that Indian firms are capable of coping with market pressures at home and taking advantage of global opportunities as well. But it also shows, with few exceptions, that Indian firms still remain dependent on foreign technology and markets. The final part concludes with a general assessment of corporate capitalism in the larger liberalizing environment.

A note on methodology

This study covers the reform period beginning in the early 1980s rather than in 1991, the year when sweeping changes were introduced. The reform process, though halting, produced some remarkable corporate initiatives before 1991.[9] Including the 1980s allows us to capture the path dependency associated with industrial change. The industry analysis is not based on macro-economic data but on meso-level sectoral/firm information. No profit data are presented but adoption of new technologies and expanding output (markets) are used as proxies for profit strategies. Innovative institutional arrangements, such as joint ventures, subcontracting, and cooperative buyer–supplier relations are also seen as corporate responses to changing economic circumstances. Though limited to three industry cases, the study captures the broader strategies of an increasingly differentiated Indian corporate sector. The analysis covers older, capitalist-intensive industries as well as newer skill-intensive sectors. It is a comparative study in an inter-temporal sense. This study shows that both established conglomerates and new players are integral to capitalist expansion under liberalization.

Regulation and capitalist maturity

Much of the discussion of corporate capitalism has been concerned with the relationship between big business and the capitalist economy, particularly industrial capitalism.[10] The central issue has been ownership and control in advanced capitalist economies.[11] For late industrializers, such as Japan, South Korea, and India, corporate capitalism referred to family control of *zaibatsu*, *chaebol*, and *big-business houses*, respectively, through a holding company.[12] Through interlocking directorships and the "one-set" principle a firm diversified its portfolio by horizontal and vertical integration.[13] This strategy allowed a firm to grow rapidly and hence exploit economies of scale. It also facilitated capturing market shares by spreading into a wide variety of industrial and service activities, such as steel, automobiles, shipping, and banking.

In India, too, family-controlled conglomerates emerged, nurtured inadvertently by the state. Most of these family-owned conglomerates began with the *baniya* (merchant) communities from Rajasthan and Gujarat. The Mumbai (Bombay) based Tatas of Parsee origin were an important exception. Their prosperity in the pre-independent period was based on British controlled colonial trade and war-related demands. After Indian independence in 1947, many of these families, especially those based in Calcutta, purchased British-run managing agencies at rock bottom prices. Virtually all major industrial sectors came under the control of big business houses, such as textiles, engineering, automobiles and components, shipping, steel, and chemicals. State-led import substitution strategy facilitated the diversification of conglomerate holdings. For example, engineering products (by Shri Ram), engines (by Kirloskars), jeeps (by Mahindra and Mahindra), aluminium (by Birlas), buses, trucks, and locomotives (by Tatas) came under family-controlled businesses. In the South, the TVS Group emerged as a major automotive related business house. In the North, in addition to the Marwaris from Rajasthan and Haryana, were smaller industrialists from pre-independence Punjab province. As refugees from Pakistan, initially they benefitted enormously from various government assistance.[14]

The pro-active role of the government in orchestrating economic change was eroded as cumbersome regulations came to dominate industrial policies. This is in stark contrast to Japan or Korea where the state did not hesitate to nurture domestic capitalists through the rigors of capitalist competition.[15] In India limited domestic and foreign competition encouraged monopolistic pricing and discouraged innovation-based growth. The primordial networks, such as kinship, caste, ethnicity, and regional ties limited the professionalization of management.[16] Under state patronage, corporate capitalism in India engendered dominance of big business, corresponding technological lethargy, and relative economic stability.

However, state-led development in a "dominant coalition" required considerable redistribution of wealth within the coalition.[17] Based on political expediency, new capitalists emerged while established conglomerates diversified their operations within the parameters of state regulation.[18] For example, the Ambani family established their highly successful Reliance Corporation in an already decaying textile industry. Politically well connected, the Ambanis began their modest operation in 1966 and grew rapidly severalfold since then. As an Indian company, Reliance has several firsts to its credit, such as raising capital abroad, earning Rs 10,000 million net profit in 1995, and being rated by Standard & Poor. Strategically, they have integrated backwards from synthetic textiles to petrochemicals for making fibers. Today it is a diversified company, with the world's largest ethylene cracker plant, and is a potential Fortune 500 entrant. With 25 per cent ownership, the Ambanis have relied on trained managers and superior technologies. They exhibit a new breed of capitalists who were quick to see commercial opportunities and cash in on them.

The established conglomerates, belonging to the various families, were successful. But few of them relied on innovations for their commercial success. The Calcutta-based Marwari groups used their jute mills as cash cows, ultimately obliterating them from the local industrial map. Both Birla's and Walchand's automobile manufacturing units faced similar problems of mismanagement, technological obsolescence, and industrial strife. In many instances, family feuds, such as that of the Sarabhais, balkanized the assets and undermined any consolidated entrepreneurial strategies. One important exception was the Tata Group. A highly diversified organization and committed to competitive production, the Tatas deployed professional management early on. They also resorted to innovative approaches to industrial relations. Tata's engineering capability, particularly in automotive technologies, was noteworthy. Like the Tatas, several less diversified traditional family-based corporations have also become more active with new technologies. The Jindal, Mittal, and Essar families are cases in point in the steel business. They have introduced state-of-the-art technologies and contributed to the global reorganization of steel production.

Unlike the Ambanis or the Tatas, who made their fortunes in India, the Swaraj Paul family became fed up with government controls and sought overseas commercial ventures. Operating out of London, their Caparo Industries began to acquire unprofitable metals-based units and turn them around. This was accomplished by maintaining a highly professionalized management team and using new technologies to control operating costs. Family control did not impede its ability to control businesses in a competitive environment.

The Indian corporate class is no longer rooted in the traditional family context. However, the process of transformation of family-owned business to professionally run corporations is complex, one in which the state had considerable influence. In general state-led development encouraged uneconomic production units, while firms monopolized high-cost production capacity. Both debilitated innovative capacity. Consequently many of these units are unlikely to do well with a change in the regime of regulation. At the same time, some of the profitable conglomerates responded to competition with new technologies. The gradual professionalization of management, hired as well as family-based, was responsible for such an outcome. Typically, sons will have been trained in elite business education schools in the US and UK. It appears that professionally run firms were more open to innovations and better prepared to tackle competition. Thus the critique of Indian conglomerates as being non-innovative is only partially correct. Also, if some of the family-based conglomerates and newer firms respond to new opportunities in creative ways, then the Indian corporate sector cannot be characterized as immature.

The formation of state-owned Maruti Udyog was a major departure from the prevailing family-based corporations. Not only did the arm of the state become commercially involved, but it allowed a foreign partner in a highly controlled auto sector for the first time. The establishment of this joint venture boosted industrialization in the Delhi region and supported numerous family-controlled but entrepreneurially driven automobile parts firms. With investments in infrastructure, several other sectors emerged. In numerous cases, firms are introducing new technologies as part of their competitive strategy. Many others are also adopting more creative institutional arrangements to cope with greater market forces.

It is evident that family-based conglomerates have remained dominant. However, the gradual shift in regulation, from state-led to market-based, and the emergence of new firms are likely to alter the structure of competition and generate varying responses. Those firms that have kept abreast with best-practice standards are likely to perform better in the new environment. Firms that failed to professionalize management and milked assets for short-term profits are unlikely to be competitive today. In either case, different industrial sectors will devise different strategies to compete, depending on technological competence, degree of competition, barriers to entry, and the like. Profit strategies will be influenced less by conglomerate control and more by technology-induced competitive strategies. The technological backwardness of Indian capital is therefore likely to be offset by foreign know-how. Institutional arrangements favoring foreign capital participation, such as joint ventures, foreign equity, and subcontracting are expected to be part of the Indian corporate map.[19] With economic openness, capitalist regulation becomes "coalitions of aligned interests".[20] National capital engages foreign partners and vice versa, sharing "common structurally based interests".[21] Primordial networks, such as family, remain important and leveraged but continue to be eroded as corporations must respond to accumulation opportunities and constraints thrown open by liberalization. The internationalization of the Indian economy suggests corporate initiatives to govern itself. Such self-regulation is dictated by both the liberalization process and by the maturity of Indian corporations.

The dynamic relationship between capitalist maturity and the changing regime of regulation is presented in Figure 5.1. As statist import-substitution-industrialization shifts toward more market-oriented policies, relative prices are altered differentially. Indian firms are compelled to respond to new opportunities and constraints at home and abroad. As each sector and individual firms face different options for tackling market forces, their profit strategies also vary. The actual corporate responses can be ascertained only by an empirical analysis. However, given our understanding of capitalist maturity and the increasing heterogeneity of the Indian industrial groups, we can anticipate increasingly technology- and export-based competitive strategies.

Liberalization and corporate strategies: three case studies

Entrepreneurialism in the Indian steel industry

Until recently, the Indian steel industry has been quintessentially a state-led monopoly. The Steel Authority of India Limited (SAIL) and

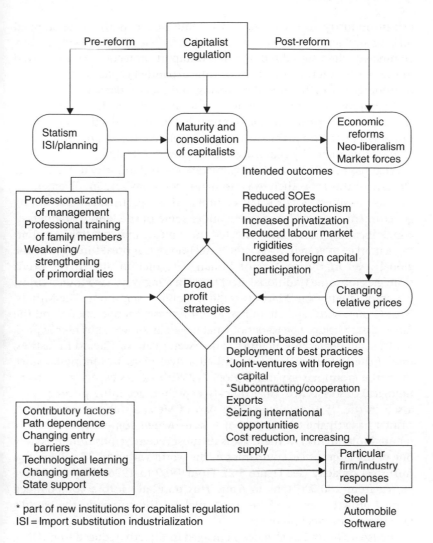

Figure 5.1 A stylized interpretation of corporate responses to economic liberalization

Tata Iron and Steel, part of the huge Tata conglomerate, have been the main producers. Both were geared toward serving the national market. With little competition, neither of them has been technologically dynamic. The rest of the industry was composed of small, technologically inefficient, electric furnace (EF) units.[22] With deregulation the share of private industry rose relative to the state sector as the state stopped making any new investments in the industry. The EF units were virtually eliminated when subsidized power and import protection were removed in the 1980s. A few relatively new firms expanded capacity using newer technologies, which reduced financing and market barriers. These were vastly improved EF units with new thin-slab casting technologies. A few smaller units opted for the conventional, cost-effective mini-blast furnaces bought from the Chinese. One relatively obscure firm rose to global prominence by acquiring existing foreign steel.[23]

What has been the role of conglomerates in steel industry restructuring? Outside of the Tatas there was no major conglomerate involvement in the steel business. A few small EF units, which profited from re-rolling government produced steel, were under some of the family holdings of conglomerates. These units reflected the typical *baniya* strategy, exploiting a market of scarcity.[24] However, technological breakthroughs at the global level in the context of Indian deregulation altered the profit strategies for some traditional steel firms in a big way. Two Indian firms, which originate from Marwari trading families, stand out: The Mittals' Ispat Group, with separate Indian and international operations, and the Ruias' Essar Group. The leader of Ispat began as a lowly, but highly profitable, scrap dealer in Calcutta.[25] Like Swaraj Paul of Caparo Industries, one of the Mittal brothers established a steel plant in Indonesia. Since then, the group has expanded globally. With excess capacity and technological obsolescence, Ispat quickly exploited declining prices of steel assets in the US and elsewhere. As part of Mexico's liberalization, Ispat cashed in with the acquisition of a state-owned company. The highly reputed Inland Steel in the US was its most recent acquisition. It is now one of the largest steel companies in the world with over 15 million ton (mt) steel capacity (see Figure 5.2). From 1989 to 1996, shipments have grown from 280,000 tons to 6 mt. This translates into a compounded annual growth rate of 55 per cent, making the company the world's fastest growing steel producer.

The Ispat Group has also been engaged in directly reduced iron (DRI), a superior scrap substitute for EF units. By 1990, Ispat already had 4 per cent of 18 mt of *global* DRI production.[26] DRI is suited to thin-slab casting, an efficient process that allows the desired shape (near net shape) to be obtained directly from molten steel. In India, Mittals' Nippon Denro Ispat Ltd (NDIL) began with a galvanizing line in 1984 and today produces over 3 mt of cold rolled steel with nearly 40 per cent of galvanized output (a high value-added product). It also launched some color coating, India's first, as unmet demand for consumer durables took off

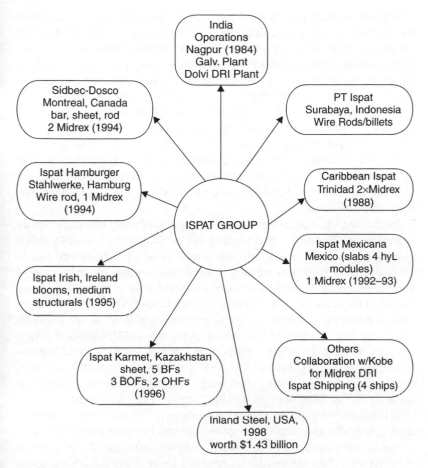

Figure 5.2   Ispat International's expanding global steel business

with economic reforms gradually introduced since the 1980s.[27] NDIL is also adopting new technologies in creative ways. With its new 1.6 mt DRI project, NDIL will also be using a traditional and expensive blast furnace, new two twin-shell EFs and two state-of-the-art SMS (German) thin-slab casters. Blast furnace iron is of higher quality and hence its products are likely to meet stringent market requirements for flat products. To ensure success, NDIL has reproduced the US-based NUCOR's Hickman plant layout and Crawfordsville's product quality. Both are considered to be global reference plants.

The Essar Group, part of the Ruia family, rivals the Ispat Group. From its trading roots, the Ruia family began with port-related construction projects. A natural extension has been to petroleum-related off-shore construction. The availability of off-shore natural gas led the Essar Group to set up the world's largest gas-based hot briquetted iron (HBI) project. Like DRI it is a substitute for scrap to be used by its state-of-the-art downstream operations for 2 mt of hot rolled coils. Its steel operation has Level II automation, indicating an advanced computerized system for process and product controls. HBI is also sold to third parties at home and abroad. Essar is integrating backward by producing iron oxide pellets for making HBI. Today, Essar is diversified but remains anchored in infrastructural services, such as shipping, oil, power, and telecommunications.

Besides the Ispat and Essar Groups, the Jindal family has launched an aggressive steel project. From trading in Calcutta in steel, ghee (clarified butter), pipes, and waste cloth, the Jindal family has branched out to more complex steel making units. Steel pipes, strips (to make pipes), and stainless steel were the principal products. One of the sons has continued to focus on steel, developing his own cost-effective EF technology. Several new steel projects are in the pipeline, the most recent being an integrated steel project in Karnataka using the COREX process. There are only three other COREX units in the world. Jindal is installing two state-of-the-art C-2000 COREX modules for producing hot iron which then will be processed into steel with conventional steelmaking technologies.[28] This combination eliminates very expensive blast furnaces, thus lowering investment and operating costs.[29] This process is environmental-friendly and surplus gas generated can be converted to energy.

The recent changes in the Indian steel industry signal the growing maturity of Indian capitalists. In systemic terms, they are adopting the "high road to capital accumulation" rather than profits based on simple manufacturing and monopoly trading. This is clear from the diversification of family holdings and the recent vintages of technologies adopted. Thus an ailing industry, dominated by the state and inefficient private units, has been transformed into a dynamic one with process innovations and computerization. As a profit strategy, these families in the steel business have systematically integrated their upstream and downstream operations. For example, the Mittal and Essar Groups are not just expanding steel production but also manufacturing the raw materials for it. By combining older technologies with new ones in strategic ways, Indian businesses are exhibiting their technological mettle as well. The entrepreneurial approach to technology adoption and hybridizing them, reveals a growing technological sophistication. These firms have altered the very nature of capitalist regulation in India – from a large oligopolistic, state-dominated steel industry to a more flexible and competitive one. Their receptivity to innovations is a far cry from steel hoarding and technological lethargy. They serve to illustrate the technological acumen of traditional *baniya* families and how they are coping with new commercial opportunities.

New firms and changing strategies in the automobile industry

In the early 1980s, when reforms were initiated, the Indian automobile industry witnessed significant restructuring.[30] A new firm Maruti Udyog Limited (MUL) was established as a joint venture (JV) between the Government of India and Suzuki Motors. Within a decade the small, technologically backward industry was transformed into a high-growth, dynamic one. The entry of MUL in the context of reforms generally weakened the grip of conglomerate branches in the industry. Also as a new firm with no legacy problems, MUL's profit strategy was influenced by Japanese practices, such as subcontracting. This encouraged fostering new suppliers and strengthening existing ones. With MUL the Indian automotive sector as a whole witnessed considerable expansion (Table 5.1). In 1980, about 181,000 vehicles were produced, 17 per cent of which were passenger cars. In 1997, the corresponding figures stood at 1.0 million and 41 per cent respectively.[31] In 1997–98, MUL boasted an 86 per cent car market share.[32]

How is the restructuring of the auto industry related to competitive corporate strategy? The establishment of MUL wreaked havoc on the original three national car producers. Only Hindustan Motors (HM), part of the Birla conglomerate and Premier Automobiles (PAL), part of the Walchand group, survived with a total market share of only 9 per cent. HM's plant located near Calcutta was a typical *baniya* operation, milking the assets without major reinvestment and retooling. A sheltered market and unstable industrial relations did not help either. The Mumbai-based PAL was similar but had the added distinction of late introduction of professional management and internal family squabbles. Rather than be driven into oblivion, both HM and PAL defensively licensed technologies from Mitsubishi Motors and Nissan respectively. Later they formed joint ventures with General Motors and Peugeot of France. Even after these new joint ventures, their combined share of the passenger car market rose only marginally, to 11.4 per cent. It is evident that profit strategies have shifted toward greater reliance on foreign technologies, low volume, and higher value-added vehicles where the margin is

Table 5.1   Changing market structure of the Indian automobile industry (%)

	1980	1985	1988	1993–94	1997–98
Passenger cars					
MUL	–	47.5	59.6	72	86
PAL	45#	28.5	22.9	12	4
HM	55#	23.5	17.2	13	8
TELCO	–	–	–	3	1
Total (numbers)	30,538	102,456	159,941	207,658	401,002
LCVs: 3–5 tons GVW					
Matador	55.9	55.2	41.2	30.7	9@
TELCO 407	–	–	29.7*	53.8	53 (3–8 tons)@
Mahindra-Nissan (JLCV)	–	4.8	7.0	4.8	5@
Total (numbers)	15,758	23,068	28,859	35,819	
LCVs: 5–6 tons GVW					
3 JLCV units	–	100.0	85.5	50.9	14@
TELCO 608	–	–	14.5**	49.1	13@
Total (numbers)	–	1,386	12,853	16,351	65,069 (all LCVs)
Components production					
Total (million rupees)	5,318	9,746	15,427	39,430	120,317
Percentage change##	–	45%	58%	156%	205%

GVW = Gross Vehicle Weight; JLCV = Japanese Light Commercial Vehicle unit; ## = from corresponding previous period stated in table; # = 1981 figure; * = production started in 1986; ** = production started in 1987; @ = % share of total LCVs.

Sources: Automobile Components Manufacturers Association, *Facts & Figures*, various issues. Kathuria, op. cit., n. 41, Table 5.5, p. 127.

higher. This has been the typical response of existing producers as well as some of the newcomers, with the latter having none of the legacy problems.

Unlike the experience of the steel industry, MUL has single-handedly reorganized the auto industry, relying on technological and institutional innovations. It aggressively expanded the capacity, retooled for new products, and institutionalized cooperative arrangements with its suppliers. The production of automotive components has increased dramatically, from Rs 5 billion in 1980–81 to nearly Rs 120 billion by 1997–98 (see Table 5.1). To understand how the supplier industry kept up with new investments in the auto industry, an examination of buyer–supplier arrangements is necessary. In the past, government policy supported a few large vendors and numerous uneconomic units through its small-scale industry program, resulting in a high degree of vertical integration.[33] Instead of making parts in-house, MUL, following Japanese practice, subcontracted them. Over time, MUL systematically internalized the external market linkages with its suppliers.[34] This strategy overcame supply bottlenecks, reduced costs, and increased productivity without undue cost escalation.[35] MUL provided an assured market for its suppliers and shared its technical expertise with its subcontractors to secure competitively priced parts. The recognition of mutual vulnerability influenced MUL's profit strategies, from simple monopolistic pricing to continuous upgrading of products via vendor development. Subcontracting and joint ventures were an institutional response to gain access to modern know-how and business practices in an expanding market.

Successful vendor development began with local content regulations.[36] Suzuki was instrumental in introducing some of its Japanese suppliers to Indian vendors. Indian entrepreneurs, many of them engineers trained in the US, became dedicated MUL suppliers. In some cases Japanese equity was involved, facilitating the transfer of Japanese manufacturing know-how to a market with little internal competition. Many of these suppliers were located next to the MUL plant, with a few of them within MUL's factory premises in the joint-venture complex.[37] Close proximity to the buyer eliminated the problems of treacherous roads and poor communications infrastructure and facilitated part deliveries several times a day on a just-in-time basis.[38] It also allows for sharing of equipment.[39] Such buyer–supplier relationships lowered costs by ensuring uninterrupted supplies of quality parts.

Vendor development was fostered through MUL's active participation. Its small equity in Sona Steering and Sona's technical and financial collaboration with Koyo Seiko, which is also Suzuki's supplier, has contributed to Sona's expansion and diversification. Sona Steering doubled its production by introducing increased automation and Japanese style cellular production system.[40] Changes in shop-floor practices contributed to better inventory management, while waste reduction and reorganization of the production process to eliminate bottlenecks yielded higher cost efficiency. This interpenetration of Japanese firms with Indian firms as buyers and sellers has generated positive externalities and greater reliability of the entire supply chain. Several Indian vendors are now "original equipment" manufacturers for MUL's products, and in some instances, for example Sona Steering, exporters as well.

The success of MUL and its supplier base has attracted more foreign firms. Honda-SIEL, Mahindra-Ford, DCM-Daewoo, Tata-Mercedes and a 100 per cent Hyundai (of Korea) subsidiary are some noteworthy ventures. There are other projects in the pipeline, involving US, European, and Japanese firms. These new projects are not without their conglomerate base, such as Tata, while SIEL and DCM are parts of the Shri Ram Group. Mahindra has been an independent firm, begun by Mahindra who left Martin-Burn, a British-Bengali managing agency in the post-independence period.[41]

Of those with conglomerate connections, only the Tatas have been truly successful. TELCO was already a successful large commercial vehicle producer.[42] MUL's success and the entry of foreign firms attracted TELCO as well. It entered the car and utility vehicles market, capturing 9.2 per cent of the combined market in 1997–98. TELCO also entered the light commercial vehicle market in a big way with 60 per cent of the market and maintained its grip on the truck and bus segment with 66 per cent.[43] The participation of foreign firms did not rout domestic firms in the CV segment as is evidenced by TELCO's market shares. The exit of Toyota and Nissan in the LCV partnerships and the sluggish performance of Swaraj-Mazda, another Japanese LCV joint-venture, suggest the operating difficulties in India, which even global leaders find difficult to cope with.

The radical transformation of the auto sector can be attributed to the creation of new firms, such as MUL and its suppliers, foreign technology, and institutionalized cooperation between buyers and sellers. Capitalist maturity is evident from successful joint-ventures, backward integration, and entrepreneurial talent unleashed by the growth of the industry. For the first time automotive exports are becoming important to the sector. MUL exported 26,000 cars in 1995–96, roughly 10 per cent of its output.[44] Auto component exports, estimated to be under $300 million in 1996–98, doubled since 1994–95, and are expected to grow considerably. Local content is high at 70 per cent for cars and 90 per cent for commercial vehicles. Productivity is also rising. Vehicles per worker has increased from 5.2 in 1991–92 to 8.6 in 1994–95.[45] The four-wheeled segment, including tractors, is expected to reach 1.3 million units in 2002–03, with 43 per cent passenger car output.[46]

Profit strategy in this industry has been based on new products, new alliances with foreign capital, and institutionalized cooperation among buyer–supplier firms. Kinship ties, though important, have not undermined this strategy. For example, the dominance of the TVS family group in a range of components production was possible through technology imports. General Motors is now an important client for TVS. Sona Steering has integrated backward with several Japanese partners and installed the Chairman's son to run Sona Okegawa, a subsidiary of Sona Steering and a joint venture with Mitsubishi Materials. The chairman himself, hailing from a traditional "jeweler" family and trained in the US as a mechanical engineer, is the son-in-law of Raunaq Singh who leads Bharat Gears. The interpenetration of family ties has not deterred the induction of professional management, especially when these organizations have been free from legacy problems. TELCO's success is a case in point. However, the inability of HM and PAL, belonging to more traditional conglomerates, to cope with new competition underscores the importance of professional management and receptivity to innovations. Profit strategy not based on best-practice systems, technological and organizational, is likely to result in technological obsolescence and managerial incompetence.

Software exports: spillovers of capitalist maturity?

The development of the Indian software sector is a reflection of the larger internationalization process. Economic reforms have brought Indian software service providers closer to their foreign counterparts. The relatively cheap supply of skilled workers, resulting from government policy, has been absorbed by the burgeoning global – mainly US – demand for software services. The increasing innovative capability among Indian software firms is also drawing in foreign companies to develop software in India. The sector as a whole is highly profitable because of low-cost skilled labor. The relative absence of the state in this sector should not lull us to ignore the critical role the Indian government has played in skill development.[47]

Riding the wave of information technology diffusion, the Indian software industry in the last decade has grown rapidly. This growth was largely driven by export expansion, pursued by the industry and supported by the government. Between 1980 and 1997–98, exports expanded from $4 million to $1.75 billion.[48] The compounded annual growth rate of software exports between 1992–93 and 1997–98 was over 50 per cent in dollar terms and 57 per cent in rupee terms. Based on recent surveys, software exports are expected to touch $50 billion in 2008. Nearly 60 per cent is directed to the US market. While this is a sizeable market share from the Indian side, the share of Indian exports to the total US market was less than 2 per cent. The domestic software market is estimated to be over $1 billion, and considerably more if in-house software activity is taken into account. This is the only industry in India in which export volume is greater than the domestic market.

The relationship between economic reforms and rising exports is not a simple one. Many factors have influenced Indian software exports, chief among them is global growth in software demand. The clustering of micro-electronics-based technologies in increasingly information-driven economic evolution has prompted heavy dependence on software. However, the rapid response of Indian firms to lock into this opportunity was supported by publicly funded physical and social infrastructure and the government's export promotion programs. The availability of English-speaking technical personnel and the provisioning of high-speed data communication links allowed the industry to enter this market with relative ease. Over time, the government has supported the industry with free trade zones, Software Technology Parks, zero import duties on software, and a 100 per cent exemption of export profits.[49]

To what extent is this activity a sign of capitalist maturity? A breakdown of the major software exporters shows that most firms were established in the 1980s, a decade of reform initiatives (Table 5.2). A number of these firms have no links to major industrial houses or foreign partners, suggesting the presence of preconditions for entrepreneurial activity. Although the top exporters are not new firms, software activity was new for most of them. Most industry leaders were engineers, educated abroad, and began their career in traditional businesses or big business houses. Early entrants, such as Tata Consultancy Services (TCS), and later Pentafour, Tata Infotech, and Patni had advantages but several new firms quickly made their presence felt. HCL Consulting, the third largest exporter, and a new firm, is part of Hindustan Computers Ltd. It was formed in 1975 by a few entrepreneurially inclined engineers from the staid Delhi Cloth Mills. NIIT, another important exporter, was created in 1981 and is also a member of the HCL group. WIPRO and Infosys were also established in 1981, with the latter considered to be one of the India's best run companies. WIPRO was spun out of a trad-itional family business specializing in cooking oils.[50] The recent departure of a fifteen-year WIPRO veteran to form Mindtree Consulting suggests the increasing entrepreneurial vibrancy of the Indian software sector.

The ability of Indian software firms to seize commercial opportunities abroad was partly an outcome of state policy. The dislodging of IBM by the populist Janata (People's) Party government created the space for establishing domestic-oriented software service companies. The public sector Computer Maintenance Corporation (CMC) was such a firm.[51] CMC's mammoth railway reservation project was a major boost to the Indian software industry. Many employees of IBM also formed small companies and others joined Indian companies such as ORG Systems. The technical institutes generated a large number of graduates, which began to enter the software sector as both employees and entrepreneurs.

Table 5.2   The Indian software industry in 1997–98

Company	Year established	Software employees	Annual exports (Rs m)	Annual revenues (Rs m)	Export share (%)
Tata Consultancy Services	1968	9000	955.27	1083.63	88.15
WIPRO Ltd	1981	3000	388.94	481.65	80.75
HCL Consulting Ltd	1994	1500	345.50	345.50	100.00
Pentafour Software	1976	750	271.75	284.56	95.50
NIIT Ltd	1981	1150	258.38	325.40	79.40
Infosys Technologies	1981	1889	250.94	257.66	97.39
Satyam Computer	1987	1700	178.12	178.49	99.79
Tata Infotech	1978	2489	171.00	211.75	80.76
Patni Computer	1978	1300	137.58	137.58	100.00
DSQ Software	1992	1058	116.78	116.78	100.00
IBM Global Services	NK	1090	115.32	242.86	47.48
Cognizant Technology	1993	888	113.17	113.17	100.00
International Computers	1986	900	108.66	108.87	99.81
Mahindra British Telecom	1988	650	99.24	99.53	99.71
Information Management	1990	685	92.71	97.66	94.93
Mastek Ltd	1982	566	84.27	91.79	91.81
L&T Information	1997	800	81.27	87.57	92.81
Silverline Industries	1992	800	77.89	77.33*	NA
Citicorp Information	1989	446	75.12	54.50*	NA
Siemens Information	1992	580	72.08	117.36	61.42

* = 1996–97; NK = not known; NA = not applicable.

Source: National Association of Software and Service Companies (NASSCOM), op. cit., n. 47, 1999, p. 24, 1998.

Over time, easy entry allowed the Indian software sector to provide low cost services in the world market.[52]

Unlike the steel and auto industries, the Indian software sector is new. The presence of large business houses is limited and their participation has been dictated by diversification of conglomerate activity. This suggests further the maturity of the Indian industrial class. TCS, Tata Infotech (formerly a UNISYS joint-venture), and others such as Tata Interactive Systems, Tata Technologies, and Tata Elxsi are all part of the Tata Group. TCS is the largest exporter with 15 per cent of the top 20 firms' total exports. The Tata Group is a mature conglomerate, specializing in manufacturing and services as well. Software development has been a natural extension of such service-based firms as TCS. Its in-house technological strength is well-known. Thus its partnership with IBM Global Services is no surprise. Others, such as WIPRO and HCL, with hardware business could logically diversify into software business. Several other firms in other sectors, such as Mahindra, L&T, Siemens, and Citicorp have operations in automobiles, fabrication, electrical machinery, and banking services respectively. But outside the Tata Group, most software firms are not within the big house orbit. The successful new Indian exporters with a software focus have been NIIT, Infosys, Satyam, DSQ, and Mastek. International Computers, part of RPG Enterprise, is a joint venture with Japanese, British, and American capital. Many other smaller companies have infusions of foreign capital, either as 100 per cent subsidiaries of foreign companies or from non-resident Indians.

Software exports resulting from entrepreneurial initiatives and diversification of existing business reflect a changing profit strategy. The profit strategy takes on a deeper meaning when the composition of India's software exports is examined. The bulk of Indian exports (58.7 per cent) comprised on-site services, while a third was off-shore services. The remaining 11 per cent was grouped under products and packages. On-site services require Indian personnel to be physically present. Indian firms or brokers recruit personnel on behalf of a foreign (US) client, which subcontracts the services. The work carried out has involved low-value, mostly non-innovative tedious tasks, such as coding and testing. Thus far, India's exports of on-site services have not been on the cutting edge.[53] Similarly, off-shore services, such as multinationals setting up subsidiaries in India, have taken advantage of low-cost, skilled workers for exporting services to their parent company. The software export business is so lucrative that even owners of traditional businesses, such as textile mills, have gone into recruiting and training workers for foreign clients. Numerous spin-off firms have emerged. However, these new firms typically follow traditional on-site services pattern. Thus the surge in exports can be seen as a linear expansion of manpower without corresponding increase in deepening skills. The specialization of Indian firms in software services is largely due to the ease of entry in a market *niche* that has high returns and low risks. Profitability and business expansion is sustained by linearly adding more people to the workforce. As foreign subsidiaries are treated as cost centres and not profit centres, the local unit cannot capture the market value of services provided. The reliance on foreign markets (through exports of services) discourages the industry from undertaking more remunerative but riskier packaged products.

Software is a high technology, high-skill activity. However, there are several challenges for the Indian software industry. In the early 1990s, Indian software productivity was considered to be about 30 per cent that of the US.[54] It is only now that firms are beginning to institute internationally recognized standards in software development. In January 1999, there were 109 firms with ISO 9000 or SEI certification, that is, about 36 per cent of the top 300 companies or 21 per cent of NASSCOM's membership. Certification by itself is not a reflection of innovativeness but rather a systematization of procedures to assure quality that could potentially lead to more value-added work. However, a weak domestic sector in the context of (or because of) undue reliance on foreign markets has locked in the Indian sector at the low-end of the software value chain. Additionally, rapid growth in software service exports could undermine India's cost competitiveness if additional skills are not generated. It is not clear if the competition for a limited pool of skilled workers by foreign firms and the resulting local salary inflation and high labor turnover will force firms to switch to more value-added work.[55] As long as the export market continues to remain lucrative, Indian software firms are unlikely to diversify into higher value-added services.[56]

The Indian software industry's profit strategy is export competition. Competitiveness of this sector is dictated by the low cost of skilled labor. Numerous firms are part of this sector with a conspicuous absence of conglomerate firms. The Tata Group is an exception. There has been significant entrepreneurial activity in this sector. This sector is also promoted by the government, despite industry claims to the contrary. Capitalist maturity is exemplified by the emergence of new firms. Their strategy has focused on the lucrative export market. Their success is a complete departure from "export pessimism" and domestic orientation prevailing under state-led regulation. However, it is amply clear that without the preconditions created and the on-going support provided by the state, this sector would have found export competition difficult. At the same time, the response of this sector to commercial opportunities can be interpreted as the on-going consolidation and differentiation of the Indian capitalist class.

There are serious structural impediments, including the clout of large markets and foreign firms, to more innovative efforts. Lucrative export markets could also foreclose an alternative, more innovative, high road to capital accumulation. India's innovative capability could change if more of the developmental work is done in India and Indian firms are able to diversify their foreign markets.[57] India's reliance on the lucrative export market may be undercutting its long-term innovative capability even as greater international interactions enhance local managerial skills.

Conclusion

The evolution of these sectors reveals the changing face of Indian corporate capitalism. However, it is not a break with the past. The growth of Indian trade-based capital under the British was consolidated and differentiated under the protective umbrella of the state in the pre-reform period. New capitalists emerged in the continuing redistribution of state largesse within the dominant coalition. Family firms remained important and political/personal connections were crucial in their expansion under a regulatory regime. Monopoly control of markets remained the principal strategy of most firms, which also dictated their diversification strategies. However, the gradual professionalization of management, including family members, fostered industrial learning and sharpened modern commercial knowledge. With changes in the regulatory regime, Indian capitalists were well-positioned to respond to new opportunities and constraints thrown open by reforms. The backlog of Indian technology and increased competition prompted Indian firms to seek foreign technology (steel, auto), foreign equity (auto, software), and foreign markets (software). Liberalization has also allowed Indian capitalists to venture abroad, not only deepening sectoral integration but also contributing to an increasingly mature and differentiated capitalist class.

The three sectors display a variety of corporate responses to liberalization, dictated by changing objective conditions. Declining barriers allowed smaller, entrepreneurial steel firms to adopt recent innovations, while Ispat International's earlier exposure to foreign markets contributed to its multinationality. This evolution is a significant departure from rent-seeking activities found under small-scale private firms in the pre-reform period. The Indian automobile sector has undergone even greater transformation. The distinctive features of the industry's evolution have been its internationalization and the creation of new institutional arrangements. Profit strategies have been based on long-term, buyer–supplier relationships, patterned after the Japanese subcontracting system. Exports indicate that quality has improved. The paradox has been the key role that the Indian government has played through its ownership in MUL, undermining established firms. Typical corporate strategy has been to form joint ventures and obtain foreign know-how and capital. The software sector has flexibly articulated itself with the global industry through exports of services – on-site and off-shore. This sector has been characterized by the emergence of new firms.

Profit strategies of Indian corporations have varied. The steel sector responded to increased competition with new technologies and foreign acquisitions. Joint ventures, institutionalized cooperation, and access to organizational and production know-how contributed to the expansion of the automobile industry. The software industry has been profitable because of its export orientation. Such diversified strategies suggest the maturity of Indian capitalists, which also result from the growing heterogeneity of Indian capital. Ispat, MUL, and Infosys are not part of large business houses. Their ownership ranges from traditional private capital, state and multinational capital to new entrepreneurial (and employees') capital respectively. Essar's steel project, Birla's joint venture with General Motors, and Tata's foray into software exports are examples of traditional conglomerate expansion and diversification. However, the secular deterioration of Birla's and Premier Auto's older units and the continued success of Tata in the auto industry reflect the importance of early professionalization of management and its ability to flexibly adjust corporate profit strategies. One clear trend has been the general internationalization of the corporate sector. Virtually all profit strategies have engaged the external sector as sources of technology, export markets, and foreign assets.

The differentiation and the growing sophistication of the Indian corporate sector is still constrained by several structural bottlenecks. Domestic demand continues to be limited by poverty and inequality. The ability to capture high value-added export markets is constrained by access to technology and multinational competition. The revision of demand forecasts in the auto industry and the difficulty in moving into more complex software exports are cases in point. Nevertheless it is important to recognize that changes in the form of capitalist regulation are forcing corporations, traditional and otherwise, to actively seek out market-conforming profit strategies. Such institutional changes must be interpreted as necessarily accompanying the maturity and heterogeneity of Indian capitalists. Corporate capitalism is increasingly self-governed with a diversity of institutional arrangements. Most noteworthy are inter-firm, institutionalized cooperation, joint-ventures, and government support for exports. Thus, liberalization need not translate into individualistic, arms-length, market responses. Rather kinship ties and political connections will continue to augment market responses. As we have seen, changes in the form of capitalist regulation have prompted unconventional (by Indian standards) collective and individual corporate responses. These actions are consequences of both increasing capitalist maturity and increasing heterogeneity of the corporate sector. The internationalization of the Indian economy can only add to the contingency of outcomes and the complexity of strategies available to Indian firms. Selective reforms, cooperative business–government partnerships, and a long-term innovation-driven commercial strategy are likely to enhance Indian corporate competitiveness in the future.

Acknowledgments

Primary fieldwork for the steel, auto, and software industries was supported by the Founders' Endowment Fund, University of Washington, Tacoma (1996), Fellowships, Fulbright Program for Faculty Research Abroad (1991) and American Institute of Indian Studies (1992), and a Senior Fellowship, American Institute of Indian Studies (1998) respectively. I would like to thank the numerous firms, government institutions, and individuals in India who willingly shared their views on these industries. Janette Rawlings, as always, provided substantive and editorial comments. I am grateful to all these institutions and individuals. The usual caveats apply.

Notes

1 An example of institutional change would be to increase the domestic market by weakening the power of landlords in the countryside. Structural change would entail capturing foreign markets by reducing technological dependence.
2 The state continues to command the largest firms. Even in the 1990s, six of the top ten companies were under the state. *Business India*, November 3–16, 1997.
3 There have been other (illiberal) outcomes accompanying reforms. Religious and ethnic strife and environmental degradation seem to take on more grotesque forms in contemporary Indian political economy.
4 The Indian capitalist class was already quite mature in 1947. See R. Sau, "The development of monopoly capital in India", in B. Berberoglu (ed.), *Class, State and Development in India* (New Delhi: Sage Publications, 1992) pp. 157–84. See also Drèze and Sen (1998: 179–80) for their view on Indian entrepreneurial talent. See also A.P. D'Costa, "The long march to capitalism: India's resistance to, and reintegration with the world economy", *Contemporary South Asia*, vol. 4 (1995) no. 3, pp. 255–85; R.W. Stern, *Changing India: Bourgeois Revolution on the Subcontinent* (Cambridge: Cambridge University Press, 1993); A. Vanaik, *The Painful Transition: Bourgeois Democracy in India* (London: Verso, 1990).
5 I use "internationalization" rather than "globalization" to avoid the vacuousness associated with the latter term. See for example R. Jenkins, *Transnational Corporations and Uneven Development: The Internationalization of Capital and the Third World* (New York: Methuen & Co., 1987); P. Hirst and G. Thompson,

Globalization in Question: The International Economy and the Possibilities of Governance (Cambridge: Polity Press, 1998); R. Wade, "Globalization and its limits: reports of the death of the national economy are greatly exaggerated" and R. Boyer, "The convergence hypothesis revisited: globalization but still the century of nations?", in S. Berger and R. Dore (eds), *National Diversity and Global Capitalism* (Ithaca: Cornell University Press, 1996) pp. 60–88; 29–59.

6   See T. Banuri (ed.), *Economic Liberalization: No Panacea, The Experiences of Latin America and East Asia* (Oxford: Clarendon Press, 1991).

7   R. Boyer, *The Regulation School: A Critical Introduction* (New York: Columbia University Press, 1990) (translated by Craig Charney); M.H. Best, *The New Competition: Institutions of Industrial Restructuring* (Cambridge, MA: Harvard University Press, 1990).

8   Some details on the floundering process of liberalization in the 1980s and 1990s respectively can be found in A. Kohli, *Democracy and Discontent: India's Growing Crisis of Governability* (Cambridge: Cambridge University Press, 1992); V. Joshi and I.M.D. Little, *India's Economic Reforms 1991–2001* (Delhi: Oxford University Press, 1998).

9   See J. Scott, *Corporate Business and Capitalist Classes* (Oxford: Oxford University Press, 1997).

10   J. Scott, *Corporations, Classes and Capitalism* (London: Hutchinson, 1985); M. Zeitlin, *The Large Corporation and Contemporary Classes* (New Brunswick, NJ: Rutgers University Press, 1989).

11   A.H. Amsden, *Asia's Next Giant: South Korea and Late Industrialization* (New York: Oxford University Press, 1989).

12   S. Tsuru, *Japan's Capitalism: Creative Defeat and Beyond* (Cambridge: Cambridge University Press, 1994) pp. 76–7.

13   Information on family firms has been obtained from various recent issues of *Business India*.

14   For example, see Amsden and Best, op. cit., n. 11 and n. 7 respectively.

15   See S.A. Kochanek, *Business and Politics in India* (Berkeley: University of California Press, 1974) for the relationship between business associations and politics.

16   P.K. Bardhan, *The Political Economy of Development in India* (Oxford: Basil Blackwell, 1984).

17   Sau, op. cit., n. 4.

18   Institutionalized cooperation and subcontracting relations as cultivated in northern Italy and Japan and their diffusion are discussed in M. Piore and C. Sabel, *The Second Industrial Divide* (New York: Basic Books, 1984); F. Pyke, *Industrial Development Through Small-Firm Cooperation: Theory and Practice* (Geneva: International Labour Office, 1992); M. Kenney and R. Florida, *Beyond Mass Production: The Japanese System and Its Transfer to the US* (New York: Oxford University Press, 1993). For the Indian case see A.P. D'Costa, "Economic governance in the Indian automotive industry: flexible institutions for mass production goals" (mimeograph, 1999).

19   Scott, op. cit., n. 9, p. 146.

20   J.R. Hollingsworth, P.C. Schmitter and W. Streeck (eds), *Governing Capitalist Economies: Performance and Control of Economic Sectors* (New York: Oxford University Press, 1994) p. 270.

21 EF units melt and purify scrap. With heavy dependence on electricity, EF units were initially confined to small volumes of high-value metals, such as aluminum refining and specialty steels. The diffusion of EF units has been limited by superior metallurgical qualities of steel produced with integrated ore and coal-based blast furnace technology. Consequently EF units have been historically relegated to producing low value-added long products, mainly bars, wire rods, and small shapes for the construction market. Only since the 1980s has EF technology gained a reputation that borders on the cutting edge. See A.P. D'Costa, *The Global Restructuring of the Steel Industry: Innovations, Institutions and Industrial Change* (London: Routledge, 1999).

22 Ibid., Chapter 7.

23 Indian EF units have been very small. Nearly 100 per cent of the EAFs were under 10 ton capacity. See S.R. Basu, P.K. Bose, and K.K. Mehrotra, "Entrepreneurs signal new era for India's minimills", *Metal Bulletin Monthly* (December, 1987). In 1989–90 there were 179 units that produced an average of only 17,500 tons per year. See G. Etienne, with J. Astier, H. Bhushan, and D. Zhong, *Asian Crucible: The Steel Industry in China and India* (New Delhi: Sage Publications, 1992) p. 77. Only one unit at that time had a capacity of 250,000 tons. Rising scrap prices, the basic raw material for EF units, induced low capacity utilization. These units consumed inordinate amounts of electric power. There was pilferage of electric power, tax evasion, and price gouging in the controlled market. Far from being innovative, the overall Indian EF segment has been technologically backward and commercially rent-seeking.

24 Today Ispat International employs a global team of over 15,000 committed and highly skilled steelmakers, engineers, analysts and managers.

25 J. Schriefer, "An empire of direct reduced iron and steel", *New Steel* (August, 1996), p. 42.

26 Personal interview, NDIL, Calcutta, June 1996.

27 It is strategically similar to DRI in that it bypasses expensive blast furnace-based hot metal. However, it also has the advantage of small size and choice of downstream process. For example, the hot metal produced by COREX can be charged either into an EF or into the basic oxygen furnace of an integrated mill. The process does not rely on coking coal (hence expensive coke ovens) and large-scale blast furnaces.

28 Recent estimates show COREX-BOF as the most expensive route, followed by the traditional BF-BOF and DRI-EF, in that order. See R. Sengupta, "The Indian steel industry: investment issues and prospects, Part II: Technology Choice and Investment" (New Delhi: Information and Credit Rating Ltd, 1995).

29 A.P. D'Costa, "The restructuring of the Indian automobile industry: Indian state and Japanese capital", *World Development*, vol. 23 (1995) no. 3, pp. 485–502.

30 Automotive Components Manufacturing Association (ACMA), New Delhi, 1997–98, p. 10.

31 Numerous automotive firms based in Delhi, Bombay, and Chennai (Madras) suggested that MUL's success was due to its first-mover advantages (meeting newly imposed fuel-efficiency standards) and government patronage (barring new entrants) (interviews conducted during September–November 1991). However, being a firstcomer meant meeting local content requirements and

stringent Japanese quality standards. Given a weak supplier base, MUL's viability called for creative initiatives to overcome supply bottlenecks.

32 D. Narayana, "The motor vehicle industry in India" (Trivandrum: Centre for Development Studies, Occasional Paper Series, 1989) p. 17.

33 R.N. Langlois and P.L. Robertson, *Firms, Markets and Economic Change: A Dynamic Theory of Business Institutions* (London: Routledge, 1995); J.R. Tauile, "Notes on dynamic flexibility, cooperation and economic efficiency", in A.K. Bagchi (ed.), *New Technology and the Workers' Response: Microelectronics, Labor and Society* (New Delhi: Sage Publications, 1995) p. 32; M. Aoki, "The Japanese firm in transition", in Y. Kozo and Y. Yasuba (eds), *The Political Economy of Japan, Volume 1: The Domestic Transformation* (Stanford: Stanford University Press, 1987) pp. 263–88. There were other factors as well, such as stable paternalistic labor-management systems. See A.P. D'Costa, "An alternative model of development? cooperation and flexible industrial practices in India", *Journal of International Development*, vol. 10 (1998) no. 3, pp. 301–21.

34 For example, in the past the Indian firm Mahindra and Mahindra, an established monopoly in utility vehicles, has been at the mercy of several sole supplier of parts (interview with Mahindra & Mahindra Staff, Mumbai, October 1991).

35 Under the now defunct phased manufacturing programme (PMP), anywhere from 75 to 90 per cent local content had to be attained within seven years.

36 General Motors, the world's largest auto firm, is planning a best-practice plant in Brazil with many of its suppliers under the same roof (New York Times, April 21, 1999).

37 Jay Bharat and Bharat Seats deliver components on a daily basis (D'Costa, op. cit., n. 21). Machino Plastics supplies plastic panels, made from molds supplied by MUL, every four hours or four times in a two-shift day. This also has been Suzuki's practice as found in Canada where CAMI, a GM–Suzuki joint venture, obtained plastic-injected molded parts from supplies every four hours. See J. Morris, "A Japanization of Canadian industry?", in D. Drache and M.S. Gertler (eds), *The New Era of Global Competition: State Policy and Market Power* (Montreal: McGill-Queen's University Press, 1991).

38 Machino Plastics, making molded components, uses MUL's maintenance equipment if needed. When they are not available Machino Plastics can rely on the support of other joint ventures, such as Swaraj Paul's Caparo Industries (a joint venture with MUL for making steel pressed parts) (interviews with Machino Plastics Staff, Gurgaon, June 1996).

39 Sona Steering Chairman's address at ACMA Annual Meeting, New Delhi, 1994. Sales nearly doubled between 1994 and 1996 (from Rs 656 million to Rs 1219 million) without any increase in manpower, with sales per worker increasing from Rs 1.58 million to Rs 2.92 million (Sona Group Company Documents, 1996).

40 Mahindra and Mahindra, long-time Indian producer of utility vehicles has collaborated with Chrysler, Peugeot, Nissan, Ford, and now defunct Willys. It has aggressively introduced cellularization (interview with Mahindra & Mahindra, Mumbai, 1991, 1996). It brought in the UK-based Lucas Engineering Systems "to change the company's manufacturing methods to contemporary Western and Japanese styles" (*Business World*, 1994, p. 13; *Business Today*,

November 5, 1995). Such "Business Process Re-engineering" entailed retooling, cellularization, and other shop-floor innovations to increase output and productivity.

41   S. Kathuria, *Competing through Technology and Manufacturing: A Study of the Indian Commercial Vehicles Industry* (Delhi: Oxford University Press, 1996); S. Lall, *Learning to Industrialize: The Acquisition of Technological Capability by India* (London: The Macmillan Press, 1987).

42   The other major players in this segment are Ashok-Leyland, with British and non-resident Indian capital (Hindujas) and Volvo of Sweden. Recently Ashok-Leyland set up a joint venture with Italy's Iveco.

43   *Shipping Times* (Singapore, April 1, 1997, p. 2).

44   H. Oba, "The impact of liberalization on automobile industry in India: is Indian automobile industry competitive?", paper presented at the seminar on *The Emergence of the Indian Economy in the Asian Perspective* (Chiba University of Commerce, Japan, December 7, 1996, Table 5).

45   ACMA op. cit., n. 30, p. 92.

46   See P. Evans, *Embedded Autonomy: States and Industrial Transformation* (Princeton: Princeton University Press, 1995).

47   National Association of Software and Service Companies (NASSCOM), *The Software Industry in India: A Strategic Review* (New Delhi: NASSCOM, 1998, 1999).

48   Ibid., 1999, pp. 29–30.

49   Evans, op. cit., n. 46, p. 171; Dataquest, December 31, 1999.

50   J.M. Grieco, *Between Dependency and Autonomy: India's Experience with the International Computer Industry* (Berkeley: University of California Press, 1984).

51   Infosys Technologies, the sixth largest exporter, began with a mere $300 dollar initial investment.

52   R. Heeks, 1996, *India's Software Industry: State Policy, Liberalisation and Industrial Development* (New Delhi: Sage, 1996). The Y2K problem, although commercially worth several hundred billion dollars, by itself is not a technology frontier moving problem. It requires a large pool of workers, tediously identifying date fields, fixing them, and testing the fixes.

53   P. Sen, "Software exports from India: a systemic analysis", *Electronics Information & Planning* (November, 1994), pp. 55–63.

54   Labor turnover is 30 per cent. Salary increases, it could be argued, reflect increasing value-added services. However, given the high degree of low value-added on-site services and off-shore work, without significant design and project management capability such rapid salary increases can only be counterproductive.

55   There have been some recent successes. For example, Indian engineers at the Texas Instruments' Bangalore center designed a digital signal processor (DSP) that could be used in a wide range of consumer durables, digital cameras, robotics and other industrial applications. N-Core, an information technology design services company, has licensed its modem software and speech compression technology to Mitsubishi, LG Semicon, and several US firms. Similarly WIPRO sold an IPR (a synthesizer core) to a reputed Japanese computer peripheral manufacturing company. The assignment included interfacing WIPRO's logics with the Japanese client's logic, a jump

from routine programming to staying ahead of industry conventional standards.

56 A.P. D'Costa, "Technology leap-frogging: the software challenge in India", presented at the 2nd *Conference on Technology and Innovations* (Lisbon: Fundação Gulbenkian Calouste, August 3–5, 1998).
57 Ibid.

6

State and Capital in Pakistan: The Changing Politics of Accumulation

Ali Cheema

In line with most of South Asia, the Pakistani model of industrialisation has been state-centric. Since independence, the Pakistani State has been at the centre of creating 'transfers' through an array of policy interventions aimed to induce industrial accumulation. While the state appears to be retreating from this model in the face of globalisation, there is still no robust explanation for the failure of this model in the Pakistani context.[1] This chapter is an attempt to write the obituary of the state-centric model in Pakistan in order to conceptualise the role of the state that is necessary to steer Pakistan out of its present economic crisis. The underlying presuppostion of the chapter is that, to understand the complexities of the current role of the state it is important first to understand the structures out of which it is born.

State-centric models of accumulation in South Asia are akin to Marx's notion of 'primitive accumulation'.[2] The emerging capitalist sectors of these economies have been critically dependant on forcible state 'transfers' from non-capitalist sectors, which provide essential resources for the creation and sustenance of capitalist enterprise. It is well understood that 'primitive accumulation' may or may not be consistent with a successful capitalist transition (Habib, 1995; Khan, 2001). This has, indeed, been the case in Pakistan. The main problem for the state-centric model of accumulation in Pakistan has been its *inability to sustain high-rates of accumulation alongside high rates of productivity growth* (Table 6.1). This is contrary to the outcome of 'primitive accumulation' in certain East Asian economies,[3] where forcible state 'transfers' resulted in stimulating both high rates of growth of accumulation and productivity. On the

Table 6.1 Key growth rates in Pakistan's manufacturing sector (annual growth rates)

	Output (%)	Total factor productivity (TFP)* (%)	Capital stock (%)
1960–70	10	5.1[4]	7.3
1978–88	9.6	−0.9	10.3

*TFP is estimated by the following equation: TFP growth = GDP growth − labour input growth − capital input growth. It measures the 'efficiency' component of growth by capturing that part of the growth which cannot be explained by the growth of factor inputs.

Source: Kemal (1978), Sayeed (1995).

contrary, in Pakistan, rates of productivity growth have waned. Manufacturing productivity, which grew buoyantly during the sixties, slowed down significantly during the eighties (Table 6.1).

Furthermore, both the rate of accumulation and output growth, which maintained a healthy trend during the eighties, have slowed down tremendously during the nineties (Table 6.2). This chapter attempts to provide an explanation for the inability of the Pakistani state to foster high rates of *efficient accumulation* over the recent decades. We analyse this issue using the case study of Pakistan's key manufacturing sector, 'spinning'. We revisit this topic, as prior explanations appear to be lacking. The standard explanation, based on poor policy choice,[5] cannot explain why state policy was consistent with both high rates of accumulation and productivity during the sixties.[6] In fact, in this chapter we argue that there was not much change in the magnitude or nature of policy-transfers for the spinning sector between the sixties and the

Table 6.2 Capital accumulation and output growth in Pakistan (annual growth rates)

	Gross fixed capital formation (total manufacturing) (% p.a.)	Gross fixed capital formation (large scale manufacturing) (%)	Output growth (total manufacturing) (%)	Output growth (large scale manufacturing) (%)
1980s	8.42	8.2	8.2	8.1
1990–1995	−1.13	−2.8	5.5	4.4

Source: Economic Survey of Pakistan (1984–85, 1999–2000).

eighties. In spite of this, productivity growth plummeted in the latter period. The explanations based on looting, corruption and rent-seeking are equally lacking.[7] These explanations encounter two problems. Firstly, again they cannot explain why processes of rent-seeking and corruption resulted in efficient accumulation during the sixties. Secondly, they cannot explain the manner in which these processes lowered the efficiency of accumulation during the eighties and nineties. While we do accept the importance of rent-seeking and corruption as possible explanations, we feel that such explanations, to be useful, must reveal the manner in which these processes inhibited efficient accumulation during the eighties and nineties. Instead, we argue that in order to understand the role of these processes as constraints on efficient accumulation, the changing context of political power and state organisation during the eighties and nineties must be mapped out.

Mapping out the relationship between the structure of (rent-seeking) and the efficiency of accumulation is important from both a theoretical and an empirical perspective. Recent developments in the theory of corruption and rent-seeking have shown these processes to be consistent with both efficient and inefficient accumulation.[8] This is contrary to the perspectives provided by neo-classical political economy.[9] According to this literature, corruption (which is not differentiated from rent-seeking in any substantive way) reduces the efficiency of accumulation through a wasteful allocation of resources, by discouraging innovation[10] and by distorting competition.[11] Khan (2000b) points out that these perspectives are limited as they assume the outcome of rent-seeking: the 'rent' unequivocally causes a social loss. However, in many cases 'rents' create social benefits by stimulating incentives for innovation, learning, socially beneficial cooperation and for the internalisation of externalities. In this perspective the 'rents' associated with state-centric approaches may well be necessary to stimulate accumulation in developing economies.

The success of East Asian industrial policy[12] has also revived an interest in identifying factors and conditions that can differentiate successful from unsuccessful state-centric experiments in developing countries. The East Asian case shows that the outcome of rent-seeking and corruption may take the form of learning/innovation 'rents', which provide essential incentives for dynamic efficiency by lowering information costs in credit markets and by allowing technological externalities to be internalised.[13]

It is also clear that analysing the changing institutional context of state intervention and the political context surrounding state-centric 'transfers' is essential, if we are to explain variations in the efficacy of the state-centric model. This is necessary from a theoretical standpoint as well. After all, if 'state-created transfers' are to increase social welfare, they must raise the costs of undertaking actions that stunt investment, innovation and learning. The relevant cost is the loss of the 'transfer' in the event that the required action is not forthcoming from the beneficiaries of policy. Therefore, for these 'transfers' to be effective this cost has to be invoked by the state credibly committing to removing the 'transfer'. However, the success of the state in *ensuring enforcement* cannot be assumed on an *a priori* basis unless a particular state is welfare promoting and is above societal interests. Both these conditions are unlikely to be met in reality.[14] Therefore, if we are to adequately analyse reality we must factor in the political economy context in which state intervention in specific periods is embedded. This chapter aims to do precisely this in the context of Pakistan's industrialisation experience.

This chapter argues that the slowdown in the process of *efficient* accumulation, in Pakistan, is attributable to the emergence of *decentralised corruption* in the eighties, which arose on account of: (a) the factionalisation of the capitalist class, (b) the growing political power of the intermediate class[15], and (c) the fragmentation of the state structure. This chapter explores the impact of *decentralised corruption on efficient accumulation* in a particular sector – spinning – that typified and led Pakistan's economic development. These issues are examined by comparing the differential effect of corruption on efficient accumulation during the sixties and the eighties–nineties. Both periods[16] witnessed significant 'state-transfers' in favour of private capital in order to induce accumulation. Furthermore, practices of corruption and rent-seeking underlay accumulation in both periods. The relative efficacy of primitive accumulation in the sixties as compared to the eighties–nineties needs to be explained in this context.

My point of course is not to argue that corruption is acceptable, either strategically or ethically, if it promotes efficient accumulation. For sure, one does not want to give up the possibility that accumulation would have been more efficient and vigorous in the absence of corruption altogther. That said, it needs to be acknowledged that corruption and rent-seeking are realities in the developing world, the complexities of which have been inadequately analysed by the neo-utilitarians.

This chapter is divided into six sections. The first section 'Posing the question' sets out the context. The second section 'Changes in the nature and magnitude of state "transfers" in Pakistan' argues that an explanation for differences in the efficiency of accumulation between our periods cannot be sought in differences in the nature or magnitude of 'state-transfers'. This section also points out that significant rent-seeking and corruption underlay state intervention in both periods. The third section 'Is efficient accumulation consistent with corruption (rent-seeking)?' reviews the theoretical relationship between different forms of corruption and the possibility for efficient accumulation. The fourth section 'Differential efficiency of corruption (rent-seeking) in Pakistan' maps out the changes in the organisational and political power of the capitalist and urban intermediate classes, as well as the nature and organisation of the state, in particular the bureaucracy. This section argues that the emerging structure of *decentralised* rent-seeking and corruption became inconsistent with efficient accumulation strategies during the eighties–nineties. It shows that this emerging structure reduced efficient accumulation by directly impacting sectoral productivity growth. It did this by encouraging the entry of low productivity firms and entrepreneurs and by bailing out entrepreneurial failure. The sixth section 'Conclusion' presents the conclusions.

Posing the question

Table 6.3 reveals three important facets about the effect of spinning sector policy during the sixties and the eighties–nineties period. Firstly, accumulation was very rapid in both periods. This is clearly revealed by the high growth rates of capital stock. In fact, if anything the growth rate of the capital–labour ratio was much more buoyant during the eighties and nineties than during the sixties. Secondly, value-added growth maintained a very healthy trend during both periods. Thirdly, while efficiency, measured by the rates of growth of total factor and capital productivity, matched the buoyancy of accumulation during the

Table 6.3   Growth rates of key spinning sector variables (in per cent per annum)

	1960–70 (% p.a.)	1981–94 (% p.a.)
Value added	12	14.8
Net capital stock	7	14.6
Employment	6	8.4
TFP	5.3	2.8
Capital productivity	6	0.2
Labour productivity	5	6.4
Capital–labour ratio	1	6.2

Source: Kemal (1978),[17] Cheema (1999).

sixties (see TFP and capital productivity in Table 6.3) this was not the case during the latter period. Table 6.3 shows that the eighties–nineties period saw a waning of both capital productivity and total factor productivity growth rates. This clearly suggests that state intervention in Pakistan was consistent with patterns of *efficient accumulation* during the sixties, but this correspondence had broken by the eighties and nineties. During the latter period we witness *inefficient accumulation*.[18]

Explanations for these patterns based on the exhaustion of technological possibilities do not take us very far. One possible explanation for low-capital productivity growth during the eighties–nineties is *the setting in of diminishing returns to capital on account of rapid accumulation without technological change*. Similarly, an explanation of lowering TFP growth rates would be consistent with the possible exhaustion of technological possibilities, by the eighties, as the sector approached the world technology frontier explain? Both these explanations do not hold in Pakistan's case as there was considerable scope for upgrading the technology in the spinning sector during the eighties (Cheema, 1999). Estimates on the age structure of machinery show that in 1978, 50 per cent of the installed machinery was more than 10 years old, while another 25 per cent was between five and ten years old (APTMA, 1977, p. 60). This clearly shows that significant potential for technological upgradation remained during the eighties, which is sufficient to rule out the explanations based on the exhaustion of technological possibilities. Therefore, we must look elsewhere for an explanation of the divergent performance of state intervention in Pakistan.

Changes in the nature and magnitude of state 'transfers' in Pakistan

As mentioned earlier the standard explanation for the declining efficacy of state intervention in Pakistan has been based on changes in state policy.[19] It is argued that policy in the sixties was more liberal and less distortionary than spinning-sector policy in the eighties–nineties period. This claim is based on a number of observations. Firstly, it is suggested that during the sixties the state was able to create incentives for exports through a system of multiple exchange rates that favoured manufacturing exports. Secondly, there was a liberal allocation of subsidised state-credit to fuel accumulation. Thirdly, cotton prices were kept fairly close to open market prices.[20] Finally, it is suggested that on the whole the import policy regarding industrial machinery and intermediate goods was fairly liberal, except during the few years after the Indo-Pakistan war.[21] A combination of these factors is thought to provide an explanation for efficient accumulation during the sixties.

As opposed to this the eighties are argued to reflect a more distortionary policy regime. Firstly, the import policy regarding industrial machinery and intermediate goods is argued to be less liberal? more illiberal. Secondly, and most importantly, it is argued that the spinning sector has been provided with a 'distorted' incentive through the availability of cotton at below world prices. These distortions are viewed as the Achilles' heel of the eighties policy regime. In the remaining part of this section we provide a comparative assessment of the policy tools used by the state during the sixties and the eighties–nineties. Our argument is that although there might be marginal differences in the 'tools' used, nonetheless, the overall direction and magnitude of state 'transfers'[22] in favour of the sector are very similar. If this is the case, then differences in policy *alone* cannot provide an explanation for the relative decline in the efficacy of state intervention in Pakistan.

Policy in the sixties

The following policy-created 'transfers' underlay the rapid accumulation within the spinning sector during the sixties: (a) availability of subsidised raw material and (b) availability of subsidised credit and cheap foreign exchange. These 'transfers' were accompanied by policies that kept the price of machinery close to the international level and deregulated entry into this sector. It is worth spending some time discussing the magnitude and form of these 'transfers', along with the structure of dispensation.

The key raw material of the textile industry has been domestic cotton. This accounts for over 80 per cent of operating costs. The state subsidised the use of this raw material through three policies. Firstly, it allowed the export of cotton at the overvalued official exchange rate, which meant that domestic producers obtained cotton at below a notional free market price (Amjad, 1982). Secondly, it levied an export duty on cotton (APTMA, 1977). This again forced the price of cotton below its international price, although the duty was steadily lowered and maintained at Rs 10 per bale from the mid-sixties. Hamid, Nabi and Nasim (1990) estimate that the joint effect of these interventions resulted in domestic cotton prices being 40 per cent lower than world prices on average during the sixties.

Thirdly, the state provided a price subsidy to textile exporters through the *Export-Bonus Scheme*. Exporters whose commodities were covered by the scheme received a voucher equal to a certain proportion of the value of their exports; the proportion was determined by government policy. The voucher entitled the holder to purchase an equivalent amount of foreign exchange to be used for import of items on the bonus list. This voucher was tradable on the secondary market. Given the stringent foreign exchange and import controls, such vouchers usually sold at a premium of 150–180 per cent of their face value, thereby providing a subsidy for textile exporters (Amjad, 1982). These interventions turned the terms of trade in favour of textile manufacturers during the Second Five-Year Plan (1960–65). However, evidence suggests that by the latter half of the period the terms of trade advantage had weakened. During the sixties, the ratio of cotton to yarn prices declined at a rate of 3.5 per cent p.a. and this effect was reversed during the Third Five-Year Plan (1965–70).[23]

The state also created 'transfers' through the financial sector. It did this by providing foreign exchange to import industrial machinery at the cheap official exchange rate and by dispensing loans on favourable terms. The rate of interest charged on these loans was 30 per cent of the scarcity value of capital (Amjad, 1982). This considerably influenced the profitability and financial position of spinning entrepreneurs. Easy access to these subsidies was provided for textile manufacturers through the Pay-As-You-Earn (PAYE) scheme and by disbursing foreign exchange loans and grants provided by multilateral agencies through state-run financial institutions namely, the Pakistan Industrial Credit and Investment Corporation (PICIC) and the Industrial Development Bank of Pakistan (IDBP). These schemes covered over 65 per cent of investment financing during the sixties. Commercial banks that were privately owned only financed working capital. Amjad's (1982) estimates clearly show that access to subsidised foreign exchange loans explains in large part the differences in investment behaviour across textile firms.

Amjad (1982) shows that the web of investment controls did not really apply to the textile industry. He points out that the textile industry was *de facto* subject to no investment or licensing controls during the sixties. Furthermore, the *Bonus Voucher Scheme* ensured access to machinery imports on liberal terms. As pointed out, under this scheme an exporter received *in addition* to the amount of rupees converted at the official exchange rate, 'bonus vouchers', which entitled him access to foreign exchange at the official exchange rate. The voucher could also be used to freely import items on the bonus list. Alongside this, a large number of textile imports were put on the 'free list', which were not subject to administrative controls. These schemes ensured that there were no entry barriers and that machinery imports were available at near world prices.

This discussion clearly shows that state 'transfers' played a critical role in stimulating accumulation in the sector. The 'transfers' were at the expense of cotton growers, taxpayers and consumers.

Policy in the eighties–nineties

State 'transfers' were critical in stimulating accumulation even during the eighties–nineties period. Again the key 'transfers' were made through the state's cotton pricing and credit policies. The seventies saw a drastic cut in policy-created 'transfers' in favour of spinning capitalists. Furthermore, assets of these capitalists in other manufacturing sectors and in banking were nationalised. These factors as well as other macroeconomic shocks resulted in initially declining and then very stagnant rates of growth of output, investment and exports in the spinning sector. Once in power the new military regime set about to establish 'transfers' in order to stimulate accumulation in the sector. A well-organised system of 'transfers' was well in place by the mid-eighties (Cheema, 1999).

The main 'transfer' again came at the expense of the cotton sector. Cotton prices were set below international prices through the use of the export duty and by placing a ceiling on domestic cotton prices. Over the eighties the former tool gained importance as the means for creating the 'transfer'. Cheema (1999) shows that the 'transfer' turned the terms of trade in favour of textile manufacturers during the eighties. However, as in the sixties, by the latter half of the period the terms of trade advantage had weakened. During the eighties the ratio of cotton to yarn prices declined at a rate of 2 per cent p.a. and this effect was reversed after the nineties.[24]

Subsidised credit was the second set of 'transfers' that underlay policy during the eighties–nineties. The conduit of this 'transfer' was no longer only the state-run financial institutions but also commercial banks that had been nationalised under Bhutto (1971–77). The aid dividend from the Soviet–Afghan war had created significant foreign exchange liquidity for the 'state' to make liberal 'transfers' to industry. Cheema (1999) shows that real long-term lending to the spinning sector was dispensed at a very liberal rate. Again the rate of interest on long-term loans was only 40 per cent of the open market price of capital.

Alongside these 'transfers', the state lowered entry barriers for the sector and provided access to machinery imports at near world prices. In the early eighties, investment into the sector was subject to controls. However, these controls were dismantled by the mid-eighties. During the eighties–nineties period a number of duty exemption schemes were provided for the import of machinery into the sector. These schemes ensured access to machinery at near world prices. As in the sixties 'transfers' to the spinning sector were at the expense of cotton growers, taxpayers and consumers.

The discussion in this section shows that there were no major differences in the type or 'magnitude' of transfers during the sixties and the eighties–nineties period. Therefore, differences in policy choice as an explanation for the differential efficiency of accumulation between the sixties and the eighties–nineties does not take us very far. The only difference in policy outcomes was the reversal of terms of trade in favour of the cotton growers during the early- to mid-nineties.[25] However, the change in terms of trade alone cannot explain differential performance if industry had been placed on a path of sustainable capitalist accumulation after more than thirty years of 'primitive accumulation'. In our view, the explanation has to be sought elsewhere; it has to be *sought in the inability of the state to mitigate the challenges posed by re-distributive demands from a growing number of political factions and to retain effective control over a fragmenting and increasing corruptible bureaucracy.*

Rent-seeking and corruption in spinning

Before outlining an explanation for the relative efficacy of state intervention it is important to understand the structure of corruption and 'rent-seeking' that emerged during the sixties and the eighties–nineties. Although rent-seeking and corruption underlay state 'transfers' in both the sixties and the eighties–nineties period, nonetheless, evidence suggests that there was considerable difference in the manner in which these practices were organised in each period.[26]

During the sixties, corruption and rent-seeking were organised on the basis of individual contact and individualised economic payoffs between business and state officials, and through individual capitalists' representation on the board of policy committees and state-run financial corporations. The main players in this game were a small number of business houses, the higher echelons of an exclusive, hierarchical, tightly knit and rule-based bureaucracy and a few key politicians, including the President (see the fourth section). It is interesting that despite their 'political power' landlords did not emerge as significant players in the contests over state 'transfers' to industry.[27]

As opposed to this, the organisation of corruption and rent-seeking was much more complicated during the eighties–nineties period. The creation, maintenance and dispensation of 'transfers' became subject to political negotiation between the ruling parties and/or the army,[28] an array of cross-class political factions and a rump of the sixties' business groups. The bureaucrat remained an important cog in the wheel of dispensation; however, his authority became contingent upon the political alliances he could muster rather than as a member of a tightly knit rule-based bureaucracy. Therefore, political endowments of different individuals and groups became an equally, if not more, important asset on the basis of which state 'transfers' were negotiated. The ability to make purely economic payoffs no longer guaranteed access to or maintenance of state 'transfers'. The transition from the earlier to the latter form of rent-seeking/corruption is discussed at length in the fourth section.

Is efficient accumulation consistent with corruption (rent-seeking)?

Before proceeding with a detailed historical analysis it is useful to assess different hypotheses regarding the relationship between different structures of corruption/rent-seeking and the efficiency of 'primitive accumulation'. The Pakistani evidence can be used to assess and/or broaden some of the hypotheses suggested by the political economy literature.[29]

There is now a growing appreciation in the political economy literature that processes of corruption and rent-seeking are consistent with examples of both *efficient* and *inefficient* accumulation. An array of theoretical hypotheses have been used to explain differential growth outcomes of corruption and rent-seeking in specific historical contexts.[30] In order to contextualise the argument presented in this chapter, the following issues are reviewed in this section: (a) the relative efficiency of economic versus political corruption, (b) the effect of enduring state-business networks on the efficiency of accumulation, and (c) the correlation between the extent of state centralisation and the efficiency of accumulation.

In the simplest sense, corruption is seen as part of a Coasean bargaining process in which state officials and capitalists bargain their way to an efficient outcome.[31] Bardhan (1997) argues that there is always an efficient outcome in a bribery game with competitive bidding by firms for a state-created 'rent'. This is because the 'rent' is awarded to the highest bidder, and it is the lowest-cost firm that can afford the largest bribe.[32] In fact, this result would hold even if there was two-firm bidding provided no 'tacit' or 'explicit' collusion arises between them. In a similar vein, Khan (2000b) argues that a minimal condition for efficient corruption is that the economic spending power of bribers is proportional to their economic gains from corruption. However, inefficiency may result if the official is influenced by considerations other than the size of the bribe (for example, a bias towards certain clients or political constituencies). With the state as the dispenser of 'transfers', it is more than likely that the political power of different bribers will be a crucial variable in bribery games. In this case, the efficiency outcome of corruption is not obvious, as political power need not be proportional to agents' economic spending power. This suggests that structures of corruption that reward economic spending power are less likely to be prone to inefficiency than structures that reward political power and/or political endowments. Of course the important caveat is that greater economic spending power must not limit competitive bidding, because structures that allow bribers to collude need not be efficient.

An important limitation of these arguments is that bribery games have an inter-temporal dimension, which these models do not consider. Minimum conditions for corruption to be efficient in a dynamic context include: the economic spending power of agents must be proportional to agents' net present value from corruption, and state officials must have long time horizons (Khan, 2000b). The latter condition ensures that state officials reward bribers offering maximum economic returns over time. These conditions are likely to be met in corruption structures where the bribe-givers and bribe-takers exchange bribes repeatedly over time, and/or if future gainers can borrow cheaply on the basis of their future gains. If there is no repeat play and/or if capital markets are imperfect then the game may well be won by agents offering higher short-term payoffs. In this case the result is not consistent with efficient accumulation. Evans (1995) argues that repeat play is more likely in social structures where considerable investment has been made in establishing an enduring business–government network. Where the network is weak, both sides come to the corruption game in order to maximise their short-term payoffs, which may well rule out inter-temporal private and social surplus maximisation.

Shleifer and Vishny (1993) argue that in general, centralised corruption has less adverse consequences for efficiency than decentralised corruption.[33] The former is akin to a hierarchical and well-knit state structure, while the latter corresponds to a fragmented state structure, where independent agencies attempt to maximise *only* their proceeds from corruption. Their model deals with the case where each state agency supplies complementary goods or services and can create bribes for itself by restricting supply. In this model a 'prisoner's dilemma' emerges as each agency maximises *its own* bribes, while taking the quantity of goods/

services supplied by others as a given. The outcome is *inefficient* in the case of a fragmented state as the bribe set by each agency is too high and the total amount of goods/services provided is too low from society's viewpoint. A centralised state is more *efficient* as it increases supply, in order to maximise total profits (by internalising the inter-agency price externality), which in turn makes society better off. However, as Khan (2000b) shows, even fragmented states can be efficient if agencies coordinate actions in a repeated game. This would happen if 'the payoffs from coordination are large compared with the payoffs from noncoordination, the time discount of officials is sufficiently low ... and ... agencies are not involved in protracted conflicts over how the spoils should be shared' (p. 133).

The efficiency results of all these arguments require both bureaucrats and capitalists to have long-time horizons in an inter-temporal game. The time horizon of state officials is in part a reflection of the vulnerability of both the state leadership and of individual bureaucrats, which in turn will depend on the political weakness of the state and its agents respectively. Strong political opposition and weak legitimacy of state leadership will increase the incentives to take the money and run. Similarly, officials' incentives to maximise short-term payoffs will increase if they are more susceptible to being 'politically' moved around or sidelined. Finally, the time horizon of capitalists will be a function of the rate of entry of 'transfer seeking coalitions' into the corruption market. A high rate of entry would increase the uncertainty of retaining a 'transfer', as the cost of excluding a large and growing number of contestants becomes prohibitive (Khan, 2000b). As Rose-Ackerman (1997, p. 43) points out 'A fundamental problem in such situations is the potential for an upward spiral of corruption', which increases the uncertainty associated with maintaining the size of the 'transfer'. Therefore, fragmented and unstable political coalitions will result in each briber trying to maximise his short-term payoff even if this is at the expense of long-term private and social gains.

The salient points of this discussion are summarised in Table 6.4, which suggests that inefficient accumulation is more likely in corruption structures that:

- reward political and not the economic spending power of players (Ai and Bi do not hold);
- involve a fragmented and weak state (Bii, Ci and Cii do not hold);
- consist of weak business–government networks (Biv does not hold);
- shorten the time-horizon for bidders (Biii does not hold).

Table 6.4 Corruption structures and efficient accumulation

Corruption structure	Conditions for efficient accumulation	
A. Static bidding game	(Ai)	Economic spending power determines the success of obtaining the 'transfer'
	(Aii)	No tacit or explicit collusion between bidders
B. Intertemporal bidding game	(Bi)	Ai holds in an intertemporal context
	(Bii)	State officials have long time horizons – contingent on <ul><li>Weak political opposition and strong legitimacy of state leadership</li><li>Low level of political interference in the appointment of state officials</li></ul>
	(Biii)	Bidders have long time horizons – contingent on <ul><li>Stable and consolidated factions bidding for 'transfers'</li></ul>
	(Biv)	Enduring state-business networks
C. Multiple rent-seeking agencies	(Ci)	Centralized and hierarchical state or
	(Cii)	Tacit coordination between state agencies

This discussion suggests that, *ceteris paribus*, fragmented and decentralised structures of corruption have a higher probability of resulting in inefficient accumulation.[34] Keeping this discussion in mind we can now evaluate the Pakistani evidence in order to explain the differential efficiency of corruption between the sixties and the eighties–nineties period.

Differential efficiency of corruption (rent-seeking) in Pakistan

The discussion in the third section enables us to assess the historical evidence in order to identify factors that explain the declining efficiency of corruption in the Pakistani case. In particular we show how changes in the structure of corruption, that is, the fragmentation of the state and the growth of 'transfer-seeking' coalitions, resulted in inefficient accumulation during the eighties–nineties period.

The sixties

During the sixties there were two types of players in the corruption game,[35] a small number of business groups and the higher echelons of an exclusive, hierarchical, tightly knit and rule-based bureaucracy along with a few key politicians. Here we detail the structure of corruption that emerged as a result of the interaction between these two sets of players. This discussion will also show that the Pakistani state's objective to promote industrialisation cannot be seen as evidence of state capture by the capitalist class, whose political power was relatively weak. Instead, it was a reflection of a relatively autonomous state's recognition for survival (Alavi, 1983; Jalal, 1990).

Monopoly houses

Until the early eighties the capitalist class which dominated the spinning industry was largely organised around the monopoly houses of the sixties (Cheema, 1999). These houses are characterised by family ownership under a centralised decision-making authority, usually the patriarch of the family, and consist of several legally separate companies engaged in highly diversified activities. Furthermore, there is no separation of ownership from control in the case of these houses.[36] An important sociological feature of these houses is that they belonged to migrant trading communities, which had settled and conducted business in urban areas of United India outside the areas which came to constitute Pakistan (Papaneck, 1972; Amjad, 1983). During the sixties, when the Pakistani state conducted its first experiment with centralised and coordinated industrial policy, these houses had easy access to the institutional structure of the state. Industrial policy was defined by an authoritarian regime which relied on the executive to set up a coordinated and centralised set of state-created incentives to boost *private sector* manufacturing productivity and accumulation.[37] An important form this *institutional access* took was the formal representation these 'houses' had on the boards of state-run financial institutions, which were the main disbursers of long-term loans to the manufacturing sector. About a third of directors of important state-run financial institutions such as the *Pakistan Industrial Credit and Investment Corporation* (PICIC), the *Investment Corporation of Pakistan* (ICP) and the *National Investment Trust* (NIT) were from these houses.[38] An outcome of this corporate structure was that industrial assets became concentrated in the hands of 44 monopoly houses who controlled 48 per cent of gross fixed assets of the large-scale manufacturing sector in 1970 (Amjad, 1982). These houses were also the main beneficiaries of loans disbursed by the two major Development Finance Institutions (DFIs) run by the state, PICIC and *Industrial Development Bank of Pakistan* (IDBP). In the case of the textile sector, Amjad (1983) shows that these 44 houses controlled 50 per cent of the production in this sector in 1970.

The access enjoyed by monopoly houses to key state agencies was contingent on the patronage of the executive bodies. The political and electoral power of the industrial class remained weak during the sixties. Cheema (1999) estimates that apart from the 1965 election, which was based on a managed franchise where the state disqualified a number of political groups from contesting the election (Jalal, 1990), the sixties houses never had effective representation in the electoral system.[39] In terms of their ethnic background, these groups belonged to Kathiawar, Gujrat and Chiniot. Before the Partition these groups had settled in Calcutta and were not rooted in the political parties that operated in the areas that constituted Pakistan.[40] Nor were these houses rooted in the migrant groups that mobilised in support of the Muslim League. It is not surprising that in his detailed study Papaneck (1962) found weak political linkages and low levels of political motivation among this group. Therefore, economic spending power became the only effective tool available to this group to influence state policy. Their weak political organisation constrained them from bringing effective political pressure to bear upon the state's industrial policy.

State structure

The second set of players consisted of state agents responsible for the allocation and disbursement of 'transfers' to the capitalist sector. The weakness of the legislature in pre- and post-independence Pakistan resulted in the bureaucracy emerging as a key player with control over formulation and administration of key policies related to the manufacturing sector. During its early history Pakistan was primarily governed by ordinances and not through legislative acts.[41] Although in theory ministers were superior to central secretaries, however, in practice the latter dominated.[42] It is well documented that Ayub gave considerable freedom of action to a few trusted ministers and to his top civil servants, while he only acted as the final arbiter of disputes between them.[43] Furthermore, civil secretaries of key ministries had direct access to Ayub and the provincial governors. The army, while a beneficiary of state 'transfers', was not directly involved in state economic policy formulation and administration.[44] The key agencies in charge of policy formulation and dispensation were the National Economic Council (NEC), the Planning Commission and the Ministries of Commerce, Finance and Industry, which were administered by the bureaucracy. The bureaucracy also controlled the operations of the Development Finance Institutions (DFIs) that were the main conduit for long-term financing during the sixties. The state structure thus got consolidated under the aegis of the Pakistani bureaucracy by the sixties.

The centralised, well-knit and rule based structure of the Pakistani bureaucracy ensured effective centralisation and coordination in administering state policy during the sixties. The central bureaucracy was dominated by the CSP[45] cadre – a lineal descendent of the ICS. The dominance of this cadre is reflected by the fact that during the sixties CSP officers held 93 per cent of the posts in the central bureaucracy. Moreover, promotion possibilities, training facilities and allowances favoured this cadre, which gave it a disproportionately higher prestige and social status relative to other cadres.[46] As in the case of the ICS, this cadre insulated itself from political control by exclusively controlling the selection, training and posting of its members. This control gave the cadre cohesion and made it a tightly knit group. Its small numbers further strengthened its cohesion. Even as late as 1969 the entire cadre consisted of no more than 500-odd members monopolising coveted posts in district administration, the provincial and central secretariats.

Structure of corruption and rent-seeking

Corruption and rent-seeking during the sixties took two forms. Firstly, it was based on individual contacts and individualised economic payoffs between members of the 44 business houses and members of the central bureaucracy. Secondly, as mentioned earlier it was based on greater institutional access for individual business houses to state-run financial institutions. Feldman (1970) documents the extensive system of patronage based on exchange relations using gifts, hospitality, social connections and bribery that developed between the bureaucracy and businessmen when Karachi was Pakistan's capital. Once Islamabad became the capital, specialised agencies were set up by individual business groups to liaison with the bureaucracy. These liaison offices were largely manned with influential ex-military and government officers, who adorned the role of 'contactors' between business and the state. However, the main mode of influence for individual business still remained individual economic payoffs to key state officials. A handfull of political intermediaries were cut into this arrangement in their role as middlemen, to whom initial licenses and permits were allotted for further sale to business houses.[47] Kochaneck (1983) argues that this pattern of corruption allowed long-term links to develop between individual business houses and the upper echelons of the central bureaucracy as they negotiated repeatedly, either through individualised payoffs or through institutional links. Citing many examples, he shows that given the weak political power of the capitalists, power was stacked in favour of the bureaucracy (pp. 234–73); that group or class action was seldom invoked in lobbying the state through political parties; and more importantly access to state 'transfers' were seldom acquired through the use of business associations.[48]

The structure of corruption that emerged during this period can be categorised as a repeated bribery game being played on the basis of economic spending power between a consolidated and centralised bureaucracy and a small number of individual business houses.[49] Our theoretical discussion suggests that it is more than likely for this structure of corruption to be consistent with efficient accumulation, as a consolidated and centralised bureaucracy would reward players promising high economic payoffs in a repeated game. The crucial questions are: (a) what unravelled this structure of corruption and rent-seeking in future decades, and (b) In what way did the new structure lower the efficiency of accumulation.

The transition years

The nature of bargaining between capitalists and the bureaucracy changed considerably during the seventies, as a result of Bhutto's civil service and industrial policy reform, which laid the foundation for nationalisation of industry. This section argues that these changes profoundly affected the structure of corruption/rent-seeking, and hence the strategies adopted by different players. In the fifth section, we show that the new structure of rent-seeking and corruption set incentives that lowered the efficiency of accumulation.

Monopoly houses

The formation of the PPP (Pakistan People's Party) government in the seventies (which had pledged a manifesto commitment to reduce industrial concentration), the creation of Bangladesh[50] and the nationalisation of the economic assets of these houses crushed their economic power. Amjad's (1983) study shows that 11 out of the top 26 houses lost more than 50 per cent of their assets in this period. The private sector was no longer considered the main agent of industrialisation and the emphasis of the state's industrial policy shifted towards developing public sector industries. These events show how weak industrialists were politically. The new beneficiary of state policy was the public sector, as a result the share of the public sector in large-scale manufacturing investment increased from 13 per cent in 1972–73 to 78 per cent by 1976–77. These factors raised the costs of institutional access for the monopoly houses.

The final blow to the *institutional access* of the monopoly houses came with the civil service reform which the PPP government undertook. As pointed out earlier the sixties houses were able to influence state agencies because of their representation on state-run financial institutions, and on account of their informal networks with members of the elite Civil Service of Pakistan (CSP) cadre. The abolition of the elite CSP cadre on the 20th of August 1973 meant that the monopoly houses no longer had an effective patron. In the new structure, the older strategies of influence-seeking and corruption no longer remained effective. The fracturing of the consolidated hierarchy of the bureaucracy resulted in tensions and inadequate cooperation between different, compartmentalised civil service cadres (World Bank, 1998, p. 1).

State structure

The structure of the state was changed by political decree when the PPP undertook its Civil Services Reform in 1973. The approximately 500 CSPs who had stood at the helm of an administrative machinery of over 500,000 members were amalgamated with other cadres into a hierarchical but mobile framework of 22 pay scales, and the separate provision for entry into an elite corps was terminated. The well-knit hierarchy of the bureaucracy was broken as the new provisions allowed lateral entry and vertical and horizontal movement between cadres. These provisions enhanced political control over the bureaucracy and curtailed the influence of the CSP cadre within the central bureaucracy. In 1969 CSPs held 93 per cent of all posts of joint secretary level and above, however, by 1973 CSPs accounted for only 43 per cent of these posts and this number fell further to 36 per cent by 1982.[51] The main beneficiaries of this opening up were members of the army and the Federal Unified Grades (FUG).[52] These changes fragmented the bureaucracy and it no longer remained a tight-knit and exclusive body.

Noman (1988) points out that the PPP was not only successful in curbing the power of the elite CSP, but the new recruitment to the bureaucracy became an instrument of political patronage for PPP supporters which changed the nature of the bureaucracy.[53] For example 17 per cent of the lateral entrants recruited in 1973 had not been assigned a post by as late as 1975. Furthermore, once General Zia assumed power he dismissed 40 per cent of Bhutto's lateral recruits on grounds of irregular appointments.[54] These examples give a flavour of the importance political patronage had assumed in the running of the bureaucracy during the seventies.

The nationalisation of the banking sector during the seventies extended political control over the entire financial sector. Political control was strengthened by weakening State Bank of Pakistan's (SBOP) regulatory and supervisory role through the creation of the Pakistan Banking Council (PBC), which became the operational controller of banks. The Federal government retained the right to select the members of PBC, and through the PBC it had effective control over the appointments of boards of individual banks. This change heightened the political control over credit 'transfers' to industry. However, these changes also increased state fragmentation, which compounded the shortcomings in the regulatory and supervisory system. The regulation and supervision of financial institutions and banks was shared by three agencies, the Ministry of Finance, the PBC and the SBOP, each with overlapping jurisdictions. This resulted in conflicting interests and perverse incentives associated with a fragmented state structure.

Sayeed (1995, p. 95) argues that 'the bureaucratic reforms as well as the initial phases of nationalisation created room for members of the intermediate class to enter into arenas which were hitherto the exclusive preserve of the elite'. Therefore, in order to understand the structure of corruption that emerged in the eighties–nineties, it is important to understand the political development of the intermediate class and the role it played in influencing the state's industrial policy.

Urban intermediate class mobilisations in Pakistan

There is a consensus in the literature on South Asian political development regarding the role played by the 'intermediate class'. Raj (1973) and Bardhan (1984) consider this class to be an important part of the dominant coalition of classes[55] which competes over state-controlled surplus in India. Different definitions have been used in the literature to define this class. For the purposes of this study we define the *urban intermediate class* to include the urban lower middle classes, the educated both professionally employed and unemployed, traders and medium/small industrialists.[56] We include the last group, because work on its origins in the Pakistani case shows that it evolved from segments of the rural and urban intermediate classes.[57]

Although there is some disagreement regarding the nature of demands articulated by this class and its organisational structure, a consensus exists over its historical emergence. The main argument is that in the Indian subcontinent, British colonialism gave the intermediate class an organisational role in society, accommodating its members as administrators and political and social leaders (Khan, 1989; Alavi,

1983).[58] Jalal (1990) shows that at the time of partition, while Pakistan inherited 18 per cent of the population of United India, it had less than 10 per cent of the industrial base and just a little over 7 per cent of industrial employment facilities. The majority of the population worked in the rural areas. As a result at the time of partition the three dominant elites in Pakistan were the large landowners, migrant industrialists and that part of the Muslim middle class that ran the state apparatus. However, the importance of the urban intermediate class was less at the time of partition. The growth in the urban intermediate class in post-Partition Pakistan occurred on account of two factors, the transfer of Muslim refugees from United India in the early fifties[59] and, more importantly, the rapid growth of urban towns and cities in the Punjab during the sixties.[60] The rapid growth of the agricultural sector due to the green revolution created a demand for an agricultural servicing and small manufacturing sector, which developed the urban areas of the Punjab and, in turn, created incentives for rapid migration of the rural population to these areas.[61] By the late-sixties the urban areas of the Punjab had become important focal points of the mobilisations against Ayub Khan's authoritarian regime. An important feature of the new groups entering the ranks of the urban intermediate class was that they relied on private sector accumulation through trade and small to medium industry[62] (Aftab and Rahim, 1986), although a large part still clamoured to be accommodated within the state apparatus (Alavi, 1983). Burki and Baxter (1975) have shown that the PPP vote in the 1970 elections was largest in those areas of the Punjab where the mobilisation against Ayub was the highest, and particularly in those districts of the province where the level of urbanisation was high and growing. As these were the areas with the fastest growth of the urban intermediate class, this evidence suggests that the *political bargaining power* of this group had increased by the late-sixties.

A large part of this mobilised urban intermediate class belonged to Punjab and Sindh, and was accommodated by Bhutto's PPP government in the bureaucracy[63] and the public sector industries.[64] However, the massive financial crisis the PPP government faced on account of the partition of Bangladesh and the OPEC oil shocks of the early seventies restricted the government's ability to incorporate all parts of this inter-mediate class. As a result, Bhutto's government sought to reduce the economic power of a part of the intermediate class it had mobilised, including medium-scale industrialists and traders from urban Punjab. To further its purpose, the government nationalised over 26 vegetable *ghee* units in 1973 and, subsequently, 4000 rice husking, cotton ginning and flour milling units situated all over the country. This move alienated not only the owners of these mills but also a large part of the trading class. The trading class lost out, firstly because there was a high degree of interlocking between the small-scale industry and traders (Alavi, 1990, p. 30). Secondly, the government set up the Cotton (CEC) and Rice Export (RECP) Corporations of Pakistan, thereby establishing a government monopoly over the export of these crops and eliminating the role of private sector exporters. These nationalisations, hence, abolished the avenues of surplus appropriation for traders and medium scale industrialists. Given the high level of political mobilisations of this group, this precipitated political mobilisations against the Bhutto government in urban Punjab, in which the small-scale traders and entrepreneurs organised alongside students, shop keepers and disgruntled regional elements (Sayeed, 1995).[65]

Sayeed (1980) shows how the mobilisations did not happen on a class basis but through organising cross-class factions on the basis of *biradari* (caste), locality-based identities and religion. Organisers and members of different political factions were offered payoffs by political parties and the army in return for the ability of these factions to deliver organisational power at least cost for the higher leadership.[66] The sixties monopoly houses allied themselves with these factions as financiers of political campaigns and street agitation (Kochaneck, 1983). These factions loosely grouped together to form the Pakistan National Alliance (PNA), which emerged as the major opposition party to Bhutto's government. Therefore, by the time General Zia-ul-Haq[67] declared his coup in 1977, that part of the urban intermediate class which included private sector medium industrialists, traders, transporters, and so on was highly politically mobilised but was as yet not *institutionally accommodated* in the scheme of state 'transfers'.

Therefore, the eighties and nineties came to be characterised by 'corruption contests' between multi-class political factions and a fragmented state structure administered by an institutionally weakened bureaucracy. By the eighties political factions comprising the urban intermediate class and the capitalists emerged as the new 'transfer-seekers' in the corruption game.

The new structure of corruption and rent-seeking: the eighties

One of the first moves of the Zia government to placate these multi-class factions was to give the private sector pride of place in future national policy.[68] The government also sought to increase the economic confidence of the sixties monopoly houses by giving them access to state policy. Consultation channels between the All Pakistan Textile Mills Association (APTMA), which was dominated by monopoly houses during this period, and the state were re-established.[69] However, APTMA was only given a consultative role, the *institutional access* it had enjoyed during the sixties was not re-established.[70] The ability of monopoly houses to negotiate with the state came to be based on their personalised links with key officials, their ability to buy key officials, and/or their links with key political factions and the army.

Key beneficiaries of the new structure of corruption were organisers and members of the cross-class factions mobilised by the urban inter-mediate classes and their clients.[71] Two factors facilitated the increase in the *political bargaining power* of these factions. Firstly, to create legitimacy for his martial law the Zia regime organised Local Bodies[72] elections in 1979 and 1983. Since elections for the national and provincial legislatures were not held until 1985, and members of political parties were restricted from contesting elections for local bodies, urban and rural councillors were the only elected representatives in the polity. The absence of political stalwarts resulted in intermediate class-led factions capturing urban local bodies under the Zia regime, with large develop-mental funds at its disposal which allowed it to entrench itself.[73] As these were non-party elections they further cemented the fragmented nature of political 'influence-seeking'. Secondly, medium-sized capitalists and traders who emerged as an essential part of the core of urban political factions were able to capture Chamber of Commerce politics at the Punjab and the federal level.[74] This became an important mechanism to enter national politics for small and medium sized capitalists and traders, who emerged as key members of these fragmented political factions.[75]

By the 1985 elections, these two channels of *political consolidation* had become important stepping stones to provincial and national-level politics for organisers of urban intermediate class-led factions. During this period, a number of important chamber members emerged as important political figures including the exiled ex-Prime Minister, Nawaz Sharif. In 1985, of the 249 Punjab Members of the Provincial Assemblies, no less than 124 were sitting councillors and by 1993, it is estimated that more than 70 per cent of members of the Punjab and National Assemblies started their political careers from local bodies.[76] The channels of access opened up by chamber politics and the accom-modation of factions in local bodies resulted in the consolidation of a new breed of 'transfer seekers' in the national assembly since 1985. This new breed was organised on the basis of fragmented and decentralised cross-class factions in order to access state 'transfers'. The active part of the sixties houses still sought influence through the use of economic spending power. However, economic graft was no longer restricted to funding individual members of the bureaucracy and key ministers in government but also included financing key political factions in dominant political parties[77] and the army. However, members of the sixties houses faced a significantly changed and hostile system. They could no longer exclude the organisers and members of political factions and their clients from accessing state 'transfers', in particular industrial credit. At times they needed the support of influential factions to maintain their own access to state 'transfers'.

The ability of these factions to organise transfers was strengthened by the politicisation of the bureaucracy that followed Bhutto's civil services reform. Zia's government made no attempt to reverse the reforms. Despite radical and wide-ranging recommendations from the Civil Services Reform Commission, Zia chose to strengthen the status-quo. His reforms were superficial and consisted of abolishing lateral recruitment, increasing reservations for military personnel in the bureaucracy and halting direct recruitment to the Officer Management Group. In fact, the army chose to use the weakened hierarchy of the bureaucracy to induct its own officers and to increase its own control over surplus allocation. In the Zia period 10 per cent of vacancies in the federal bureaucracy were reserved for army officers, who became permanent members of the bureaucracy. The regional bias in favour of Punjab was, if anything, strengthened as the army was dominated by Punjabis. Furthermore, the authority of the bureaucracy was weakened through the use of provisions allowing horizontal and vertical movement of bureaucrats across cadres. This became an important mechanism for shedding bureaucrats who refused to play ball, and was used by not only the army but also by subsequent political governments. This weakened the power of the bureaucracy considerably. World Bank (1998, p. 2) notes that ' . . . the civil service has become increasingly politicised and open to intervention by specific political interests in routine decisions such as appointments, transfers and promotions of individual civil servants . . . '. However, an individual bureaucrat still retained power but now his power was contingent on the strength of the political faction backing him in office. The fragmentation of the bureaucracy's hierarchy further weakened its institutional power. Lastly, post 1985 there has been a proliferation of the number of ministers and ministries, which has further fragmented the structure of the state (World Bank, 1998).[78] This is partly a reflection of the need to accommodate a growing number of 'transfer-seeking' factions into the scheme of state patronage. In turn, a fragmented state allowed easy access to decentralized networks, between 'transfer seekers' and key officials from the bureaucracy, army and/or political parties, at various levels of the state.[79] Since, the system itself had become porous, it made it easier for individual bureaucrats to cultivate their own clients, in exchange for economic bribes or political protection.

What emerges from this discussion is that the structure of corruption had changed during the eighties–nineties period. It became a game played between fragmented and decentralised cross-class factions bidding for state patronage, and a fragmented state structure dispensing 'transfers' across sectors and individuals. Our discussion in the third section suggests that this kind of corruption structure is most detrimental for efficient accumulation. In the fifth section we will show that in Pakistan decentralised corruption was, indeed, responsible for lowering the efficiency of accumulation during the eighties–nineties period.

Decentralised corruption and inefficient accumulation

The fifth section substantiates two propositions. Firstly, *decentralised corruption* created significant upward mobility into the ranks of the industrial class, by allowing members of the urban intermediate class easy access to state 'transfers' and especially state credit. Secondly, the accumulation incentives of the *decentralised corruption* regime were directly responsible for the decline in spinning sector productivity during the eighties–nineties period.

We begin by showing that the political ability of factionalised 'transfer-seeking' coalitions to capture state-credit resulted in significant upward mobility into the ranks of the capitalist class. One way to measure upward mobility is by the number of new entrants that are able to break into the capitalist sector. In so far as new entry is consistent with a change in the overall social profile of entrepreneurs, that is from non-capitalists to capitalists, this can be argued to create means for both economic and social upward mobility. Table 6.5 shows that the availability of 'state credit' resulted in significant new entry into the spinning sector.

Column (2) shows that the entry of new companies grew at an increasing rate during the mid-to-late eighties and the early nineties. The rate of entry was particularly fast during the early-to-mid-nineties. Columns (3) and (4) show that not only did new companies enter the sector, they were also able to wrestle away market shares from incumbent companies. This suggests that there was a significant degree of economic

Table 6.5 Measures and causes of economic mobility in the spinning sector

Period	Gross entry rate (p.a.) (%)	Market share of incumbents (%)	Market share of entrants (%)	Incumbents share in state credit (%)	Entrants share in state credit (%)
1981–85	1.8	95	5	97	3
1986–90	4.5	77	23	79	21
1990–94	11.0	63	37	53	47

Source: Cheema (1999).

upward mobility into the sector during the eighties–nineties. Finally, columns (5) and (6) show that access to state credit provided an important means for 'underwriting' this upward mobility. The proportionate access of entrants to state credit doubled during the last two policy periods.

However, the question still remains whether these changes in the rate of entry and access to state credit were consistent with changes in the social profile of entrepreneurs. Table 6.6 tells a revealing story. It shows that the main beneficiaries of changes in the ownership pattern were not the established industrial groups. Instead, by 1994 single-company entrepreneurs had doubled their share of spinning capacity from 27 per cent in 1981 to 45 per cent in 1994, or from 66 companies in 1981 to 234 companies in 1994. These new entrants were much smaller in size,

Table 6.6 Ownership profile of spinning entrepreneurs

	Percentage of installed capacity owned by different groups		
	1981 (%)	1990 (%)	1994 (%)
Industrial groups established before 1979	47	56	39
Industrial groups established during the eighties	26	13	17
Single-company entrepreneurs	27	31	45

Note: All companies belonging to an industrial group or to one of its family members have been consolidated as 'industrial group ownership'. If a family has split up into different groups then this has been taken into account.

Source: Cheema (1999).

the average size of a single-company mill being 14,500 spindles in 1994, while an industrial group mill averaged 24,000 spindles. Cheema's (1999) survey of the social background of single-company new entrants reveals that 44 per cent were originally ginners, 11 per cent were ex-government servants, 28 per cent were urban professionals and 17 per cent commercial agents or traders. In short, a large proportion belonged to the ranks of the urban intermediate class. Interestingly, most of these Greenfield entrants were people with experience in trade but little or no experience in manufacturing. The social origins of this group are very different from the established industrial groups. The latter belong to migrant trading communities, who had settled and conducted business in urban areas of United India outside the areas that came to constitute Pakistan. The new entrants, however, are from the heartland of the Punjab (Table 6.7).[80] The regional bias in entry is, perhaps, an outcome of the regional bias in the state structure. This evidence suggests that *decentralised corruption* allowed the emergence of a new breed of industrialists, who had links with the heartland of urban Punjab, and were politically integrated within the system.

Cheema's (1999) detailed productivity estimation shows that this new entry was an important cause for the declining TFP growth in the spinning sector during the eighties–nineties period. There are many causes for the fall in productivity, such as declining capacity utilisation due to rising cotton costs, slowdown in demand and so on. However, careful analysis reveals that during the late eighties and early nineties the entry of low productivity firms reduced productivity growth by 7 per cent per annum. This suggests that the *decentralised corruption* significantly lowered the efficiency of accumulation.

The question is why did rapid entry into the spinning sector cause a decline in sectoral productivity? After all, entry signifies an increase in competition, which, if anything, should have strengthened the incentives for efficient accumulation. We would argue that the answer is to

Table 6.7   Regional distribution of spinning capacity

	1981 (%)	1990 (%)	1994 (%)
Punjab	43	54	67
Sindh	52	43	30
NWFP	5	3	3

Source: Cheema (1999).

be found in the system of state 'transfers' combined with the distorted incentives provided by *decentralised corruption*.

Access to cheap cotton and cheap state 'credit' meant that all new entrants were socially insured from any kind of risk-taking. Entrepreneurs' access to political protection ensured them against the risk of failure or environmental shocks, and enabled them to shift the cost of poor management and inefficiencies onto the state-run financial sector. The financial sector bore these costs by providing bailouts and credit rescheduling to ailing and failed firms.[81] This political insurance meant that entrepreneurs would not bear the costs of short-term and inefficient behaviour. The structure of *factionalised and decentralised corruption* created uncertainty for individual 'transfer seekers', as their access to 'transfers' was contested by excluded political factions.[82] This made it rational for them to prefer strategies that maximise short-term, rather than long-term, payoffs. It is, therefore, no surprise that many such strategies were adopted by a significant proportion of new entrants. These included: over-invoicing machinery and taking equity out of the enterprise, poor machinery and project choice, over-leveraging their company, diverting operating surpluses to consumption by under-declaring profits and by consuming rather than reinvesting profits. *Decentralised corruption* coupled with a fragmented state structure had shortened the time horizon of state officials. The ability of officials to retain key posts came to be based on political protection and not an objective set of institutional rules. Similarly, appointments and promotions were not based on objective-performance monitoring but on the ability of individual officials to sustain political protection. It was, therefore, rational for officials to accommodate 'transfer-seekers' offering the highest short-term payoffs, even if these agents were blatantly unproductive. Ths system of incentives eroded the state's ability to monitor the performance of companies and to discipline inefficient beneficiaries, which is essential for the efficient working of 'state-centric' models.[83]

This is not to suggest that all entrepreneurs were inefficient; however, a significant portion of new entrants were and this caused a decline in sectoral productivity. Furthermore, this inefficient entry into the ranks of the capitalist class created significant negative externalities for the dynamic entrepreneurs in the sector. By 1995, the sad story of state-intervention was eloquently told by a leading dynamic spinner, Mr Farooq Sumar. He wrote, 'When we come to the industry it has to be said that our "Pajero culture" has created a saturation of spinning mills as a result of which Sheikhupura road has become the graveyard of spinners. Ill conceived investment by all and sundry including politicians, drug racketeers, landlords etc. in cahoots with a highly corrupt nationalized financial sector, have wrecked the viability of the spinning industry... Thus precious resources of a poor country have been locked up – I am afraid even lost – in a useless investment' (*Business Recorder* 15/04/1995). By the nineties it had become evident that Pakistan's structure of *decentralised corruption* had become incompatible with efficient accumulation, thereby sounding the death knell to the state-centric model in Pakistan.

Conclusion

In this chapter we have argued that the differential efficiency of accumulation between the sixties and the eighties–nineties period cannot be explained by differences in the nature and extent of policy intervention. Furthermore, we have shown that in both periods rent-seeking and corruption underlay the scheme of state-led accumulation. An explanation of the differential efficiency of accumulation has been sought in the changing nature of rent-seeking and corruption between the sixties and the nineties.

During the sixties the structure of corruption was consolidated and centralised. It set incentives for a centralised bureaucracy to reward capitalists offering the highest economic spending power in an intertemporal context. This structure was sustainable as it was based on repeat play between a small bureaucracy and a numerically small, and politically weak, capitalist class. Repeat play emerged in the system because of the consolidation of institutional and social networks between a centralised bureaucracy and individual capitalists. The *de facto* outcome of this structure was that it promoted efficient accumulation.

This structure unravelled during the seventies because of two reasons. Firstly, the civil service reforms of the seventies weakened and fragmented the state. Secondly, there was a fragmented growth of politically mobilised 'transfer-seeking' coalitions that were bidding for state 'transfers'. The structure of *decentralised corruption* was institutionalised by Zia-ul-Haq, who incorporated these fragmented factions in the state structure and further unravelled the rule-based nature of the state. We have shown that the new structure of *decentralised corruption* ended up shortening the time horizons of both state officials and the new 'transfer-seekers'. This set incentives for both sides playing strategies that maximised short-term payoffs, even if they came at the expense of long-term efficiency. One consequence of this structure was that state-credit allocation to industry no longer *necessarily* benefited the efficient firms. As a result, there was significant entry of low productivity firms in the sector, which reduced sectoral efficiency. Matters were made worse by loss-making firms' ability to negotiate political bailouts. In short, by the eighties–nineties the structure of rent-seeking and corruption had become inconsistent with efficient state-led accumulation.

A recognition of the constraints imposed by the new structure of corruption has led some analysts to argue that the state must be shut down. Therefore, privatisation, deregulation and liberalisation have become the *mantras* of the reformers. While the role of the state has to be clearly reduced in certain areas, a complete withdrawal, given the current predicament of Pakistan, should clearly be ruled out. After all, the state must, at a minimum, deliver law and order, including the protection of property rights. Moreover, even in a market-based economy the state has to play a regulatory role. Given the current political structure, there is no guarantee that the state would be able to efficiently provide even these services. Therefore, it is essential that the new reform agenda reviews the state's model of industrialisation, and emphasises the reform of the state's political and institutional structure.

Acknowledgments

The author benefited greatly from discussions with Dr M.H. Khan, Syed Shahid Hussain, Dr F. Bari, Dr A. Sayeed, Dr B. Vira, Ms S. Blankenburg and Dr A. Mian. He would like to thank Mr B.M. Siddique for assistance with the background research and editing.

Notes

1 This is especially pertinent as similar models succeeded in East Asia (Jomo and Khan, 2000; Stiglitz and Yusuf, 2001).
2 Khan (2001) defines 'primitive accumulation' as 'accumulation which is not based on capitalist production but which is essential for the capitalist transition since it provides the initial resources for the creation of capitalist property and for setting up capitalist enterprises' (p. 591).
3 In particular South Korea and Taiwan (Cheema and Chang, 2002).
4 Kemal's (1997) estimates show that the average change in manufacturing TFP growth between 1992 and 1997 was –0.6 per cent.
5 Noman (1992), Hamid (1992) and Little *et al.* (1970).
6 Kemal (1978) and Ahmed (1980).
7 Hussain (1999) and Hasan (1998).
8 For a rigorous discussion see Khan (2000a,b). An in-depth literature review can be found in Bardhan (1997) and Rose-Ackerman (1997).
9 Posner (1975), Kreuger (1974) and Bhagwati (1982).
10 Murphy *et al.* (1993).

11   de Soto (1989).
12   Stiglitz and Yusuf (2001), Chang and Cheema (2002), Wade (1990) and Amsden (1989).
13   Khan (2000b), Chang and Cheema (2002).
14   A fact pointed out by Adam Smith in 1776.
15   For a definition see the fifth section.
16   As opposed to this, the 'transfers' to private sector capital in general and the spinning sector in particular had dried up during the seventies, on account of Bhutto's anti-private capital policies. It is for this reason that we focus only on the sixties and the eighties–nineties.
17   Mookherjee (1995) finds a similar result for Indian industrialisation. That is, Indian industrialisation has also been associated with low rates of both capital productivity and total factor productivity growth.
18   Kemal's data are for both composite spinning and weaving units as well as for specialised spinning units. This is because the bulk of spinning mills during the sixties were composite mills, although yarn constituted a major share of mill output. Cheema's (1999) data also contains a mix of both types of mills. However, during the eighties these mills were more or less only producing yarn. This was not the case during the sixties; therefore, the bias of comparing mills with a slightly different product-mix remains in this data.
19   This assertion is usually not backed by in-depth comparative policy analysis. Only Sayeed (1995) has attempted an in-depth exercise and his conclusions are similar to the ones presented here. Noman (1992) provides the data to show that policy intervention was comparatively more efficient during the sixties. However, he does not provide an adequate explanation for this observation. His argument is a clear case of ex-post rationalisation, that is, sixties policy was more efficient because industrial growth was comparatively more efficient during the sixties.
20   APTMA (1977).
21   Amjad (1982).
22   Or 'rents'.
23   During 1965–70 the ratio of cotton to yarn prices increased by 1 per cent p.a.
24   During 1990–95 the ratio of cotton to yarn prices increased at a rate of 5 per cent p.a.
25   On the politics of this, see Cheema (1999).
26   Kochaneck (1983), Amjad (1982) and Feldman (1972) give a detailed account of the method of lobbying and liaison employed by the business community during the sixties. Cheema (1999), M.Z. Khan (2001), World Bank (1998), Kochaneck (1996) and Sayeed (1995) describe the way in which rent-seeking and corruption were employed by the business community during the eighties–nineties period.
27   There were many reasons for this. Firstly, political collective action was weak among this group. This is evidenced by the large-scale inter-party defections that involved landlords and occurred during the fifties parliamentary period. This weakness pre-empted them from effectively contesting central government policy. Secondly, as agrarian policy was a provincial subject, it set incentives for economic policy capture by this class at the provincial level of government. Thirdly, landlords have traditionally been excessively

shy in making industrial investments even when offered liberal incentives by the state, especially in the fifties.

28   Depending on the period under consideration.

29   For an in-depth analysis see Khan and Jomo (2000).

30   Khan (2000a,b) and Shleifer and Vishny (1998).

31   Leff (1964) and Boycko *et al.* (1995).

32   Beck and Maher (1986) and Lien (1986) have shown that, under plausible assumptions, the efficiency consequences of competitive bribery are reproduced even when there is imperfect information about the bribing capacity of competitors.

33   On a related discussion see Rose-Ackerman (1997).

34   Although, if decentralized corruption unravels distortionary entry barriers it may be social welfare increasing.

35   It needs to be pointed out that our concern is solely with corruption/rent-seeking over the dispensation of 'transfers' to the capitalist sector.

36   Amjad (1982).

37   On descriptions of this policy set-up and its effects see Kemal (1978), Ahmad (1980), Amjad (1982) and Sayeed (1995). The discussion on spinning sector policy has already been covered in the second section.

38   Amjad (1982).

39   Cheema (1999) shows that by the 1985 election the proportion of industrialists in national parliament had increased considerably, but as we will show below this was a very different industrial class.

40   Papaneck (1972).

41   Between 1947 and 1958 the Assembly passed 160 laws, while the executive issued 376 ordinances. During the sixties the Assembly met only 221 days and again most action was taken by executive ordinance (Kochaneck, 1983, pp. 58–9).

42   Kennedy (1987).

43   Kochaneck (1983).

44   Lt. General S.G.M. Peerzada, Yahya Khan's chief military advisor is quoted as having said, 'We took the blame last time when everything was done by civilians. This time we will do everything and take the credit too!' (Kochaneck, 1983, p. 54). Alavi (1983) makes a similar point.

45   Civil Service of Pakistan.

46   As Kennedy (1987, p. 32) puts it, 'This glamorous career pattern was made possible by the constitutionally-sanctioned system of reservation of posts for CSP officers . . . '

47   Amjad (1982, pp. 147–151).

48   Although by the mid- to late-sixties individuals and groups with close alliances to the military and the bureaucracy had broken into the ranks of the capitalist class; however, Amjad (1982, p. 150) shows that their numbers remained quite small.

49   Consisting of no more than 50 families (Amjad, 1983).

50   Monopoly houses lost both private assets and a large internal market as a result of the creation of Bangladesh.

51   Kennedy (1987), Chapter 4.

52   FUG comprised all other cadres except the police cadre and the CSP cadre.

53   Noman (1988, p. 62) shows that as a result of these changes between 1973 and 1977, the Establishment Division accepted 1374 officers into the

bureaucracy, approximately three times as many as would have been
accepted through the CSP channels.

54 Kennedy (1987).

55 In Bardhan's typology, the other members of the dominant coalition
include the industrial and trading capitalists and the large landowners.

56 Alavi's (1990, p. 165) notion of the salariat class defined as 'a section of the
urban middle class, those with educational qualifications and aspirations of
jobs in the state apparatus, the civil bureaucracy and the military' is used to
explain the growth of the state apparatus to accommodate this class, as well
as contests over credentials such as educational quotas, and so on, which
allow access to state employment.

57 Zaidi (1999).

58 Khan (1989) argues that the structure of colonial rule and the pivotal leadership
of members of this class in anti-colonial and nationalist struggles allowed
this class to develop a high degree of ability in organising political and
social mobilisations. He sees its organisational ability as based, firstly, on
high levels of education, articulation and wealth relative to the multitudes
of workers, peasants and the poor and, secondly, on their relatively greater
numbers compared to capitalists and large landlords. A measure that captures
the relative political bargaining power of this group in the South Asian
context is its leadership and organisational role in creating multi-class political
factions (Khan, 1989).

59 Burki (1980) shows that the refugees constituted 46.3 per cent of the urban
population of Pakistan's 19 largest cities in 1951.

60 Burki (1974) and Sayeed (1995).

61 Burki (1974) argues that the population of towns and cities in the Punjab
increased by over 50 per cent between 1961 and 1972 (p. 754). He defines
large cities as urban areas with a population of 100,000 and towns as urban
areas with a population between 5000 and 100,000.

62 In 1971–72, only 27 per cent of the urban employed were characterised as
manufacturing workers. The remainder fell into the categories 'Service
Sector Employees, Professionals, Self-employed' which are the occupational
categories that define the ranks of the urban intermediate class (Pakistan's
Statistical Yearbook, 1994).

63 Shafqat (1999) shows that since Bhutto's civil service reform, most of the
recruits into the civil service have been from the urban middle classes,
largely consisting of children of government servants (clerk to a high ranking
officer), offspring of professionals (doctors, lawyers, and so on) and progeny
of agriculturalists.

64 Kennedy (1987) shows that as a result of the 1971 civil service reforms urban
Sindh and Punjab came to be over-represented in the bureaucracy.

65 Sayeed (1980, pp. 163–75) provides detailed evidence on traders and
merchants organising and financing the urban agitation in the country after
the 1977 elections.

66 Khan (2002, pp. 594–5) argues that 'The organizational power of a faction
depends on its ability to field its supporters, from mobilizing them for local
elections to bringing them out to impose costs on opponents, in many cases
through organized violence'.

67 General Zia-ul-Haq's martial law regime lasted from 1977 to 1985.

68 Although the Zia government did not conduct any further nationalisation, it stuck to Bhutto's original nationalisations.
69 This is well documented in the early eighties issues of the Annual Reports of the All Pakistan Textile Mills Association (various issues).
70 Civil bureaucrats dominated the boards of state-run financial institutions during this period and the boards lacked effective representation of industry.
71 That is, people who cultivate links with factions or support them in order to get access to state 'transfers'.
72 Local bodies were the lowest tier of representative government, below the provincial legislature.
73 Zaidi (1999, p. 431) and Niazi (1994, p. 10).
74 Kochaneck (1996).
75 The federal and provincial chambers were historically controlled by medium-sized industrialists and traders (Kochaneck, 1983). The monopoly houses had not controlled these chambers, largely because they had direct access to the state in the sixties. The dominance of medium and small business in chamber politics was reinforced by the introduction of compulsory membership during the sixties, which placed this sector in an overwhelming numerical majority. Cheema (1999) shows that in 1983 only 4 out of 27 members of the governing body of the Lahore Chamber of Commerce were from the monopoly houses of the sixties, and in 1989 only 3 out of 35 members were from these houses.
76 Zaidi (1999, p. 439) and Warraich (1994, p. 11).
77 While conducting fieldwork in 1995 the author was told, by many members of the sixties houses, that they were making significant 'transfers' to the political funds of key members of both the Pakistan Peoples Party and the Pakistan Muslim League.
78 The World Bank (1998, p. 1) study observes that 'Tensions and inadequate cooperation between different, compartmentalized civil service cadres... spread through the middle layer'.
79 It is not surprising that state corruption became such an important issue in Pakistani society by the nineties. World Bank (1998, p. 2) notes that 'Corruption... pervades all three branches of government: the executive, the legislature and the judiciary'.
80 The largest increase in installed capacity, during this period, was around Lahore, followed by Faisalabad and Multan.
81 M.Z. Khan (2001) estimates that in 2001 the size of the non-performing loan portfolio of banks equalled 4 per cent of GDP.
82 An example of this is that, once in power, each ruling party made it a point to bring corruption cases against its opponent factions.
83 Khan (2000a), Chang and Cheema (2002).

Bibliography

Aftab, K. and Rahim, E. (1986) "The Emergence of a Small Scale Engineering Sector: The Case of Tubewell Production in the Pakistan Punjab", *Journal of Development Studies* 23(1):60–76.
Ahmad, M.A. (1980) *Productivity, Prices and Relative Income Shares in Pakistan's Large-Scale Manufacturing Sector, 1958–70*. Unpublished dissertation, University of Oxford.

Alavi, H. (1983) "Class and State in Pakistan", in H. Gardezi and J. Rashid (eds), *Pakistan: the unstable state*, Lahore: Vanguard Press.

Alavi, H. (1990) "Authoritarianism and Legitimation of State Power in Pakistan", in S. Mitra (ed.), *The Post Colonial State in South Asia*, London: Macmillan.

All Pakistan Textile Mills Association (APTMA) (1977) *Study of the Cotton Textile Industry in Pakistan*, Karachi.

Amjad, R. (1982) *Private Industrial Investment in Pakistan 1960–70*, Cambridge University Press.

Amjad, R. (1983) "Industrial Concentration and Economic Power in Pakistan", in H. Gardezi and J. Rashid (eds), *Pakistan: The Unstable State*, London: Zed Press.

Bardhan, P. (1984) *The Political Economy of Development in India*, Oxford: Basil Blackball.

Bardhan, P. (1997) "Corruption and Development", *Journal of Economic Literature* 35:1320–46.

Beck, P.J. and Mahar, M.W. (1986) "A Comparison of Bribery and Bidding in Thin Markets", *Economic Letters* 20:1–5.

Bhagwati, J. (1982) "Directly Unproductive, Profit-seeking (DUP) Activities", *Journal of Political Economy* 90:988–1002.

Boycko, M., Shleifer, A., and Vishny, R. (1995) *Privatizing Russia*, Cambridge, Mass.: MIT Press.

Burki, S.J. and Baxter, C. (1975) "Socio-Economic Indicators of the People's Party Vote in the Punjab: A Study at the Tehsil Level", *Journal of Asian Studies* 34.

Cheema, A. (1999) "Rent-seeking, Institutional Change and Industrial Performance: the effect of regulation on the productivity growth performance of Pakistan's spinning sector 1981–1994", PhD dissertation submitted to the University of Cambridge, Sidney Sussex College, Cambridge.

Cheema, A. and Chang, H.J. (2002) "Technology, Trade and Industrial Policy for Developing Countries: an institutional, political and technological view", *Journal of Economics of Innovation and New Technology*, X(1&2) upcoming; The United nations University, INTECH (#2001–8).

De Soto (1987) *The Other Path: the invisible revolution in the Third World*, Harper & Row, New York.

Evans, P. (1995) *Embedded Autonomy – States and Industrial Transformation*, Princeton: Princeton University Press.

Feldman, H. (1970) *Karachi Through a Hundred Years*, Karachi: Oxford University Press.

GOP (1985) *Economic Survey of Pakistan 1984–85*.

GOP (2001) *Economic Survey of Pakistan 1999–2000*.

Habib, I. (1995) "Process of Accumulation in Pre-Colonial and Colonial India", in I. Habib (ed.), *Essays in Indian History: towards a marxist perception*, New Delhi: Tulika.

Hamid, N. (1992) "Industrial Incentive Structure: a need for reform", in A. Nasim (ed.), *Financing Pakistan's Development in the Nineties*, Lahore: Oxford University Press.

Hamid, N., Nabi, I. and Nasim, A. (1990) *Trade, Exchange Rate and Agricultural Pricing Policies in Pakistan*, Washington DC: World Bank.

Hassan, P. (1998) *Pakistan's Economy at Crossroads: past policies and present imperatives*, Karachi: Oxford University Press.

Hussain, I. (1999) *Pakistan: the economy of an elitist state*, Karachi: Oxford University Press.

Jalal, A. (1990) *The State of Martial Rule: the origins of Pakistan's political economy of defense*, Cambridge: Cambridge University Press.

Jomo, K.S. and Khan, M.H. (2000) *Rents, Rent-Seeking and Economic Development: theory and the Asian evidence*, Cambridge: Cambridge University Press.

Kemal, A.R. (1978) *An Analysis of Manufacturing Industries in Pakistan: 1958–68*. Unpublished PhD dissertation, University of Manchester.

Kemal, A.R. (1997) "Employment and the Manufacturing Sector of Pakistan", *Report for the Planning Commission of Pakistan*, Islamabad.

Kennedy, C. (1987) *Bureaucracy in Pakistan*, Karachi: Oxford University Press.

Khan, M.H. (1989) *Clientelism, Corruption and Capitalist Development: an analysis of state intervention with special reference to Bangladesh*, Unpublished PhD dissertation, Faculty of Economics and Politics, University of Cambridge.

Khan, M.H. (2000a) "Rents, Efficiency and Growth", in K.S. Jomo and M.H. Khan (eds), *Rents, Rent-Seeking and Economic Development: theory and the Asian evidence*, Cambridge: Cambridge University Press.

Khan, M.H. (2000b) "Rent-Seeking as Process: the determinants of its inputs, outputs and net effects", in K.S. Jomo and M.H. Khan (eds), *Rents, Rent-Seeking and Economic Development: theory and the Asian evidence*, Cambridge: Cambridge University Press.

Khan, M.H. (2001) "Class, Clientalism and Communal Politics in Contemporary Bangladesh", in K.N. Panikkar, T.J. Byres and U. Patnaik (eds), *The Making of History: essays presented to Irfan Habib*, New Delhi: Tulika.

Khan, M.Z. (2001) "Assessment of Bank Supported Reforms in the Banking Sector", Islamabad, *mimeo*.

Kochaneck, S. (1983) *Interest Groups and Development: business and politics in Pakistan*, Karachi: Oxford University Press.

Kochaneck, S.A. (1996) "Ethnic Conflict and the Politicization of Business", in C. Kennedy and R.B. Rais (eds), *Pakistan: 1995*, Lahore: Vanguard Press.

Krueger, A. (1974) "The Political Economy of the Rent-Seeking Society", *American Economic Review* 64:291–303.

Leff, N.H. (1964) "Economic Development Through Bureaucratic Corruption", *The American Behavioral Scientist* 8(2):8–14.

Lein, D.H. (1986) "A Note on Competitive Bribery Games", *Economic Letters* 22:337–41.

Little, I.M.D., Scitovsky, T. and Scott, M. (1970) *Industry and Trade in Some Developing Countries: a comparative study*, London: Oxford University Press.

Mookherjee, D. (ed.) (1995) *Indian Industry: policies and performance*, Delhi: Oxford University Press.

Murphy, K.M., Shleifer, A. and Vishny, R.W. (1993) "Why is Rent-Seeking so Costly for Growth", *American Economic Review, Papers and Proceedings* 83(2):409–14.

Niazi, M.A. (1994) "Local Bodies: the history", *The Daily News on Friday*, 30 September.

Noman, A. (1992) "Liberalisation of Foreign Trade and International Competitiveness", in A. Nasim (ed.), *Financing Pakistan's Development in 1990s*, Lahore: Oxford University Press.

Noman, O. (1988) *Pakistan: a political and economic history since 1947*, London: Kegan Paul International.

Papaneck, G. (1962) "The Development of Entrepreneurship", *Economic Review* 52(2):46–66.

Papaneck, H. (1972) "Pakistan's Big Business: muslim separatism, entrepreneurship, and partial modernization", *Economic Development and Cultural Change* 221(1):1–32.

Posner, R. (1975) "The Social Cost of Monopoly and Regulation", *Journal of Political Economy* 83:807–27.

Raj, K.N. (1973) "The Politics and Economics of Intermediate Regimes", *Economic and Political Weekly* (7 July 1973).

Rose-Ackerman, S. (1997) "Corruption and Development", *Annual World Bank Conference on Development Economics*, The World Bank, Washington, DC.

Sayeed, A.U. (1995) *Political Alignments, the State and Industrial Policy in Pakistan: a comparison of performance in the 1960s and 1980s.* Unpublished PhD dissertation, Faculty of Economics and Politics, University of Cambridge.

Sayeed, K.B. (1980) *The Nature and Direction of Political Change in Pakistan*, New York: Praeger.

Shafqat, S. (1999) "Pakistani Bureaucracy: crisis of governance and prospects of reform", *The Pakistan Development Review*, Pakistan Institute of Development Economics (PIDE), Islamabad, pp. 995–1017.

Shleifer, A. and Vishny, R. (1998) *The Grabbing Hand: government pathologies and their cures*, Cambridge, Mass., London: Harvard University Press.

Shleifer, A. and Vishny, R. (1993) "Corruption", *Quarterly Journal of Economics*, 108:599–617 (collected in *The Grabbing Hand*. Harvard University Press, 1998).

Stiglitz, J.E. and Yusuf, S. (eds) (2001) *Rethinking the East Asian Miracle*, New York: Oxford University Press.

Wade, R. (1990) *Governing the Market*, Princeton: Princeton University Press.

Warriach, A. (1994) "Local Elections, National Impact", *The Daily News on Friday*, 30 September.

World Bank (1998) "Pakistan: a framework for civil service reform in Pakistan", *Report on Poverty Reduction and Economic Management, South Asia Region* (Report No. 18386-PAK), World Bank.

Zaidi, S.A. (1999) *Issues in Pakistan's Economy*, Karachi: Oxford University Press.

7

Corporate Capital in Contemporary Sri Lanka

Don K. Embuldeniya

In 1977, the newly elected United National Party government initiated a program of sweeping economic reforms that changed the face of the Sri Lankan economy. The impetus for economic reform was multi-fold: growing internal and external financial imbalances, increasing rates of unemployment, and so on. In this context, reforms were seen as a major stimulus to strengthening the balance of payments, improving industrial production, increasing employment, and expanding private sector-led economic activities. The reforms, aimed at transforming the highly state controlled economy, to a more liberalized one, resulted in the rapid growth of large-scale firms and a relative diversification of industry. During the transition from state capitalism to a more liberalized economy over the past two decades, conglomerates have taken credit for an increasing proportion of sales, profits and assets within the country. While global factors played a part in country's economic transformation, this chapter focuses on internal economic factors. While some argue that Sri Lanka's economic reforms have been motivated by a desire to appease international financial institutions and secure outside assistance, this chapter strives to provide a look at the internal impetus for change and an outline of Sri Lanka's economic transformation since 1977.

Introduction

In nearly every country in South Asia, economic reforms and liberalization policies are being considered and implemented. While many countries were forced to adopt economic reforms in the 1980s due to changing economic circumstances, Sri Lanka embarked on its program of reforms in the late 1970s in response to growing domestic concerns with the economy. At issue were a broad concern for deficit reduction, the search for increased tax revenue and the containment of inflationary pressures. It can be argued that the thrust of the reforms adopted in 1977 by the government was three-fold:

(1) to decrease state controls affecting transactions and to eliminate price distortions emanating from these controls;
(2) to expand the economic space available to the private sector for its operations; and
(3) to change the focus of economic activity from an inward-orientation to an outward-orientation.[1]

The adoption of economic reforms in 1977 represented a frontal attack on the "state capitalist" system of the 1970s. This attack entailed freeing the private sector from state control, integrating the national economy with global markets and creating a less interventionist development strategy. The reforms were expected to tackle the problems of economic distortions by changing the incentive structure. The movement toward a liberalized national economy was accentuated by a steady expansion in private sector-led activities. The success of the reforms has been evidenced by significant growth in the corporate sector in Sri Lanka. Additionally, the newly formed and reformulated private sector-led economic activities introduced new values and institutional arrangements that were conducive to continued economic growth and expansion.

Understanding the character of the Sri Lankan corporate sector in the context of economic reforms is particularly important for several reasons. First, in terms of both policy-making and the political and economic effects of policies, the transformations in the corporate sector cannot be separated analytically from the broader policy processes built around economic reforms. The concern for reform of the corporate sector is part of a broader concern for deficit reduction, the search for increased tax revenue, and the containment of inflationary pressures. Second, it can be argued that the increasing salience of the private sector erodes the power and autonomy of the nation-state by redistributing economic decision-making power to a broad spectrum of private actors. Prior to 1977, the Sri Lankan state often sought to insulate the economy from international as well as national sources of instability, with varying degrees of success.[2] According to many analysts, government today has little choice but to privatize state-owned enterprises and rigidly pursue stable macro-economic policies.

The immediate issues of equity and social justice have tended to dominate the discussion of the Sri Lankan economy. Although they have profound political and economical consequences, the large-scale firms that have come to dominate the post-1977 Sri Lankan economy have received very little analytical attention. The primary goal of this chapter is to fill the current void in analytical attention regarding the impact of economic reforms on the corporate sector. This study frames its analysis with the following questions: what is the nature and outcome of economic reforms? What is the character of large-scale firms in Sri Lanka? What qualitative changes can be seen as a result of these firms in the post-1977 era? And, what factors account for these transformations? Given the severe limits on data, this chapter does not attempt to propose a new grand theory or a comprehensive analysis of the new Sri Lankan corporate sector. Instead, it provides a preliminary outline of the post-1977 changes in the Sri Lankan economy.

This chapter is organized as follows: followed by the first section "Introduction", the second section "Background to 1977 policy reforms" provides a background to 1977 economic reforms and briefly enumerates their contents. The third section "Economic reforms and structural change: post-1977 economic outcomes" presents an evaluation of economic reforms. The fourth section "The corporate sector and economic reforms: the post-1977 experience" provides a preliminary analysis of the implications of economic reforms on the corporate sector. The fifth section is on "The state of the economy and reforms from 1997 to 2002". The sixth section "In lieu of a conclusion" will provide some concluding remarks.

Background to 1977 policy reforms

During the early 1970s, like many other Third World political economies, the Sri Lankan economy experienced the impact of several adverse developments in the international economic environment, notably the oil price shocks, the steep rise in international interest rates, and the decline in prices of its raw material exports. Compounding these external shocks were inadequate domestic economic and financial policies, pursued by successive governments since the independence in 1948. Their convergence resulted in large and growing domestic and external financial imbalances. As Table 7.1 reveals, between 1970 and 1975, the external debt grew sharply, rising from 12.7 per cent of GDP in 1970 to 34.1 per cent of GDP in 1977.

Table 7.1   Selected economic indicators, 1965–77 (in million rupees)

	1960	1970	1971	1972	1974	1975	1977
Exports	1,831	2,033	2,039	2,016	3,503	3,969	6,570
Imports	1,961	2,295	2,100	2,199	4,770	5,196	6,061
Trade balance	−135	−262	−61	−183	−1,267	1,227	509
GDP	N/A	13,187	13,209	13,631	14,585	14,987	16,078
GDP growth	N/A	4.2	0.17	3.19	3.16	2.76	4.19
External debt	N/A	1,499	1,870	2,650	2,919	3,703	10,590
As % of GDP	N/A	12.7	14.7	19.3	13.5	15.4	34.1
As % of exports	N/A	73.7	91.7	131.4	83.3	93.2	161.1
Investment-GDP ratio	14.1	18.9	17.1	17.3	15.7	15.6	14.4
Savings-GDP ratio	11.2	15.7	15.1	15.7	8.2	8.1	18.1

Source: IMF, *International Financial Statistics* (various issues); World Bank, *World Development Report* (various years).

In 1977, unlike many other heavily indebted countries, however, Sri Lanka was not faced with a severe "economic crisis". This is indicated by the figures in Table 7.1. During the 1970–77 period, GDP had grown every year and investment/savings ratios remained relatively constant (Table 7.1). This trend even continued during 1974 and 1975, when the first oil shock had led to acute shortages of goods. In the early 1970s, the country's economic performance was largely determined by changes in the terms of trade. As the terms of trade improved in 1976 and 1977, the rate of economic activity picked up. Adding to this relative buoyancy was both tourism and the migration of Sri Lankans to the Middle East for employment. These have emerged as clear points of relative economic growth.

After 1977, under the rubric of structural adjustment programs (SAPs), the newly elected United National Party (UNP) government embarked on a comprehensive restructuring of the economic policies which had evolved over the previous three decades.[3] The new policy regime was purportedly aimed at revitalizing the agrarian sector, improving industrial production, increasing employment, raising domestic savings and investment, and strengthening the balance of payments in the medium term. The Central Bank of Sri Lanka termed the new package of reforms "a sweeping departure from tightly controlled, inward-looking, welfare-oriented economic strategy to a more liberalized, outward-looking and growth-oriented one".[4]

The key elements of the new ensemble of economic policies involved investment incentives to foreign and domestic capital, a shift in the composition of public spending, and a liberalized international trade policy, premised on export-led growth. Economic growth, however, was only one of its objectives. As noted by the then Minister of Finance and Planning, Ronnie de Mel, the others included: (1) the expansion of employment; (2) the rehabilitation and expansion of the nation's capital stock; and (3) a progressive improvement in the country's balance of payments. The Minister explained that:

[t]his last objective is necessarily a long term one. In the short term increased foreign assistance is essential to bridge the current account deficits arising from the high levels of investment required for the other objectives to be accomplished.[5]

All the measures adopted were proclaimed as designed to reinvigorate the stagnant economy. For the governing regime, this package of measures constituted a fundamental shift in government's approach to economic management, from one of intervention and control, to one of guiding the economy toward a course of rapid and self-sustaining growth.[6] The government vested its hopes in three main macro-sectors, which were to provide the major stimulus to growth and employment: export-oriented manufacturing, an ambitious rural and urban development program, and the Accelerated Mahaweli Program, a vast scheme to bring large areas under irrigation and generate rural employment.

Post-1977 economic liberalization took place in the context of extensive public sector expenditure. In a theoretical sense, this may be an example of substantive contradictions between different components of Sri Lanka's reform agenda. From the point of the neo-classical economic model that underpins reforms, these interventions produce economic distortions; but, according to the government, these resources were allocated partly in explicit support of economic liberalization. Although there were differences over some specific policies, international financial institutions and donor agencies justified such public investments as means of facilitating the government to undertake further structural reforms and supporting a pro-Western regime which was committed to a neo-liberal economic agenda.[7]

Economic reforms and structural change: post-1977 economic outcomes

The acceleration in the processes of capital formation, economic growth and employment creation achieved in the initial phase of liberalization package was rather impressive. The rate of annual growth between 1975–77 and 1977–78 doubled (see Tables 7.1 and 7.2). The underlying weaknesses of the policy package, however, began to surface gradually. The economy continued to be saddled with deficits on a number of accounts. There were sharp increases in imports without equally rapid growth in exports. Trade and current account deficits were high. On the side of exchange earnings, revenues from exports of goods and services were favorable factors. Although this involved high return flows of foreign exchange, their contributions to net exchange earnings were rather limited (see Table 7.2). Consequently, annual budget deficits continued to remain large. The problem of budget management became increasingly difficult. Contributing to this problem was a large increase in the defense expenditure since the 1980s. In 1977 defense expenditures represented only 0.6 per cent of the gross domestic product (GDP),

Table 7.2   Selected macro-economic indicators, 1978–98

Year	GDP growth (%)	Gross domestic investment (% GDP)	Gross domestic savings (% GDP)	Exports (% GDP)	Imports (% GDP)	External debt service ratio*
1978	8.7	20.0	14.8	34.8	39.5	15.5
1979	6.1	25.8	13.3	33.7	45.7	13.0
1980	6.1	33.7	12.1	32.2	54.8	13.3
1981	5.5	27.7	11.2	30.4	46.5	16.9
1982	5.1	30.7	12.7	27.4	46.3	18.6
1983	4.9	28.8	13.3	26.3	41.4	21.9
1984	4.1	25.8	17.5	29.0	35.0	17.5
1985	4.9	25.8	14.2	26.0	38.0	21.0
1986	4.3	23.6	12.0	23.7	35.3	26.2
1987	1.5	23.3	12.8	25.1	35.6	27.5
1988	2.7	22.8	12.1	26.1	36.8	28.6
1989	2.3	21.7	12.2	27.2	36.7	24.2
1990	6.2	22.6	14.6	30.1	38.1	17.8
1991	4.6	22.9	12.8	28.7	33.8	18.5
1992	4.4	24.3	15.0	31.7	41.0	17.1
1993	7.7	25.6	16.0	33.7	43.3	13.8
1994	5.1	27.0	15.2	33.8	45.6	13.0
1995	5.5	25.1	15.5	35.9	45.5	13.4
1996	3.8	24.2	15.3	34.97	43.9	–
1997	6.3	24.3	17.3	36.5	43.6	7.74
1998	4.7	25.4	18.9	36.0	42.4	8.0

*As percentage of exports of goods and services.

Source: World Bank, *Trends in Developing Economies* (various years).

and by 1997 this figure had risen to about 6 per cent.[8] Although during this period the investment rate remained relatively high, it was achieved through a heavy dependence on inflows of foreign capital, as domestic savings remained relatively low (see Table 7.2).

On the surface, economic growth, the buoyancy in economic activity, the pace of investment and the creation of jobs led to statistically favorable impressions about the effects of the new policy regime until the mid-1980s.[9] However, the government's ambitious investment program, had gradually taken the country into a payment crisis which had acquired serious proportions by the end of the decade. The signs of this emerging crisis were visible before the actual crisis hit the economy in 1989. The global recession of the early 1980s and other factors made the mobilization of foreign aid increasingly difficult as the costs of the government's investment program rose. The acceleration of global inflation meant that even the committed foreign aid lost substantial value in real terms. In the years 1981–83, the government was compelled to take considerable amounts of commercial credit. Consequently, this produced conditions for a sharp rise in external debt service ratios within the span of the next four to five years (see Table 7.2).

Although economic growth accelerated and the creation of employment for the unemployed became rapid over the first phase of economic reforms, developments from various other angles (that is, urban bias in development planning, increasing income disparity, and so on) spurred a growing public hostility toward these policies.[10] After 1982, the performance of the economy began faltering. The economic growth rate fell continuously from 1978 onwards, from 6.3 per cent in 1978 to 4.9 per cent in 1985 and 4.7 per cent in 1998 (see Table 7.2). After 1982, the sagging economy impacted on the unemployment front as well. Unemployment, estimated to have fallen from over 14 per cent in 1978–79 to 11.7 per cent in 1981–82, began rising to over 14 per cent in 1985–86. This trend continued in 1995 and the unemployment rate came closer to the 13 per cent mark.[11]

With the introduction of economic reforms, it was expected that the existing opportunities for manufacturing could be expanded through private investments.[12] Thus, the government's economic policy curtailed any meaningful public investments in the manufacturing sector. Although the government continued to grant tax concessions and credit facilities to entrepreneurs, the development of the manufacturing sector was predominantly reserved for private initiative. Private capital was expected to bring in modern technologies, open up new frontiers in the country's desire to become an exporter of non-traditional value-added manufactured goods, and to develop the manufacturing capacity in more technologically sophisticated products such as electronics.[13] Although manufacturing growth in post-1977 Sri Lanka was substantially superior to the pre-1977 era, results were less than expected.[14] Despite the diversification of manufacturing structure, the developmental outcome in the manufacturing sector lagged behind stated expectations of policy makers, especially in terms of both value addition and linkage efforts. Although value added manufacturing accounted for 18 per cent of GDP in 1980, this rate dropped to 17 per cent by 1998.[15]

Private sector investments in manufacturing have been sporadic, and concentrated in a handful of export-oriented sectors such as textile manufacturing. In 1991, approximately 60 per cent of these products came from enterprises with extensive foreign capital participation.[16] Given the high imported input content of this sector, the net foreign exchange earnings per unit of industrial output exported remained low. Second, as a result of heavy import dependence for inputs, the overall contribution of the textile and apparel sector to the economic development process, has been disappointing – in terms of both value added and linkage effects.[17] Domestic firms have failed to establish a firm industrial base. Foreign capital participation in manufacturing has been limited to low-technology products which are intensive in the use of unskilled female labor, and, incapable of producing adequate backward linkages in the national economy. Nevertheless, this pattern is gradually changing as industries attract technologies that are more advanced.

The corporate sector and economic reforms: the post-1977 experience

Until 1977, the macro-economic policy framework had undergone little change, and there seemed to be a lack of pressure for economic reforms. Since independence, governments in Sri Lanka had intervened to finance the productive sectors. The state interventions in the productive sectors were guided by the Keynesian premise that the state may establish enterprises to launch projects which private investors might not consider financially profitable.[18] In consequence, post-independence governments superimposed a form of "state capitalism" on the national economy inherited from the colonial era. The status quo was maintained as industry enjoyed protection through quotas and foreign exchange restrictions. Labor unions looked to government to safeguard their interests, and agricultural interests seemed content with working through a system of state-controlled producer pricing.

In the interest of defeating negative terms of trade, the Sri Lankan government, especially between 1970–77, sought to establish import substitution industries. Although semi-autarchic economic policies caused concern for many entrepreneurs, nationally based manufacturing enterprises were beneficiaries of this system of foreign exchange allocations and import controls that were prevalent until 1977. However, paradoxically, negative terms of trade forced the government to introduce the import quotas that some local manufacturers had been lobbying for since the early 1960s. The system worked to the overall advantage of many manufacturers. It is fair to argue that some leading textile manufacturers attained their favored position in the domestic market through protectionist policies. Increased production for the domestic market, to some extent, made up for declining exports. As well, increased domestic production of basic inputs by state owned enterprises, also provided the private sector with cheap inputs, for example, steel and chemicals, needed for manufacturing processes.[19]

At the onset of economic reforms, the private sector...was not in practice strongly committed to economic liberalism. Private businessmen certainly wanted a reversion to much freer access to foreign exchange in order to meet consumer demands – their own as well as that of the 'market' more generally – and to replace much obsolete capital equipment. But the private sector had otherwise grown up in symbiosis with a large state sector and a relatively interventionist state, and did not generally demand any radical change in those arrangements.[20]

Simply extrapolating from this point, one would expect domestic entrepreneurs to be resistant to change and opposed to extensive liberalization of the economy. Bolstered by the opposition of labor and other affected social groups who feared human and social implications of economic reforms, the government lobbied by its external donors (that is, international financial institutions) would then appear to be the main catalyst for change. A closer look, however, exposes the way domestic interest groups actually defined their own interests and engage in the political process that facilitated economic reforms.[21] Far from being static, the interests of entrepreneurs have undergone considerable changes as economic opportunities changed. One Sri Lankan observer held up as striking the discovery through his own interviews with leading entrepreneurs that large firms did not feel really threatened by economic reforms.[22]

The orientation of the corporate sector

After the liberalization of the Sri Lankan economy in 1977, the penetration of international capital into Sri Lanka's social and economic life became increasingly thorough. Through subsidiaries, license arrangements and other links, international capital has become a significant part of the Sri Lankan political economy. Today, the representatives of international and domestic capital, for example, resident representatives of multinational corporations and corporate executives, comprise an integral feature of the Sri Lankan political, economic and social order. International capital no longer functions as an external force whose interests are represented internally by commodity exporters. International capital, now operating locally, shares with many sectors of local capital an interest in further liberalization of the economy.

For analytical purposes, the post-1977 Sri Lankan corporate sector can be loosely divided into two categories – internationalist and nationalist. Each tends to reflect a makeup grounded in formal and informal linkages to the global market system. The internationally oriented firms consist primarily of economically powerful firms which, especially after 1977, established increasing ties with international capital and markets. From the standpoint of economic influence, large firms constitute the core of Sri Lanka's international corporate class. More often than not, these internationally oriented Sri Lankan firms are linked to the industrialized West as well as the newly industrialized countries through a number of interest and institutional ties. These include joint ventures, licensing agreements, marketing arrangements, and business associations. These connections tended to wed Sri Lankan business leaders ideologically to policies furthering free international trade and capital.

By contrast, the nationalist coalition consists primarily of domestically oriented small- and medium-scale businesses. These firms comprised of entrepreneurs who engaged primarily in serving the local market. During the pre-1977 era, behind the protection of tariff barriers and import restrictions, these nationalist elements served as the backbone of the consumer goods industry. As early as 1965, several of these economic nationalists had banded together to form the National Chamber of Commerce of Sri Lanka (NCCSL), which espoused economic nationalism. They naturally favored avoiding international economic integration and sought to protect national markets and resources from external influences of the international economy. Most remained wary of international financial institutions and often spurned the government's liberalization overtures.[23] Evidence suggests that small- and medium-scale enterprises, in particular, have been marginalized by the exchange rate and trade liberalization measures. For example, cheap fabrics from South East Asian countries have flooded the market, aggravating the crisis in the textile-manufacturing sector. Duty waivers for imported fabrics, under the liberalization program, have added to this crisis.[24]

Two different types of enterprises can be distinguished in the Sri Lankan corporate sector – specialized firms and conglomerates. The specialized enterprises are firms operating in the same line of business. In Sri Lanka, small- and medium-scale firms that are involved in textile and garment manufacturing, for example, can be considered specialized firms. Conglomerates are diversified firms that are under common control operating in different, unrelated industries. "Different" means that they operate in at least two industries that are not in the same line of business. Many of these firms are publicly traded in the Colombo Stock Exchange. A number of these firms, like John Keells Holdings Ltd, function as holding companies in which the various subsidiaries operate with a high degree of autonomy. The following section assesses the degree of diversification and conglomeration in the corporate sector of the Sri Lankan economy today and identifies several of the most diversified firms.

Large firms in the post-1977 era

For the last twenty years, the growth of the corporate sector in the Sri Lankan economy has been very rapid and has exhibited the trend towards conglomeration and diversification (see Table 7.3). Although surveys carried out to evaluate the impact of liberalization on large firms in Sri Lanka are virtually nonexistent, it is possible to hypothesize potential outcomes of economic reforms by analyzing the character of large firms. In numerous instances, large firms have entered new business ventures in unrelated sectors without abandoning existing activities. For example, until the late 1970s the main activity of Ceylon Tobacco Company (CTC), a subsidiary of British American Tobacco, was manufacturing and marketing cigarettes. Since liberalization, it has added financial services, horticultural products and biotechnology into company's product base.

Judging from the sharp increase in conglomeration and diversification in the economy, it would appear that large firms had a great incentive to diversify. One explanation of why firms become conglomerates is that economies of scale may be realized. In the case of Sri Lanka, however, one may find alternative causal explanations for conglomeration and diversification. A considerable number of these explanations are located in the policies that were pursued under the umbrella of economic reforms. The restoration or, in some cases, construction of market

Table 7.3 A profile of selected publicly listed large firms in Sri Lanka

Firm	Business interests	No. of subsidiaries			Profit/loss after tax (in Rs 1000)		
		1977	1987	1997	1977	1987	1997
Aitken Spence & Co.	Hotels, travel, cargo handling, manufacturing, property development, engineering, plantation and insurance.	9	15	38	4,159	15,360	81,410
Richard Pieris & Co. Ltd	Manufacturing, plantation, distribution, property development and exports.	2	3	17	0.980	9,246	161,476
John Keells Holdings Ltd	Transportation, food and beverage, plantation, exports, leisure, financial services, information technology, property development and investment trusts.	N/A	30	59	N/A	15,351	571,688
Hayleys Ltd	Manufacturing, hotels, exports, agribusiness, engineering, travel, manufacturing, transport and management services.	6	17	33	2,682	107,869	530,013
Carson Cumberbatch & Co. Ltd	Food and beverage, plantation, hotels, real estate, airline representation, investments, information technology, brokerage services and insurance.	N/A	4	14	N/A	7,119	116,340
Lankem Ceylon Ltd	Agrochemicals, chemical products, hotels, property development and plantation.	2	4	8	3,400	1,480	355,920
Shaw Wallace & Hedges Ltd	Investment services, imports, exports and manufacturing.	6	8	4	−0.387	22.131	1.796
Ceylon Tobacco Co. Ltd	Manufacturing, marketing, exports, insurance, financial services and foliage products.	N/A	5	6	N/A	241,270	572,451

Source: Various sources.

mechanisms under economic reforms is one of the most salient reasons for the diversification of large firms. In Sri Lanka, restoration primarily entailed the reduction in regulations of capital, elimination of trade licensing, liberalization of restrictions on foreign exchange transactions, and privatization. By expanding loanable funds and facilities, and by expanding opportunities for increased income, financial liberalization has complemented trade liberalization on both demand and supply sides. In addition, since 1977 the government has granted several tax concessions to industries engaged in the production, manufacture, agribusiness and exports.

Deregulation of the economy in Sri Lanka has opened up the possibility of some of the conglomeration and diversification. It has also opened the way to the entry of firms into businesses from which they were previously excluded. This has been particularly evident in Sri Lanka's banking and financial sector. Several firms with specialized business interests like Ceylon Tobacco Co., and Brown & Co. have entered into sectors such as financial services that were previously limited to public sector financial institutions. The entry of new firms into the financial and banking sector, coupled with the rapid expansion of the activities of other financial institutions (both local and international), sets the stage for an expansion in credit. By augmenting loanable funds and facilities available to private sector investment, financial market deregulation appears to have helped large firms in the short run. In consequence, a certain amount of conglomeration and diversification appears to be partly attributable to deregulation.

Large firms which have undertaken business conversions or developed new products and technologies have moved into new fields. Firms which offered high value-added goods and services to meet market and consumer needs have enjoyed a relative improvement in their business results. Despite economic and political crisis in the region, many of these conglomerates have enjoyed a high rate of growth, and they now represent an increasing proportion of the sales, profits or assets of the Sri Lankan economy. Hayleys Limited, for instance, accounts for 1.7 per cent of the country's export income, 2.8 per cent of its domestic value addition, and 7 per cent of the country's market capitalization.[25] Furthermore, in 1997, Ceylon Tobacco Company (CTC) was the largest contributor to government revenue: CTC paid SLRs 16.3 billion to state coffers in the form of excise duty, goods and services tax, import duties, defense levy and corporate income taxes.[26]

Many of the large firms attempting to maintain their domestic production operations are boosting their competitiveness not only in the pricing side, but also in non-cost terms, for example, by upgrading their quality and technology and improving their flexibility in order to compete with overseas firms. Table 7.3 indicates that majority of surveyed companies have improved their profit margins since 1977. In order to respond to new challenges and opportunities, firms have improved their financial structures and management strengths. This has been achieved by firms using their own resources as well as external resources that have become available to them as a result of globalization.

Globalization and large firms

Large enterprises have responded to economic globalization in a variety of ways. Some firms have moved their production operations overseas, and some are maintaining their domestic operations while introducing foreign technology and procuring supplies overseas. Globalization and the changing structure of the Sri Lankan economy have led to some changes in the traditional pattern of inter-firm relations, with subcontracting relationships (especially in textile/garment manufacturing sector) within Sri Lanka becoming more fluid and the degree of cross-border specialization increasing. Some are furthering cross-border specialization and expanding exports and imports, while others are actively doing business with foreign-affiliated firms.

Since 1977, several firms have established operations overseas. A review of Sri Lankan business enterprises that have expanded overseas shows that the majority of such investments involve hotel projects in the South Asian region, and only a handful of firms with overseas operations engage in manufacturing. For instance, Aitken Spence & Co. Ltd and John Keells Holdings Ltd have made extensive overseas investments in several hotel projects, particularly in the Maldives. In addition, a number of large firms, like Haleys Ltd, have established offices in Japan, USA, Australia and Holland, and a production base in Thailand. However, no major business enterprises in Sri Lanka have established any meaningful overseas manufacturing activities. In terms of sales, domestic sales still appear to account for a large share of turnover. For example, although CTC has expanded into overseas markets mainly in Europe and Middle East, domestic sales account for about 98 per cent of its sales turnover.[27]

During the post-reform period, there has been very little cross-border purchasing of major firms. Globalization of Sri Lanka's corporate sector has occurred primarily via overseas investments in speculative instruments such as stocks. The Colombo Stock Exchange (CSE), which was established in 1985, has had marginal importance in Sri Lanka. Recently,

Table 7.4 The Colombo Stock Exchange, selected statistics 1995–98

	1995	1996	1997	1998
Annual turnover (SLRs Mn)	11,249	7,403	18,315	18,232
Domestic	5,815	3,355	10,455	11,807
Foreign	5,434	4,048	7,860	6,425
Shares traded (No. Mn)	316	227	515	634
Domestic	185	133	337	425
Foreign	131	94	178	208

Source: Colombo Stock Exchange.

however, it has experienced a rapid expansion of its equity markets. Under economic reforms, foreign investment in publicly quoted companies is permitted up to 100 per cent. The market capitalization of the CSE increased from US$0.2 billion in 1989 to US$2.0 billion in 1996.[28] Today, the CSE has 239 companies listed with a market capitalization of over US$1.7 billion. The market capitalization is approximately 12 per cent of the GDP of the country.[29] Recent CSE activities suggest that there has been a sharp increase in foreign investment in publicly quoted companies (see Table 7.4). In 1998, the total turnover was in excess of SLRs 18.2 billion of which SLRs 6.4 billion constituted foreign investment in listed shares.[30] The outcome of these speculative investments has been the increased concentration of domestically and externally generated investments in large firms' stocks and bonds.[31] For example, foreign investors own more than 52 per cent of Aitken Spence & Co.'s shares, and 55 per cent of John Keells Holdings Ltd's shares are owned by non-national investors, while the balance is spread among domestic shareholders.[32]

The state of the economy and reforms, 1997–2002

Economic growth in Sri Lanka has been uneven in the late 1990s as the economy faced a number of global, domestic economic and political challenges. The Asian financial crisis took less of a toll on the economy of Sri Lanka in 1997 than elsewhere in the region, due in part to exchange controls on the capital account and relatively low exposure to short-term foreign debt. But, by the middle of 1998, the Sri Lankan economy started to slow markedly. The economy was faced with effects of the Asian economic crisis, global recession, domestic and regional political problems, and the Russian economic crisis, resulting in sharply lower tea prices and terrorist bombings in civilian areas, especially the country's international airport. The slowdown has continued as Sri Lanka's key export industry – garments – suffered the effects of a global economic slowdown.[33]

Nuclear stalemate in India and Pakistan in May 1998 had an effect on foreign commercial and investor interest in Sri Lanka, especially on the Colombo stock market.[34] As a result of these challenges, growth moderated in 1998 to 4.7 per cent. As the depressed conditions continued into 1999, annual GDP growth rate slowed to 4.3 per cent. Sri Lanka's exports declined by 4 per cent in 1999, after twelve straight years of growth.[35] The economy is faced with a series of challenges due to increased defense spending, a higher oil bill, and a slowdown in privatization process. The government spent around about $350 million on defense in 2000. The government also increased wages and pensions of government servants in the run-up to October parliamentary elections. As a result, the budget deficit is expected to rise from an estimated 7.6 per cent of GDP to around 10 per cent of GDP.[36]

Since 2001, when the United National Front (UNF) government came to power,[37] Sri Lanka has made progress in macro-economic reforms and some financial and structural reforms that stimulate productive investment.[38] In its first state budget, the UNF government pledged to cut the budget deficit and revive the country's struggling economy. The government, which has agreed to a ceasefire with the Liberation Tigers of Tamil Ealam (LTTE), set an economic growth target of 3.5–4.0 per cent for 2002. It also planned to cut the budget deficit to 8.5 per cent in 2002, from 10.8 per cent the previous year. Reductions in public spending aimed to reduce the budget deficit from previous year's 10.8 per cent of gross domestic product to 8.5 per cent. In a bid to reverse previous year's 1.3 per cent shrinkage of the economy and achieve 3.5 per cent growth this year, the government is pushing through tax, finance and labor reforms.[39] As confidence in the government's peace initiatives and economic policies aims to boost the economy, the stock market has shot up more than 30 per cent, after heavy falls following the LTTE attack on the country's international airport in 2001.[40] According to the CSE, interim results released by 208 listed companies for the first quarter of 2002 show a significant growth in profits as against the last quarter of 2001. Profits of these companies have increased by 86 per cent from Rs 2.1 billion in the last quarter of 2001 to Rs 3.9 billion in the first quarter of 2002.[41]

Despite its long history of economic reforms, diversification of the economy away from its traditional reliance on commodity exports and low-value products remains too slow to generate a significant increase in incomes. To progress rapidly to develop a fast growing, externally oriented market-based economy, Sri Lanka's private sector has begun to implement better business strategies and the UNF government has also begun to make the necessary policy and regulatory reforms to improve the enabling environment for the corporate sector.[42] As the Minister of Economic Reforms Milinda Moragoda notes, "if financial reforms are to succeed, they should be implemented as a partnership between the government and the private sector."[43]

The UNF government has introduced a number of changes to the country's tax system to revive the corporate sector. The government has begun reforming Sri Lanka's indebted state-owned banks and loss-making state-owned enterprises.[44] It announced that a corporate tax surcharge, introduced in 2001, would be removed, and that the tax system as a whole would be streamlined. Indeed, the international financial institutions and donors had long urged the country to simplify the tax system.

The government announced that it hoped to raise $221 million through the sale of state assets in 2002.[45] The government also relaxed restrictions on foreign investment in financial services and public utilities, clearing the way for the government's privatization program. Up to 15 per cent of Sri Lanka Telecom is slated to be privatized in a public offer in 2002. The state-owned Sri Lanka Insurance Corporation is scheduled to be privatized and Ceylon Petroleum Corporation, the sole importer and refiner of oil, is being restructured before it too is privatized.[46] Other areas targeted for private investment included the construction of roads, supply of water, and electricity production and distribution. The 2002 Budget projected revenues of $218 million from state asset sales this year.[47]

According to the Central Bank of Sri Lanka, foreign investment of up to 100 per cent of the equity capital of companies could be made free of exchange controls. These changes were made in anticipation of more foreign direct investments as peace talks between the government and LTTE to end the 18-year conflict civil war showed progress. Indeed, the level of foreign direct investment plunged to $80 million in 2001 from a record of $231 million in 2000 due to political instability, a major LTTE attack on the country's only international airport, and the global economic slowdown.[48] According to the Board of Investment of Sri Lanka, Sri Lanka hopes to attract $600 million in foreign direct investment per year.[49] To achieve these objectives, the government has reduced the top rate of corporate taxation to 30 per cent in 2003, and this will be further reduced to 20 per cent in 2004.[50]

In lieu of a conclusion

The salient point of Sri Lanka's economic reforms is that they were determined by political and economic factors internal to the country. Sri Lanka's actual experience has been mixed. The reforms seem hardly to have solved many structural problems in the economy. Even with liberalization and reform mechanisms, complete abandonment of public spending has not been sustained. Nonetheless, post-1977 economic reforms have introduced a range of policies and incentives that were crucial to the further expansion of the private sector. Some of them have created opportunity structures for increasing private sector-led economic activities. Large-scale firms have taken a leading role in this process.

Given limits on data, this chapter has been unable to do more than outline the basic issues and broader patterns, presenting a limited range of evidence to enable readers to make an initial evaluation of them. This chapter, therefore, offers its readers no conclusions. Rather, this chapter should be treated as an introduction to a far more complex study. The chapter will have achieved its goal if it stimulates much needed research and evaluation among analysts and policy makers on the Sri Lankan corporate economy in the context of economic reforms and globalization.

Notes

1   In addition, the following factors also induced the decision-makers to opt for a radical liberalization program: the contemporary world-wide enthusiasm for economic liberalism, promised and anticipated support from international capital; and the strong external reserves position the government inherited. See, W.D. Lakshman, "Introduction", in W.D. Lakshman (ed.), *Dilemmas of Development: Fifty Years of Economic Change in Sri Lanka* (Colombo: Sri Lanka Association of Economists, 1997) pp. 8–12; Ronald J. Herring, "Economic Liberalisation Policies in Sri Lanka: International Pressures, Constraints and Supports", *Economic and Political Weekly*, vol. XXII (1987) no. 8, pp. 325–33; Lal Jayawardena *et al.*, *Stabilization and Adjustment Policies and Programmes, Country Study 15, Sri Lanka* (Helsinki: World Institute of Development Economic Research, 1987); Saman Kelegama, "Privatisation: An Overview of the Process and Issues", in W.D. Lakshman (ed.), *Dilemmas of Development: Fifty Years of Economic Change in Sri Lanka* (Colombo: Sri Lanka Association of Economists, 1997) pp. 456–93.

2   Pre-1977 economic policies have been well documented in literature. See, for example, Premachandra Athukorala, "Import Substitution, Structural Transformation, and Trade Dependence: A Case Study of Sri Lanka", *The Developing Economies*, vol. 24 (1981) no. 2, pp. 119–42; Paul Isenman, "Basic Needs: The

Case of Sri Lanka", *World Development*, vol. 8 (1980) no. 3, pp. 237–58; W.D. Lakshman, "Economic Growth and Redistributive Justice as Policy Goals: A Study of the Recent Experience of Sri Lanka", *Modern Ceylon Studies*, vol. 6 (1975) no. 1, pp. 64–87; L.A. Wickremeratne, "Planning and Economic Development", in K.M. de Silva (ed.), *Sri Lanka: A Survey* (Honolulu: University of Hawaii Press, 1977); Jeyaratnam A. Wilson, *Politics in Sri Lanka: 1947–1979* (London: MacMillan, 1979).

3   The UNP took over 80 per cent of the parliamentary seats (140 of 168) in 1977 general election, reducing the Sri Lanka Freedom Party (the previous governing party) to eight members and the Marxist/Communist parties were excluded entirely for the first time since the introduction of adult suffrage in 1931.

4   Central Bank of Ceylon, *Annual Report* (Colombo: Central Bank of Ceylon, 1978) p. 2; quoted in Herring, op. cit., n. 2, p. 328.

5   Quoted in Denis Goulet, *Survival with Integrity* (Colombo: Marga Institute, 1981) p. 31.

6   Sri Lanka's experience contrasts sharply with Latin America's reform experience. Drawing on reform experiences in Latin America, theorists like Guillermo O'Donnell have argued that the introduction of economic reforms proceeds in tandem with political authoritarianism. See Guillermo O'Donnell, "Reflections on the Patterns of Change in the Bureaucratic-Authoritarian State", *Latin American Research Review*, vol. 13 (1978) no. 1, pp. 3–38. Sri Lanka's reform experience cast doubt on this thesis. Despite few episodes of democratic decay, reforms in Sri Lanka were adopted within a relatively democratic political environment. For a comprehensive analysis of political pluralism and economic reforms in Sri Lanka, see Mick Moore, "Economic Liberalization Versus Political Pluralism in Sri Lanka", *Modern Asian Studies*, vol. 24 (1990) no. 2, pp. 341–83.

7   See Moore, op. cit., n. 6, pp. 354–67; World Bank, *Development in Sri Lanka: Issues and Prospects* (Washington, DC: World Bank, 1978) p. 1.

8   See World Bank, *World Development Report 1997* (New York: Oxford University Press, 1979); World Bank, *World Development Report* (New York: Oxford University Press, 1997). Since the early 1980s, the Sri Lankan government allocated a large amount of resources to military/defense expenditure. Civil war in Northern and Eastern Sri Lanka, and periodic uprisings in the island induced the government to increase the strength of the defense forces and to purchase modern military hardware.

9   The numbers of unemployed reached peak levels in the mid-1970s: In 1976, the unemployment rate exceeded one million. In the period after the economic reforms of 1977, the trend of unemployment has been downwards. The recorded unemployment rates dipped to approximately 900,000 in 1978 to 750,000 in 1995. See B.M. Kiribanda, "Population and Employment", in W.D. Lakshman (ed.), *Dilemmas of Development: Fifty Years of Economic Change in Sri Lanka* (Colombo: Sri Lanka Association of Economists, 1997) pp. 223–49.

10 Public hostility against government's economic reform program emanated from various social groups. The post-1977 emphasis on economic liberalization and export-oriented development has assumed a fundamental practical importance to the labor movement in the country. A myriad of factors – the

expansion of export-oriented industries in export processing zones, deregulation and privatization – posed unprecedented challenges and problems to a wide spectrum of labor unions in Sri Lanka. As well, post-reform economic activities were concentrated around the Colombo metropolis and in areas where large infrastructure projects were located. Spatially, this pattern of development failed to produce equitable distribution of the benefits of economic reforms. One may argue that violent political protest organized by the Janatha Vimukthi Peramuna (JVP) during 1986–89 was, at least partly, a reaction to the social impact of economic reforms.

11 Kiribanda, op. cit., n. 9, pp. 243, 246.

12 The pre-1977 pattern of industrial development in Sri Lanka exhibited both import substitution and export-oriented components. Post-independence governments often pursued a dual policy to concentrate on greater utilization of available domestic resources and to re-orient industrial production toward export markets, albeit with mixed results. For a comprehensive analysis of these policies and their outcomes, see N. Balakrishnan, "Industrial Policy and Development Since Independence", in K.M. de Silva (ed.), *Sri Lanka: A Survey* (Honolulu: University of Hawaii Press, 1977) pp. 192–212.

13 See Srimal Abeyratne, "Trade Strategy and Industrialization", in W.D. Lakshman (ed.), *Dilemmas of Development: Fifty Years of Economic Change in Sri Lanka.* (Colombo: Sri Lanka Association of Economists, 1997) pp. 367–9; Sriyani Dias, "Economic Liberalization and the Development of Manufacturing in Sri Lanka", *Asian Survey*, vol. XXXI (1991) no. 7, pp. 614–15.

14 From 1977 onward, the striking feature of the economy has been the rapid growth rates in manufacturing. The manufacturing sector grew at the impressive rates of 4.6 per cent in 1978/82 period, 6.7 per cent in 1983/87 period, 6.8 per cent in 1988/92, and 9.8 per cent in 1993/94 period, a vast improvement over the 1.1 growth rate in 1971–77 period. See Abeyratne, op. cit., n. 13.

15 World Bank, *World Development Report 1999/2000* (New York: Oxford University Press, 1999) p. 253.

16 See Premachandra Athukorala, "Foreign Direct Investment and Manufacturing for Export", in W.D. Lakshman (ed.), *Dilemmas of Development: Fifty Years of Economic Change in Sri Lanka* (Colombo: Sri Lanka Association of Economists, 1997) p. 404.

17 See Abeyratne, op. cit., n. 13, p. 376; Dias, op. cit., n. 13, pp. 618–23. However, one must not understate this sector's contribution to the economy. According to apparel industry statistics, Sri Lanka's apparel industry has almost tripled in value since 1988, to over US$1.5 billion, making it the country's premier export earner. Exports are expected to increase to US$3.5 billion in the year 2000. Currently, export of apparels accounts for over 50 per cent of the country's total exports. Sri Lanka's apparel products are exported worldwide, with the major market being the United States, which accounts for 60 per cent of the purchases followed by the European Union (EU) countries by 34 per cent. Over 600 factories employ approximately 300,000 personnel making it the largest employer in the country. See National Apparel Exporters Association, "Sri Lanka and Its Garment Industry", *<http://www.garments.lk/about1.htm >*, 1999. Although the significance of the garment industry was touted as a success story by the UNP as well as PA

governments, according to the Minister of Industries of the current PA government, Mexico and Caribbean countries are now making inroads into the US market. See K. Ratnayake, "World recession impacts Sri Lankan economy", <*http://www.wsws.org/articles/1999/apr1999/sri-a03.shtml*>, 1999.

18 See Satchi Ponnambalam, *Dependant Capitalism in Crisis: the Sri Lankan Economy 1948–1980* (London: Zed Press, 1980); Sumanasiri Liyanage, "The State, State Capital and Capitalistic Development", in W.D. Lakshman (ed.), *Dilemmas of Development: Fifty Years of Economic Change in Sri Lanka* (Colombo: Sri Lanka Association of Economists, 1997) pp. 425–55; Lloyd Fernando, "Development Planning in Sri Lanka", in W.D. Lakshman (ed.), *Dilemmas of Development: Fifty Years of Economic Change in Sri Lanka* (Colombo: Sri Lanka Association of Economists, 1997) pp. 101–26.

19 However, this does not mean all was well with the private sector. Despite some readjustment of manufacturing activity oriented towards the use of domestic resources, economic policies such as foreign exchange restrictions persistently retarded private sector manufacturing activities due to their heavy reliance on imported intermediate products and raw materials, resulting in low overall capacity utilization.

20 Moore, op. cit., n. 6, pp. 351–2.

21 The orchestration of a fundamental change in government's economic policies was not without problems. Within the government there were, of course, opposing viewpoints on many issues, especially issues implying considerable change of economic strategy. Some politicians and bureaucrats were hesitant to relinquish their opportunities for influencing decisions related to investments and subsidies. The governing UNP regime in 1977 has been divided between "reformers", in charge of the finance and trade ministries and "indigenists". For instance, the then Minister of Industries, Cyril Matthew, was one of the influential proponents of protectionist policies. Support for indigenism has, however, been rather shallow among Sri Lankan's state elites. See K.M. de Silva and Howard Wriggins, *J.R. Jayewardene of Sri Lanka, A Political Biography Volume Two: From 1956 to His Retirement (1989)* (Honolulu: University of Hawaii Press, 1994) pp. 458–9.

22 I am indebted to Palitha Wijesinghe, a former World Bank official, for this observation.

23 None of these processes, however, were static. Since 1980s, the nationalist faction of local entrepreneurs has entered into alliances with large firms and international capital through secondary linkages, for example, by becoming suppliers to multinational ventures in Sri Lanka.

24 Ratnayake, op. cit., n. 17.

25 Sunday Observer Internet Edition, "Corporate Profile: Hayleys Ltd", <*http://www.lanka.net/lakehouse/1998/07/12/bus16.html*>, 1998.

26 Lanka Monthly Digest Internet Edition, "Industry Feature Liquor and Tobacco: Crying Foul!", <*http://www.lanka.net/LMD/98sep/1md6.html*>, 1998.

27 Sunday Observer Internet Edition, "Corporate Profile: Ceylon Tobacco Company Ltd", <*http://www.lanka.net/lakehouse/1977/04/20/bus14.html*>, 1997.

28 Colombo Stock Exchange, "Overview", <*http://www.lanka.net/slweb/slstock.html*>, 1997.

29 Colombo Stock Exchange, "Market Statistics", <*http://www.lanka.net/lis12/yellow/stocks/statistics.html*>, 1999.

30 Ibid.

31 Large firms in Sri Lanka, both local and transnational corporate subsidiaries, tend to utilize locally generated savings instead of bringing in new capital from outside. In addition to borrowing funds from the local banking system, they arrange with local stock brokering firms to sell shares and bonds on the Colombo Stock Exchange. This enables them to utilize local savings instead of investing their own capital from abroad.

32 Sunday Observer Internet Edition, "Corporate Profile: Aitken Spence & Co. Ltd", <*http://www.lanka.net/lakehouse/1977/12/221/bus11.html*>, 1997; Sunday Observer Internet Edition, "Corporate Profile: John Keells Holdings Ltd", <*http://www.lanka.net/lakehouse/1998/07/05/bus09.html*>, 1998.

33 Central Bank of Sri Lanka, Annual Report 1998, <*http://www.centralbanklanka.org/1998/annual_rpt.pdf*>, 1998; Global Edge, Sri Lanka: Economy, <*http://globaledge.msu.edu/ibrd/CountryEconomy.asp?CountryID=172&Region ID=3*>, 2001.

34 Global Edge, op. cit., n. 33.

35 Central Bank of Sri Lanka, Annual Report 1999, <*http://www.centralbanklanka.org/01_n.pdf*>, 1999.

36 Central Bank of Sri Lanka, Annual Report 2000, <*http://www.centralbank lanka.org/!1der.pdf*>, 2000.

37 The current governing coalition – the United National Front (UNF), comprising the United National Party – the Tamil National Alliance and the Sri Lanka Muslim Congress won 116 seats out of 225 seats in Parliament in December 2001. As a result, Sri Lanka now has a President from one party and a Prime Minister from another.

38 Ranil Wickremasinghe, "Policy Statement by Prime Minister Ranil Wickremasinghe made in Parliament on 22nd January 2002", <*http://www.news.lk/pm's_speech.htm*>, 2002.

39 The Island, "Budget highlights", <*http://origin.island.lk/2002/03/23/*>, 2002; Ministry of Finance, "Budget 2002 Highlights", <*http://www.eureka.lk/fpea/pdf/2002/new.pdf*>, 2002.

40 BBC News, Sri Lanka's stock market booms, <*http://news.bbc.co.uk/2/hi/business/1872558.stm*>, 2002; Lanka Business Online, "Revving Up", <*http://www.lankabusinessonline.com/*>, 2002.

41 Colombo Stock Exchange, Market Performance Review June 2002, <*http://www.cse.lk/review.html*>, 2002.

42 In addition, the UNF government has also embarked on a number of trade negotiations with the view of further expanding economic reforms. A Trade and Investment Framework Agreement (TIFA) between the US government and Sri Lanka will be signed shortly to enhance US investment and trade with Sri Lanka. Negotiations are also underway for a Indo-Lanka Free Trade agreement with emphasis on investments and services. See, USAID, "USAID/Sri Lanka Annual Report FY2002", <*http://www.dec.org/pdf_docs/PDABW199.pdf*>, 2002; Lanka Business Online, "Second Bout", <*http://www.lankabusinessonline.com/*>, 2002.

43 Sunday Observer, "Call for fast track financial reforms", <*http://origin.sundayobserver.lk/2002/03/24/bus02.html*>, 2002.

44 According to Finance Ministry estimates, one third of the 225 public enterprises are suffering losses. See, Z. Ibrahim, "Brushing Up", <*http://www.lankabusinessonline.com/*>, 2002.

45 Ministry of Finance, op. cit., n. 39.

46   BBC News, "Sri Lanka to float state telecoms firm", <*http://news.bbc.co.uk/2/ hi/business/1937060.stm*>, 2002; Sunday Times, "CPC mulls selling oil complex", <*http://www.sundaytimes.lk/020428/bus.html#1*>, 2002.
47   Ministry of Finance, op. cit., n. 39.
48   Central Bank of Sri Lanka, "Recent Economic Developments: Highlights", <*http://www.lanka.net/centralbank/con_highlight_2002.pdf*>, 2002.
49   Arjunna Mahendran, "Sri Lanka's New Economic Outlook", <*http:// www.boisrilanka.org/New%20Economic%20Outlook.pdf*>, 2002.
50   Daily News, "Budget at a glance", <*http://www.dailynews.lk/2002/03/23/ new11.tml.html*>, 2002.

References

Athukorala, P., 'Import Substitution, Structural Transformation, and Trade Dependence: A Case Study of Sri Lanka', *The Developing Economies*, vol. 24 (1981) no. 2, pp. 119–42.

de Silva, K.M. (ed.), *Sri Lanka: A Survey* (Honolulu: University of Hawaii Press, 1977).

Dias, S., 'Economic Liberalization and the Development of Manufacturing in Sri Lanka', *Asian Survey*, vol. XXXI (1991) no. 7.

Goulet, D., *Survival With Integrity* (Colombo: Marga Institute, 1981).

Herring, R.J., 'Economic Liberalisation Policies in Sri Lanka: International Pressures, Constraints and Supports', *Economic and Political Weekly*, vol. XXII (1987) no. 8, pp. 325–33.

Isenman, P., 'Basic Needs: The Case of Sri Lanka', *World Development*, vol. 8 (1980) no. 3, pp. 237–58.

Jayawardena, L., *et al.*, *Stabilization and Adjustment Policies and Programmes, Country Study 15, Sri Lanka* (Helsinki: World Institute of Development Economic Research, 1987).

Lakshman, W.D. (ed.), *Dilemmas of Development: Fifty Years of Economic Change in Sri Lanka* (Colombo: Sri Lanka Association of Economists, 1997) pp. 8–12.

Lakshman, W.D., 'Economic Growth and Redistributive Justice as Policy Goals: A Study of the Recent Experience of Sri Lanka', *Modern Ceylon Studies*, vol. 6 (1975) no. 1.

Moore, M., 'Economic Liberalization Versus Political Pluralism in Sri Lanka', *Modern Asian Studies*, vol. 24 (1990) no. 2.

O'Donnell, G., 'Reflections on the Patterns of Change in the Bureaucratic-Authoritarian State', *Latin American Research Review*, vol. 13 (1978) no. 1.

Ponnambalam, S., *Dependant Capitalism in Crisis: The Sri Lankan Economy 1948–1980* (London: Zed Press, 1980).

Wickremeratne, L.A., 'Planning and Economic Development', in K.M. de Silva (ed.), *Sri Lanka: A Survey* (Honolulu: University of Hawaii Press, 1977).

Wilson, J.A., *Politics in Sri Lanka: 1947–1979* (London: MacMillan, 1979).

World Bank, *World Development Report 1999/2000* (New York: Oxford University Press, 1999).

Index